ARTHUR C. CLARKE

MODERN MASTERS OF SCIENCE FICTION

Edited by Gary K. Wolfe

Science fiction often anticipates the consequences of scientific discoveries. The immense strides made by science since World War II have been matched step by step by writers who gave equal attention to scientific principles, human imagination, and the craft of fiction. The respect for science fiction won by Jules Verne and H. G. Wells was further increased by Isaac Asimov, Arthur C. Clarke, Robert Heinlein, Ursula K. Le Guin, Joanna Russ, and Ray Bradbury. Modern Masters of Science Fiction is devoted to books that survey the work of individual authors who continue to inspire and advance science fiction.

A list of books in the series appears at the end of this book.

ARTHUR C. CLARKE

Gary Westfahl

UNIVERSITY OF ILLINOIS PRESS
Urbana, Chicago, and Springfield

Library of Congress Cataloging-in-Publication Data
Names: Westfahl, Gary, author.
Title: Arthur C. Clarke / Gary Westfahl.
Description: Urbana : University of Illinois Press, [2018] | Series: Modern masters
    of science fiction | Includes bibliographical references and index.
Identifiers: LCCN 2017049899 | ISBN 9780252041938 (hardcover : acid-free paper)
    | ISBN 9780252083594 (pbk. : acid-free paper)
Subjects: LCSH: Clarke, Arthur C. (Arthur Charles), 1917–2008.
Classification: LCC PR6005.L36 Z95 2018 | DDC 823/.914—dc23
LC record available at https://lccn.loc.gov/2017049899

To Gregory Benford,
Arthur C. Clarke's longtime friend
and my longtime friend as well

contents

ACKNOWLEDGMENTS

I first must thank these individuals who provided research materials and information—David Aronovitz; Gregory Benford; Richard Bleiler, Homer Babbage Library, University of Connecticut; Denny Lien, formerly of University of Minnesota Libraries; Katie Salzmann, Southwestern Writers Collection of Witliff Collections, Alkek Library, University of Texas, San Marcos; Nichole Zang, Special Collections Department, Library of University of Maryland, Baltimore County; and especially Andy Sawyer, Science Fiction Foundation Collection, Sydney Jones Library, University of Liverpool, and Janet Moores, Maria Mendoza, and the other staff of the Interlibrary Loan Department, Tomás Rivera Library, University of California, Riverside—all of whom invariably responded to my repeated requests for texts.

I also thank the University of Illinois Press's former director, Willis Regier, series editor Gary K. Wolfe, associate acquisitions editor Marika Christofides, and their colleagues for their assistance during the process of completing this book and preparing it for publication. Edward James, John Rieder, and Wolfe provided detailed comments that helped to improve the evolving manuscript.

Finally, I thank my family members—my wife, Lynne; son, Jeremy; daughter, Allison Westfahl Kong; son-in-law, Steven Kong; and granddaughter, Serena Kong—for supporting all of my writing endeavors.

ARTHUR C. CLARKE

By the mid-1960s Arthur C. Clarke had already produced a body of work that would forever distinguish him as a major science fiction writer. He had been enshrined as one of the genre's "Big Three," along with Isaac Asimov and Robert A. Heinlein, all writers renowned for their scientific acumen, lively imaginations, and involving narratives. Clarke novels like *Childhood's End* (1953), *The Deep Range* (1957), and *A Fall of Moondust* (1961), and Clarke stories like "History Lesson" (1949), "The Nine Billion Names of God" (1953), and "The Star" (1955), were already regarded as classics, and one of those novels—*A Fall of Moondust*—became in 1961 the first science fiction novel included in *Reader's Digest Condensed Books*. Even in the midst of the genre's celebrated "New Wave," prominent new writers were emerging, such as Larry Niven and Gregory Benford, who were avowedly following in Clarke's footsteps by producing the sort of science-oriented "hard science fiction" that Clarke had perfected. Few imagined then that Clarke's greatest accomplishments lay ahead of him.

For in 1968 there appeared Stanley Kubrick's film *2001: A Space Odyssey*, cowritten by Clarke, soon heralded as the greatest science fiction film ever made. The success of that film, and Clarke's accompanying novel, led to his new career as a best-selling author and media personality, first as a commentator during television coverage of three *Apollo* missions and later as host of three documentary series. He also published several additional novels that integrated the disparate interests displayed in earlier works and demonstrated ongoing improvement as a writer, including the award-winning *Rendezvous with Rama* (1973) and *The Fountains of Paradise* (1979) and three sequels to *2001*. Knighted by the British government in 1998 for his achievements in writing science fiction and scientific nonfiction, Clarke remained active until dying at the age of ninety, contributing to worthy projects, corresponding with colleagues via email, and writing several passages for a final novel, *The Last Theorem* (2008), completed by Frederik Pohl when Clarke's failing mind could no longer handle the demands of writing. Reviewing that novel's proofs became Clarke's final task before he died in March 2008.

To justify a new book about Clarke, one might note that while numerous articles analyze his fiction, relatively few books focus exclusively on the author: Joseph D. Olander and Martin Harry Greenberg's anthology *Arthur C. Clarke* (1977), George Slusser's *The Space Odysseys of Arthur C. Clarke* (1978), Eric S. Rabkin's *Arthur C. Clarke* (1979), John Hollow's *Against the Night, the Stars: The Science Fiction of Arthur C. Clarke* (1983), David N. Samuelson's *Arthur C. Clarke: A Primary and Secondary Bibliography* (1984), and Robin Anne Reid's *Arthur C. Clarke: A Critical Companion* (1997). These studies also tend to emphasize what are commonly regarded as Clarke's major works, routinely overlooking much of his short fiction, and all were completed before significant new works appeared. Thus, a truly comprehensive survey of Clarke's science fiction has never been produced, and this will be the first book to discuss, at least briefly, all of his published works of fiction, though only an appendix describes later "collaborations" partially attributed to Clarke but actually written entirely by the credited coauthor, as Clarke and other authors candidly admitted. (Gentry Lee said, in "Arthur C. Clarke and Gentry Lee Online Chat" [1996], "Arthur and I talk about the books, I write all the text, he reads and makes editing suggestions.") These works, along with the minimally collaborative *The Last Theorem*, are *Cradle* (1988), *Rama II* (1989), *The Garden of Rama* (1991), and *Rama Revealed* (1994), by Lee; *Richter 10* (1996), by Mike McQuay; *The Trigger* (1999), by Michael P. Kube-McDowell; and "The Wire Continuum" (1998), "Hibernaculum 46" (2000), *The Light of Other Days* (2000), *Time's Eye* (2004),

Sunstorm (2007), "Time Gentlemen Please" (2007), and *Firstborn* (2008), by Stephen Baxter.

Another rationale for a new Clarke book is the recent appearance of texts, unavailable to earlier scholars, that provide insights and information about Clarke's career, including Clarke's *Astounding Days: A Science Fictional Autobiography* (1989); Neil McAleer's *Arthur C. Clarke: The Authorized Biography* (1992), updated as *Sir Arthur C. Clarke: Odyssey of a Visionary: A Biography* (2013); a collection of Clarke's adolescent publications, *Childhood Ends: The Earliest Writings of Arthur C. Clarke* (1996); two collections of Clarke's correspondence, *Arthur C. Clarke and Lord Dunsany: A Correspondence* (1998) and *From Narnia to a Space Odyssey: The War of Ideas between Arthur C. Clarke and C. S. Lewis* (2003); and a tribute volume, *Arthur C. Clarke: A Life Remembered* (2013), featuring brother Fred Clarke's memories of the author's childhood. Though not all of these were helpful to this study, such new resources enable contemporary scholars to better examine Clarke's works.

This might be termed a legalistic justification for a new examination of Clarke: yes, it might be worthwhile to comprehensively examine his fiction in the context of additional information. But this study was primarily inspired by the belief that, despite the critical attention he has received, Clarke remains a writer who has never been properly understood. True, Clarke has been correctly celebrated for his far-ranging visions of humanity's distant future, meticulous attentiveness to the nuts-and-bolts of near future technology, wry sense of humor, and passionate advocacy for space travel. Yet scholars tend to be dismissive of Clarke's skills in storytelling, character development, and prose style, even as these steadily improved throughout his career; they have not always noted how he radically differs from other science fiction writers in several respects; and they sometimes, rather awkwardly, approach his works as traditional sorts of literature, not properly appreciating Clarke's special background as a longtime science fiction fan and aspiring scientist.

First, as a reader of *Astounding Science-Fiction* in the 1930s and 1940s, Clarke became familiar with the ideas of editor John W. Campbell Jr., who argued that the writing of science fiction should proceed in the manner of a thought experiment, as authors allow their stories to "develop in any direction that the logic of the developing situation may dictate" (Introduction 5). There is every indication that this is how Clarke plotted his stories, prioritizing the implications of his ideas over any impulse to adhere to preconceived narrative structures. Indeed, if the fragments Clarke completed for *The Last Theorem* are representative of his writing process, he would write passages in no particular order, as it suited him, and eventually assemble them in an expedient fashion. (For *The Last Theorem* he wrote a preamble set in 1945 and descriptions of events throughout the life of protagonist Ranjit Subramanian, including moments with his father during his childhood and adolescence, his first sexual experience, his decision to marry, a space flight undertaken while working for NASA, the youth of his mentally disabled son, and his wife's death.)

In addition, while young Clarke was undoubtedly exposed to literary classics during his education and assiduously read science fiction magazines, he devoted most of his subsequent reading time to nonfiction—as suggested by the fact that seventeen of the twenty fictitious books he "reviewed" in "Ego's Review" (1940) and "Coming Distractions" (1969) are nonfiction. A similar picture of his reading habits emerges from a 1993 letter to *Interzone*, wherein he reports, "My memory circuits are now so clogged with gigawords that I find it almost impossible to read fiction." He also acknowledges, "I've read only one of the winners" of the Arthur C. Clarke Award, and to knowledgeably address controversies involving the selection of Marge Piercy's *Body of Glass* (aka *He, She and It*) (1991), he only "dipped into the opening chapters" to find the novel praiseworthy (4).

For these reasons, it seems unlikely that Clarke would have undertaken to model stories on Homer's *Odyssey* or John Milton's *Paradise Lost* (1667), yet because academic scholars were much more familiar with these works than Clarke, these are precisely the sorts of readings that they were inclined to provide. At times the task of Clarke's critics is not to build upon the work of predecessors but rather to brush it aside to start afresh.

In particular, while it is true that some of Clarke's works are set in the very near future and some are set in the very distant future, critics have failed to discern their underlying similarities and dubiously concluded that there were effectively two Arthur C. Clarkes: the hard-nosed, practical Clarke, devoted to meticulously plausible descriptions of near-future technology, and the wild-eyed, mystical Clarke, prone to fuzzy, unfounded speculations about mysterious forces underlying the visible universe. Even astute readers like Peter Nicholls and John Clute fall into the trap of describing the purported

"Clarke paradox: that the man who of all sf writers of his generation was most closely identified with knowledgeable, technological Hard SF was at the same time strongly attracted to the metaphysical, even to the mystical" ("Arthur C Clarke").

In fact, Clarke was always hard-nosed and practical, but he correctly realized that anyone pondering what humanity might accomplish in the distant future, or what advanced aliens might have already accomplished, necessarily anticipates achievements and technologies that cannot be clearly explained to present-day humans—the insight conveyed by his Third Law: "Any sufficiently advanced technology is indistinguishable from magic" ("Clarke's Third Law on UFO's" 255). Thus, reading commentaries on Clarke, one might imagine that one day Clarke would be in a mundane, commonsensical mood and on another day would drift into quasi-religious ruminations on cosmic issues; actually, he wrote in a straightforward manner whenever possible but appropriately employed language recalling mysticism while dealing with futuristic matters that could only be described in such imprecise terms. As Russell Blackford correctly notes, it is *not* "mystical to ponder the far future," or "to wonder what forms of life or consciousness will one day supersede humanity . . . for there is nothing in Clarke's most visionary speculations that is inconsistent with the scientific world view on which modern technology is based" ("Future Problematic" 41). Clarke seems to be a science fiction mystic primarily because he ventures into far-ranging speculations, involving millions of years of predicted advances, more frequently than other writers.

There are other ways Clarke's distinctive fiction has not been fully appreciated. Throughout his lifetime he had a weakness for the adolescent humor of wordplay and slapstick, and while this dominates only his juvenilia, it does surface, incongruously, in some later works. As suggested, Clarke regarded his fiction primarily not as literature but as stimulating explorations of possible future developments, yet he regularly differed from other science fiction writers in addressing several of the genre's preoccupations: he thought new inventions would likely bring more problems than benefits; he suspected that after achieving regular space travel, humans might never venture beyond the solar system; he calmly accepted that humanity would become extinct in the near or distant future, or evolve into forms unimaginable to present-day humans; he anticipated the aliens we encounter would be genuinely alien, in both their physiology and psychology; he believed there existed a deep, enduring bond between humanity and the seas, perhaps stronger than the anticipated bond between humanity and space; and he examined religions not because he suspected they might be true—as he remained a lifelong atheist—but because he was curious about why humans developed religious beliefs, how they might be persuaded to abandon them, and why such beliefs might endure in defiance of expectations.

Finally, commentators routinely argue that Clarke was strong in developing ideas but weak in developing characters. However, his characters are actually not bland but merely reticent, and the isolated lifestyles they adopt—remaining distant or alienated from their original families, wives, and children, and relying primarily upon connections to broader communities and long-distance communication to ameliorate feelings of loneliness—not only represent a reflection of Clarke's own personality, as a closeted homosexual and victim of a disability, but also constitute his most important prediction, inasmuch as increasing numbers of twenty-first-century citizens are living in this manner.

In describing these characteristics of Clarke's worldview, I also summarize the contents of this book's main text, which, after a biographical sketch, surveys his humorous juvenilia and related later works; proceeds to examine Clarke's treatment of inventions, space travel, human destinies, aliens, the sea, and religion; and finally analyzes his characters. All of Clarke's stories and novels are referenced, but the major thematic chapters conclude with more thorough explorations of the novels I regard as his best works: *The Fountains of Paradise*; *Imperial Earth* (1975); *Against the Fall of Night* (1953), *The City and the Stars* (1956), and *Childhood's End*; *2001: A Space Odyssey* and *Rendezvous with Rama*; *The Deep Range* and *The Ghost from the Grand Banks* (1990); and *The Songs of Distant Earth* (1986). After a conclusion, the book describes his "collaborations" and presents an edited bibliography.

In this text, a work published by an American press for predominantly American readers, page references to novels are taken from first American editions, and American versions of book titles are employed (*Sands of Mars* [1952], for example, not *The Sands of Mars*). Quotations from *The Last Theorem* lack page numbers because they are taken not from the published novel—almost entirely Pohl's work—but from passages written entirely by Clarke that were emailed to Gregory Benford in 2006 and forwarded to me in 2015. Page references for most stories are taken from their republication in *The Collected Stories of Arthur C. Clarke* (2000); page references for stories not in that anthology are taken from their first appearances, with the exception of pieces from the *Huish Magazine* (their page references are taken from their republication in *Childhood Ends*) and "At the Mountains of Murkiness, or Lovecraft-into-Leacock" (1940) (its page references are taken from its 1973 republication in George Locke's *At the Mountains of Murkiness, and Other Parodies*). Page references for Clarke's works of nonfiction, and secondary sources, are taken from first publications.

CHAPTER 1

BIOGRAPHICAL SKETCH

The key facts about Clarke's early life have been presented in several sources: he grew up on a farm, Ballifants, in the village of Bishops Lydeard; experienced the trauma of his father's death when he was thirteen; began creative writing while attending Huish's Grammar School in Taunton, Somerset; and after graduating moved on to a civil service position in London and intense involvement in science fiction fandom. Recently available sources, however, provide additional details about youthful activities that anticipated later achievements.

From an early age Clarke was primarily interested in science. Among other activities—described in Fred Clarke's "Arthur C. Clarke: The Early Days" (1987)—he collected fossils, assembled objects with his Meccano construction set, installed an intercom system in his home, and devised an experimental way to transmit sound using light beams and photoelectric cells. But he became especially fascinated with outer space and the possibility of space travel, building telescopes, and constructing and launching small rockets. These experiences are occasionally alluded to in later fiction: both "Saturn Rising" (1961) and *Rendezvous with Rama* describe boys obsessed with astronomy who construct telescopes, and Clarke's 1938 poem "Prelude to the Conquest of Space" makes fun of his rocket experiments, as the narrator's three progressively more ambitious efforts to launch rockets all result in destructive explosions.

Still, even while looking up at the sky and speculating about its wonders, the young Clarke also spent time at his grandmother's house in Minehead and its nearby beach. In his "Foreword: Coming Home," to *Literary Trips* (2001), Clarke describes this beach as "a great crescent of sand from which I could see the distant coast of Wales, and the mysterious islands of Flat Holme and Steep Holme. Every day the tide's long withdrawal would expose a wonderland of rock pools full of alien life forms: here I would construct elaborate sand castles and await their demolition by the returning waves. This much-loved playground was the inspiration for my short story 'Transience.'" These childhood experiences laid the groundwork for his later devotion to scuba diving in Sri Lanka; indeed, Clarke concludes, "The great arc of Minehead bay . . . imprinted itself on my mind so effectively that I unconsciously sought it for the rest of my life" (ix), explaining his devotion to "Unawatuna Bay, on the south coast of Sri Lanka," which he later realized constituted his "platonic ideal—the apotheosis of my childhood playground" (x).

For biographer Neil McAleer the crucial event of Clarke's childhood was the death of his father, Charles Clarke, effectively obliging Clarke to serve as a father figure of sorts to his younger sister and two younger brothers, and perhaps establishing his lifelong pattern, noted by McAleer, of forging strong friendships with younger men. Still, Clarke indicates that he and his father were never close; in "Introduction: Of Sand and Stars" (1983) he recounts how his father once handed him a cigarette card with a picture of a dinosaur, stating this was "virtually the only memory I have of my father—a shadowy figure who has left no other mark, even though I was over 13 when he died" (10). While McAleer attributes Charles Clarke's death to lingering effects of the poison gas he was exposed to during World War I, Clarke simply says in his 1986 *Playboy* interview, "My father died prematurely of cancer" (59), and while retelling the anecdote of the cigarette card in his 2007 foreword to *The Rise of Animals*, he describes cigarettes as "the drug that killed my father" (xi), conveying that he succumbed to lung cancer caused by smoking.

While some of his comments indicate that Clarke was genuinely saddened by his father's death, his discussion of that event in *Astounding Days* suggests that he was more affected by the resulting loss of family income:

> At the age of eleven or twelve, I had graduated from the elementary school which still stands virtually unchanged in the center of Bishop's Lydeard, the small Somerset village where my father (like many other demobilized officers) had rented a farm after the end of the First World War. Unfortunately, he had little talent for business or agriculture; his previous occupation had been a Post Office engineer, and I have sometimes wondered if his background in telecommunications could have influenced my future career. . . . After Father's death in 1931, Mother continued to run the farm, augmenting its income (or neutralizing its losses) by riding lessons, breeding Cairn terriers, and taking paying guests. (9–10)

Clarke's widowed mother was not only obliged to focus her energies on finding other ways to earn money (including, in addition to those Clarke listed, cultivating a garden to raise food for her family and knitting gloves), but she also had to rely upon her children to perform chores.

While Clarke reports in *Astounding Days* that his mother "with great difficulty . . . was able to send me to Huish's Grammar School" (11), one has to assume that a majority of his fellow students came from more affluent families who could afford the necessary payments to send their children there without "great difficulty," and the young Clarke may have been painfully aware of that fact. For whatever reason, throughout his career he manifested a strong desire to earn money, which eventually led to seemingly unwise decisions. As he entered his seventies, with a steady stream of income from regularly republished novels and collections, there was no need for Clarke to lend his name to several "collaborations" he actually did not write, and these inauthentic publications tarnished the value of his name on book covers as readers and reviewers learned to ignore books credited to "Arthur C. Clarke and. . . ." One also wonders why the elderly Clarke kept picking up pocket change by writing innumerable introductions and forewords, often to unlikely books. (Long after becoming accustomed to million-dollar advances, for example, he agreed to write the foreword to my *Science Fiction Quotations: From the Inner Mind to the Outer Limits* [2005] for the paltry sum of fifteen hundred dollars.) But remembering the poverty of his youth, he may have felt compelled to keep adding to his savings, building up reserves sufficient to deal with any disaster. (Some also argue he sought to keep generating income primarily to support charitable endeavors.)

It was around the time of his father's death that Clarke first became devoted to science fiction. At Huish's Grammar School he discovered an issue of *Astounding Stories* and after reading its entire contents began collecting other American science fiction magazines. Like many youthful readers of science fiction, Clarke developed a desire to write science fiction, as evidenced by pieces in the *Huish Magazine*, and after graduating and moving to London, he quickly connected with other science fiction fans and began writing for and editing fanzines.

At this point a possible comparison of Clarke to another renowned British science fiction writer, H. G. Wells, breaks down. True, both were bright young lads interested in science who successfully struggled to rise above humble origins by writing scientific nonfiction and science fiction; both developed a passionate aversion to war and became international celebrities. But although there were other noteworthy differences in their lives—Wells grew up in a city, while Clarke lived on a farm, and Wells faced his own childhood traumas but never experienced the youthful loss of a parent—their disparate relationships with science fiction fundamentally altered the courses of their careers. Wells came of age when there was no recognized genre of science fiction, was hence obliged to devise his own approach to writing science fiction, soon concluded that such stories lacked literary merit, and accordingly devoted the bulk of his later decades to writing realistic novels. In contrast, Clarke began reading science fiction magazines as an adolescent, joined groups of science fiction fans, started writing with some knowledge of the genre and its conventions, and never expressed or evidenced any desire to abandon science fiction, which became his lifelong avocation.

All the passions viewed as central to Clarke's career—devotion to space, the sea, and science fiction; a pattern of close relationships with males; and a constant urge to make money—may be traced, then, back to his early years. But I would add another characteristic that arguably defines his life: while Clarke forged many friendships during his life, few people claimed to have known him well. In *Sentinels in Honor of Arthur C. Clarke* (2010), for example, Gregory Benford offers a telling anecdote about Clarke attending a party in New York City and spending all of his time writing a short story instead of conversing with the partygoers—defining, perhaps, his simultaneously sociable yet private nature. In part, this may be because Clarke needed to rigorously conceal one aspect of his life—his homosexuality—after recognizing his sexual orientation as a youngster. But he was similarly circumspect about other personal matters that never would have aroused moral indignation, like his apparent proclivity for writing satirical poetry. Yet this is also what makes Clarke seem, years after his death, a true man of the future.

As a London civil servant, Clarke surely performed his duties well, but his life was centered on the British Interplanetary Society and science fiction fandom. His passions for space travel and science fiction inspired articles on those topics, as well as several stories and two poems published in fanzines. However, although Clarke extols science fiction poetry in a 1938 article, "The Fantastic Muse," he never published additional poems, although one piece of evidence indicates that writing poetry remained a private avocation: a brief poem included in the text of *The Lost Worlds of 2001* (1972), "Kubrick, Stan."

Clarke's fan-oriented activities were halted by World War II, which led him into the Royal Air Force and years of work developing Ground Controlled Approach Radar, the experience that inspired the article "You're on the Glide Path—I Think" (1949) and Clarke's only realistic novel, *Glide Path* (1963). Thus, his only recorded publications in 1943 were excerpts from two letters published in a fanzine.

As the end of the war approached, Clarke began writing again—a few scientific articles, including his famous plan for communications satellites, "Extra-Terrestrial Relays" (1945)—and as a veteran could finally afford to attend college, earning a degree in mathematics and physics from King's College London and briefly working as an editor for *Physics Abstracts*. A turning point in Clarke's postwar life came in 1950 when he met photographer Mike Wilson, as Wilson's interest in scuba diving inspired Clarke to take diving lessons. Soon, underwater explorations became a regular activity, and the two men would later produce several books about the undersea world offering Clarke's prose and Wilson's photographs.

In 1946 Clarke also returned to writing science fiction, selling stories to American and British magazines, and by the early 1950s he was gaining a reputation, and considerable income, as an author. Most early earnings came from nonfiction books about space travel, beginning with *Interplanetary Flight: An Introduction to Astronautics* (1950), but his science fiction novels attracted attention as well, most notably *Childhood's End*, generally considered his first major work. While Clarke began enjoying regular visits to America, he seemed destined for a long and successful career in his native country.

Everything changed in 1952, I would theorize, due to an event usually not mentioned in accounts of Clarke's life: the arrest of British mathematician and cryptographer Alan Turing for homosexual activity. After agreeing to chemical castration as an alternative to prison, Turing reportedly committed suicide two years later. While Turing was not as renowned as he is today, news of his arrest may have reverberated throughout Britain's homosexual community, reminding them of the draconian laws against homosexuality that their government evidently remained determined to enforce, regardless of the perpetrator's social status. If aware of Turing's situation, Clarke would have recognized that, despite his own achievements, he might face similar persecution if caught in a compromising position.

Such a realization may have influenced two significant decisions in Clarke's life. First, in 1953, after meeting American divorcée Marilyn Mayfield in Florida, they almost immediately got married. McAleer insists they were genuinely attracted to each other, but Clarke undoubtedly understood that a wife would allay suspicions about his sexual preferences. In any event, the relationship ended after six months—Clarke told McAleer only that "the marriage was incompatible from the beginning" (100)—though they remained married for a decade. Second, Clarke began spending more time away from his homeland, eventually settling in Sri Lanka. Clarke publicly explained that he relocated in order to pursue his fondness for scuba diving; however, McAleer notes the move also allowed Clarke to avoid Britain's high taxes. (An amusing reference to this issue surfaces in "Venture to the Moon" [1956] as British astronauts volunteer to spend extra time on the moon solely to avoid paying taxes that year.) Yet Turing's experiences may have given Clarke little incentive to remain in Britain, and as verified in John Baxter's 1997 book, *Stanley Kubrick: A Biography* (203), Clarke relocated to distant Sri Lanka in part because its laws regarding homosexuality were less severe, and Clarke could express his true sexuality without fearing retribution.

Clarke's underwater exploits, facilitated by his new home near the Indian Ocean, led to a burgeoning focus on writing nonfiction books about the sea, though he continued writing science fiction stories and novels. This phase of his life largely came to an end in 1962, when he was temporarily incapacitated by polio (though that diagnosis remains unconfirmed); still, he continued diving as much as possible, and references to the sea remained a recurring feature of his fiction.

Another life-altering event came in 1964, when Clarke was invited by Stanley Kubrick to collaborate in writing the film *2001: A Space Odyssey*. This experience made him more famous, enabling him to garner an unprecedented one-million-dollar contract to write three novels and obtain lifelong financial security. Clarke announced his retirement after completing the third novel, *The Fountains of Paradise*, but proved unable to stop writing fiction and eventually completed six additional novels, several brief stories, and numerous articles, introductions, and afterwords.

The mature Clarke also developed an interest in doing more work in film, with mixed results. He hosted three documentary television series, contributed to a documentary about fractals, and advised director Peter Hyams regarding the film adaptation of *2010: Odyssey Two* (1982), titled *2010: The Year We Make Contact* (1984). But he also labored on proposed film projects that never came to fruition, though a few were transformed into novels: *The Songs of Distant Earth*, the Gentry Lee–written *Cradle*, and the Mike McQuay–written *Richter 10*.

In the 1990s and thereafter, Clarke worked only occasionally on novels but produced many nonfiction pieces, primarily introductions to others' books and commentaries for new editions of his older books. The year 1998 was especially significant because he was knighted by the British government, so he could proudly call himself Sir Arthur C. Clarke. Unfortunately, when the British *Sunday Mirror* published an article claiming that Clarke was a pedophile, one week before the scheduled ceremony, he requested that the ceremony be delayed until a police investigation could clear him of the charges. One effect of the article, though, was a more-or-less open acknowledgment of Clarke's homosexuality.

During his final years, although he announced in his 2003 "Foreword 1" to *To the Edge of Doom* that "I have retired" from "the field of science fiction"

(9), he sporadically worked on another novel, *The Last Theorem*, but had to abandon the project because his memory was faltering, apparently a lingering effect of post-polio syndrome. After he first approached Gregory Benford about completing this novel, the assignment was given to Frederik Pohl, and though that final novel proved disappointing, Clarke's death in 2008 was widely reported throughout the world, and many prominent individuals offered fond tributes.

While McAleer's updated biography will undoubtedly remain the standard reference on Clarke's career, other individuals who knew him well may provide additional revelations, and Clarke generated a vast quantity of private diaries that, he stipulated, could only be published thirty years after his death. In 2038, therefore, the world may learn more about this reticent individual's long and remarkable life.

CHAPTER 2

JOCULAR JUVENILIA

Clarke's writing career can be divided into two phases. As a youth writing for the *Huish Magazine* and fanzines, he produced only two stories, "Retreat from Earth" (1938) and "The Awakening" (1942), and one poem, "The Twilight of a Sun" (1939), that anticipate the somber tone and expansive imagination characterizing most of his later works. He otherwise specialized in humorous science fiction of an understandably juvenile nature, featuring parodies, puns and wordplay, in-jokes directed at friends and colleagues, wild exaggeration, and pure silliness, sometimes presented as purported nonfiction. Works published during his professional career generally were entirely different: while there were amusing stories, and serious works with touches of humor, the humor was sophisticated and understated, designed to elicit a wry smile instead of a belly laugh. As Peter Brigg notes, Clarke's mature works "featur[ed] understatement, irony, and wit" with a "delicate" touch (Olander and Greenberg, *Arthur C. Clarke* 27), comments one could not make about earlier writings.

Clarke clearly did not value the first phase of his career, including only three examples of his youthful wit—"Travel by Wire!" (1937), "How We Went to Mars" (1938), and "Whacky" (1942)—in *The Collected Stories of Arthur C. Clarke* while omitting twenty-two other pieces from that era; and the few individuals familiar with those texts would probably agree that, with the possible exceptions of "The Fate of Fu-Manchu" (1935) and "At the Mountains of Murkiness," they were justifiably ignored. Still, any comprehensive survey of Clarke's fiction must briefly discuss them, as they help to explain incongruous lapses into his earlier style that occasionally surface, particularly in works one could term Clarke's mature juvenilia—as Clarke suggested by titling one of them "Droolings from My Second Childhood: 2" (1999).

One characteristic of Clarke's juvenilia is that he eschews his own voice, adapting a false persona or mimicking another writer's style. A series of five publications in the *Huish Magazine*—"Correspondence" (1932), "Our Correspondence Column" (1933), "News from the Torrid Zone" (1933), "Letters to the Editor" (Spring 1935) and "Letters to the Editor" (Summer 1935)—are letters allegedly written by former Huish students working in inhospitable circumstances. A sixth farcical letter, "Letters to the Editor" (Autumn 1934), was supposedly written by an expert on gramophones, while other fictitious letters receive responses from editor Clarke in "Answers to Correspondence" (1934). The fanzine piece "Letters to the Secretary of an Interplanetary Society" (1941) offers purported letters responding to plans to build a spaceship, including a warning that horoscopes should be cast before embarking and the familiar complaint that the rocket will never work because in space there is "nothing . . . to push against" (17).

His first true work of fiction, "The Fate of Fu-Manchu" (attributed, like most *Huish* writings, to "Clericus"), parodies Arthur Conan Doyle's Sherlock Holmes stories, as does the second section of "Whacky." Both mock Watson's tendency to mention exotic former cases, as "Fu-Manchu" cites "The affair of the Murgatroyd Mothballs," "the case of the Pondicherry Peanuts" (33), and "the affair of the Elastic-sided Egg-cup!" (35), while "Whacky" refers to "the curious case of the Camphorated Kipper" (27). The first story also pays homage to Sax Rohmer's Fu Manchu stories as Holmes and Watson discover the Asian villain plotting to blow up the Houses of Parliament. Another *Huish* publication, *Jule Gets His: A New Super-Drama by a Well-Known Author* (1934), is a screenplay recasting characters from William Shakespeare's *Julius Caesar* (1599) as modern gangsters in New York City. In *Childhood Ends* Clarke describes "In Darkest Somerset" (1936) as "obviously a parody of the old time 'travelogues'" (72). "At the Mountains of Murkiness" begins as a parody of H. P. Lovecraft, but as the subtitle suggests, the tone shifts to that of humorist Stephen Leacock when the grotesque beings they encounter in Antarctica speak politely in English and agree to bring their guests some tea. "Prelude to the Conquest of Space" is a parody of Henry Wadsworth Longfellow's "The Arrow and the Song" (1845), describing the disastrous results after the narrator twice "shot a rocket into the air" and finally "shot a rocket into space" (20).

The puns and wordplay in Clarke's youthful writings are predictably childish. His first work of fiction, "Interview with Celebrities VIII" (1932), seeks to amuse readers with the almost incomprehensible dialect Clarke invents for a fictitious "unspoiled rustic" (1). "The Jon Bloc Soc" (1933) summarizes an imagined meeting of the school's philosophy club discussing the Greek "philosopher, Phalacius," and other figures, such as the "tyrant, Gluttenous," the "poets Livid and Simplicitus," the "historian, Fabricatus, and the dramatists Juvenile, Senile and Puerile" (11). Wordplay of a technical nature dominates "Letters to the Editor" (Autumn 1934), wherein the correspondent claims that a gramophone requires "a screened grid pentaheptode, in semi-series parallel with an indirectly operated double duo-diode triode septode" (26). In the same style, the fictitious chemicals needed to remove ink stains in "Answers to Correspondents" include "para-amino-benzoydiethyl-aminoethenol hydrochloride" (22). In "Letters to the Editor" (Spring 1935) an impossibly tall mountain is called "Mt. Hiasell" (37). "In Darkest Somerset" describes Nature Club members entering "the primeval forest of Bun-Cum" and encountering "the wildebeeste and dirtebeeste" (71).

While less commonplace, similar humor surfaces in Clarke's fanzine writings. Crew members in "How We Went to Mars" include "our chemist, Dr Badstoff" (6), "Isaac Gussbaum, our auditor," and "Eric Wobblewit, our tame humourist" (9). One review in "Ego's Review" describes a novel about the last man on Earth, "who starves to death in a canned-food factory owing to the universal destruction of tin-openers," titled "'All Is Rust' by Les Lonesome" (7–8), while another reports that "A Guide to Ancient Egypt" describes Egyptian "pleasure resorts, such as the Valley of Tombs . . . and the Great Morgue of Tummi-Ake the Bigger" (8). "At the Mountains of Murkiness" mentions "Lady Muriel Mildew" (96) and "the mad Arab, Abdul Hashish," who "wrote of the hellish valley of Oopadoop in that frightful book, the forbidden 'Pentechnicon'" (97).

In youthful fiction Clarke makes fun of people he knew—classmates and instructors at Huish's Grammar School and science fiction fans—though the jokes are not always understandable to contemporary readers. For example, when an elderly former classmate in another fictional interview, "Octogenarian Observations" (1934), recalls that "Master T. T. was young and vigorous, and Master Goodliffe was a powerful full back on the footer field" (13), one guesses that Clarke is referring to two of Huish's most elderly instructors—as partially confirmed when Clarke comments in *Childhood Ends* that T. T. is "our athletic gym master, who then seemed to me quite an old man, though he was probably in his 50's" (14). In his farcical account of how British science fiction fans conquer the postwar world and establish a utopia, "A Short History of Fantocracy—1948–1960" (1941–1942), one discerns the humor in observing that "the mathematical" George Medhurst "had been delayed by the lengthy calculations he had made in order to find the quickest route" (Part I: 9). But why the arrival of William F. Temple "driving a gipsy caravan containing his numerous offspring (including the famous Temple Triplets)" (Part I: 7) seemed funny may forever remain a mystery. And while he usually employs real names, Clarke is not above more playful references to fellow fans, as "Ego's Review" mentions "Sam Stewed" (Sam Youd, or John Christopher) and "John Lurke" (John F. Burke) (9).

Young Clarke was willing to make fun of himself, as signaled by his embrace of the nickname "Ego"; indeed, fanzine publications are usually attributed to "Arthur 'Ego' Clarke." As a character in "A Short History of Fantocracy," "Ego had naturally chosen his home as a rendezvous, oblivious to the fact that it might take the northerners months to reach it" (Part I: 7). In "Ego & the Dying Planet" (1941), a summary of the first draft of *Against the Fall of Night* probably (though not definitely) written by Clarke, he suggests his shortcomings as a writer (and perhaps subtly references his homosexuality) by wryly commenting, "It comes as something of a shock to me nurtured on pro-stf. [professional "scientifiction"] when, at the point where the Hero, by long established tradition, should meet the Girl, there merely turns up another boy!" (39).

Generally, Clarke's early fiction features broad and often silly humor. In five purported letters, he competes with himself to describe, speaking as fictional former students, the most absurdly unpleasant environments imaginable. The author of "Correspondence" is a fisherman in a bitterly cold North Sea where "the wind at present has a velocity of some 70 m.p.h.," "The temperature is about 40 degrees below zero," and the fish they catch "were frozen solid" (4). Yet a second correspondent in the Arctic Circle complains in "Our Correspondence Column" that he enjoys "a life of ease and comfort" compared to his own, truly frigid workplace, where he must "dissolve pounds of calcium chloride in my blood to lower its f[r]eezing-point sufficiently to prevent it from solidifying in my rigid veins," and radio transmissions are not clearly received, "owing to the wireless waves getting frozen on the way" (6). Problems faced by the author of "News from the Torrid Zone" stem from the incredibly hot climate of "Vyring Pan" in "British Malaria": workers employ "the powerful refrigerating plant at the rubber-mines here . . . to reduce water to its boiling point," and their "clothes . . . made of asbestos" must be changed "once an hour as the material becomes red hot!" (7). The writer of "Letters to the Editor" (Spring 1935) is doing research on Mt. Hiasell at "such an altitude that there is absolutely no atmosphere at all" (37), while "Letters to the Editor" (Summer 1935) reports the author is deep-sea diving "off the coast of British Hotchaland" and encountering strange "monsters of the deep" (40). Perhaps the most amusing thing about this series of letters is the way it concludes, with a note from an editor who has tired of its humor: "This correspondence must now cease" (41).

Still, even if they inspire little laughter, these letters command attention because they show Clarke engaged in the sort of extrapolative thinking characteristic of science fiction, pondering questions about imagined realms: How would people survive in incredibly cold or hot climates? What special problems would arise? How would they measure the temperature? (This topic keeps recurring, perhaps because it was a staple of Clarke's science classes.) It is also striking that, after considering extremely cold and warm climates, Clarke's imaginative search for other unpleasant locales leads him to an outpost effectively in space and into the ocean depths, anticipating two environments that would dominate his fictional career—but emphasizing their hardships, not their wonders and possibilities.

Clarke's early fiction visits space on other occasions, but always farcically, though he addresses the subject seriously in articles like "We Can Rocket to the Moon—Now!" (1939). In "Interviews with Notorieties—No. 1" (1936) the author visits "the Professor," who, after parachuting out of a rocket when it goes astray, hurries the interviewer into a spaceship to avoid a bill collector and flies to Mars, where he sadly discovers a plaque revealing that his rival "Hank Schwartzberger" has already reached the planet (69). Only slightly more plausible is "How We Went to Mars," wherein several scientists, after their errant experiments cause gleefully described deaths and property damage, launch a spaceship and accidentally travel to Mars, where they are greeted by human-like Martians and "found our knowledge of contemporary science-fiction invaluable, for everything with which the Martians tried to surprise us we had heard of long before" (11). Efforts to achieve space travel are also intimated at the conclusion of "A Short History of Fantocracy."

In two early stories, other new forms of transportation are treated less than seriously. "Travel by Wire!" describes how scientists develop and market a "radio-transporter" (1) that teleports people to destinations by means of radio waves or cable, though it regularly results in deaths or disfigurements. In "Into the Past" (1939) two science fiction fans in 1950 follow the instructions in a 1949 story to construct a time machine, enabling one of them to visit the recent past and obtain pristine copies of valuable science fiction magazines, though the machine finally malfunctions and strands the traveler in 1930.

Seeking lessons to draw from largely inconsequential works, one first notes a pattern of cruel humor, with people's deaths regularly described in jocular language. In "The Fate of Fu-Manchu" Watson finds "bottles and vials of strange Eastern poisons" in Fu-Manchu's laboratory and "pocketed some of them, thinking they might be useful in my practice" (35); the story concludes when Holmes and Watson calmly anticipate that Inspector Prodnose will soon "unscrew those gas-cylinders" (36) and kill himself. The final joke of *The Mystic Potion* (1935), a play written by several Huish students featuring Clarke as a character and possible coauthor, is that those brewing the potion end up dead, and one resident of Mt. Hiasell in "Letters to the Editor" (Spring

1935) dies a horrible death after being pulled through a tiny hole in his home into the surrounding vacuum. In "In Darkest Somerset," after nonchalantly noting the deaths of several porters during the expedition, the narrator notes that "after shooting the few remaining porters, we went on board" the boat that takes them home (72). One joke in "Prelude to the Conquest of Space" is that an errant rocket "blew San Francisco out of sight" (20); the narrator of "Travel by Wire!" casually describes the gruesome deaths sometimes caused by their teleportation system; the scientists of "How We Went to Mars," after accidentally destroying Parliament, escape punishment by arranging a courtroom explosion that "removed all opposition and most of Temple Bar" (5); and a wife apparently poisons her husband in "Whacky." Perhaps this indicates that young Clarke felt a certain coldness toward, and emotional distance from, people around him; one might also interpret these passages as anticipations of the mature intellect that, in stories like "The Nine Billion Names of God" and "siseneG" (1984), treats the death of the universe as an enormous joke.

The casual attitude toward death and similarly dismissive remarks about property damage in "How We Went to Mars" also suggest a willingness to condone crimes that elsewhere surfaces in other ways. One sample sentence in "French without Tears" (1934), which describes an imaginary method for rendering French sentences using mathematical symbols, is spoken by a man transparently trying to avoid paying duties on goods he is taking to another country; as noted, the inventor of "Interviews with Notorieties" does not pay his bills. *Jule Gets His* describes a modern-day Julius Caesar as a criminal controlling New York City, and the system remains in place after his death when another criminal, "Oct." or Octavian, replaces him. These works also reference questionable, if not illegal, efforts to make money: the author of "In Darkest Somerset" conspicuously mentions the store "Marks and Spenser," acknowledging this as an "advert." (71); the protagonists of "Into the Past" are retrieving magazines from the past to sell them at exorbitant prices; and the narrator of "How We Went to Mars" says little about his sojourn on Mars to encourage readers to purchase his "forthcoming book, 'Mars with the Lid Off,'" which "will be published by Blotto and Windup at 21/-"(11). These flourishes may reflect Clarke's concerns about his often precarious financial situation at the time.

A critic might pore through these stories seeking evidence about which authors were influencing this developing writer. We know Clarke was reading science fiction magazines, and their impact is conveyed in "Interviews with Notorieties" by the Professor's "vast collection of weird-looking magazines which bore titles such as 'Fantastic Fiction,' 'Science Stories,' and many other strange and lurid appellations" (68), and its story about a solitary inventor and his spaceship, a typical trope in magazine stories. "The Fate of Fu-Manchu" conveys a fondness for Doyle's Sherlock Holmes stories, later referenced in *The Songs of Distant Earth* when the investigator who pins down details of a plot to sabotage a starship "started to read" a cherished book, and "the fog rolled once more down Baker Street" (189). More broadly, one might describe characters like Alvin in *Against the Fall of Night* and Rikki Stormgren and Jan Rodricks in *Childhood's End* as detectives determined to solve cosmic mysteries. *Jule Gets His* shows that Clarke had read some of Shakespeare's plays and perhaps came to appreciate the value of tragic endings, one feature of some later fiction. "In Darkest Somerset" suggests that he enjoyed travel writing, and later novels like *Rendezvous with Rama*, *Imperial Earth*, and *3001: The Final Odyssey* (1997) have the structure of travelogues, describing leisurely journeys through exotic environments.

"At the Mountains of Murkiness" raises questions about whether Lovecraft's mythos of ancient, powerful aliens lurking unseen in the universe influenced the advanced aliens in Clarke's fiction. Nicholas Seeley, for one, discerns similarities in their works, arguing, "Both seemed haunted by a vision that for years they struggled to put in words, a vision of mankind's transience and its power; our insignificance and our possibility" ("The Wizard in the Space Station"). The story also suggests the possibility that other humorous works reflect Clarke's effort to emulate Leacock. "A Short History of Fantocracy," despite its farcical tone, conveys sincere admiration for H. G. Wells, as the leaders' "Declaration of the Rights of Fans" describes their "goal" as "the achievement of a "scientifically organised World State" and adds, "It is hoped that Mr. Wells will still be sufficiently active to assist as political advisor" (Part II: 23).

Finally, a familiarity with these early works helps to explain why some mature works display features observed in his juvenilia—fictitious letters, parodies, puns and wordplay, in-jokes and silly humor. In his first professionally published story, "Loophole" (1946), Clarke employs letters to tell a story, as most of the text consists of messages exchanged by Martians, appalled to discover that humans have mastered atomic energy, who inform the people of Earth that they can no longer send rockets into space. Two final letters, written by humans, indicate that humanity has destroyed the Martians by developing a form of teleportation to instantly transport devastating bombs to their planet. "The Longest Science-Fiction Story Ever Told" (1966) consists of a single, infinitely long letter, rejecting a "not at all original" story about an author "whose work is always plagiarised even *before* they can complete it." The letter proceeds to quote, as another example of such a story, an identical rejection letter including the same quote, a process that ellipses indicate continues infinitely. Following the ellipses, one sees an identical, concluding "Better luck next time!" and signature also being infinitely repeated (854). "Report on Planet Three" (1959) adopts the voice of a Martian scientist, dismissing the possibility of life on Earth.

Although Clarke acknowledged that Lord Dunsany's Jorkens stories were one inspiration for his own club stories featuring Harry Purvis, only two later stories and one poem qualify as outright parodies. First, Reginald Bretnor published many "Ferdinand Feghoot" stories, implausible vignettes that conclude with horrible puns, and Clarke offers his own example in "Neutron Tide" (1970), wherein, after encountering a neutron star, a spaceship is destroyed, though one item is recovered from "some unfortunate engineer's tool kit": "one star mangled spanner" (880). As suggested by its title, "Move Over, E.R.!" (2000) makes fun of the television series *E.R.* (1994–2009) and other medical dramas, briefly describing an episode with four subplots, including the "first successful operation" of "Dr Fumblefinger, the blind brain surgeon," and the "quelling" of "yet another riot in the Terminal Halitosis Ward, restive after the unfortunate Affair of the Electrified Bedpans" (67). Finally, while it never appeared separately, *The Lost Worlds of 2001* includes a parody of Samuel Taylor Coleridge's "Kubla Khan" (1816) titled "Kubrick, Stan," written during the filming of *2001: A Space Odyssey*. It begins by noting, "For MGM did Kubrick, Stan / A stately astrodome decree" while Clarke "ran / Through plots incredible to man / In search of solvency" (190) (making yet another reference to his desire to make money).

"Move Over, E.R.!" also includes examples of the wordplay found in earlier writings, including the characters "Dr Hacksaw, still smarting over his rejection from Veterinary School"; "Dr Max Rictus, holder of the prestigious Lucretia Borgia Chair of Applied Toxicology at the University of Florence"; and the "Matron-from-Hell Mrs Brimstone and resident psychiatrist Dr Twitch" (67). When Clarke again reviews imaginary books in "Coming Distractions," there are similar sorts of humor: one reviewed book is *Fifty Years Behind the Proctoscope* by Dr Eugene Augenfahrt" while another relates the story of "Heteronomous Hackworthy, found standing among 15 badly dishevelled corpses with a dripping axe in his hand" (38). The protagonist of "The Steam-Powered Word Processor" (1986), a nineteenth-century man who like George Babbage seeks to create an early computer, is "the Reverend Charles Cabbage" (930). And Clarke emphatically recalls early proclivities with "Droolings from My Second Childhood: 2," which consists entirely of two lists of purported alien creatures that space travelers "should avoid at all costs," including "The Vomitossity from Venus," "The Screaming Scum from Sinope," "The Dribbling Doom from Deneb," and "The Fulminating Follicules from Fomalhaut" (36–37).

Amusing references to colleagues are commonplace in the White Hart stories, which employ as their framework a fictionalized version of the actual gatherings of Clarke and other science fiction fans in London's White Horse pub during the late 1940s (described in Frank Arnold's "Mordecai of the White Horse"). Patrons mentioned therein include William F. Temple, Charles Eric Maine (pseudonym of David McIlwain), John Christopher, John Beynon Harris (better known as John Wyndham), and George Whitley (pseudonym of A. Bertram Chandler). At times, writers are gently ridiculed: in "Silence Please" (1950) one patron "had just lost his temper with John Christopher (we all do this at some time or other)" (246); in "Armaments Race" (1954) "Bill Temple" was "still rankling over the fact that some perfectly serious stories had just been returned by an American editor on the grounds that they hadn't made him laugh" (476); and in "The Next Tenants" (1957), when Purvis mentions a "myrmecologist," an uncomprehending Whitley asks, "A which-what?" (587).

In later novels Clarke makes humorous references to other writers. To justify the decision to keep the lunar monolith a secret, officials in *2001* cite the extreme reactions of experimental subjects who are told about the existence of aliens in a psychological research project called "Project BARSOOM" (168), the name of Mars in Edgar Rice Burroughs's Mars novels. Both *The Ghost from the Grand Banks* (21) and *3001: The Final Odyssey* (218) mention Isaac Asimov's fictional robot psychologist, Susan Calvin, as a real female scientist along with actual female scientists Ada Lovelace and Grace Hopper. The later novel's Frank Poole "often said to himself, 'I am a Stranger in a Strange Land,'" said to be "paraphrasing the title of a famous book he had read in his youth" (87)—Robert A. Heinlein's *Stranger in a Strange Land* (1961). Another writer, Brian W. Aldiss, is identified in *The Ghost from the Grand Banks* as "Lord Aldiss of Brightfount . . . President Emeritus, Science Fiction World Association" (45) (recalling Aldiss's first book, *The Brightfount Diaries* [1955]).

Clarke also refers to himself several times in White Hart stories, using one of his pseudonyms, Charles Willis, and in "The Pacifist" (1956) Willis defeats a computerized version of tic-tac-toe that ordinarily defeats human opponents—but only by cheating. "Coming Distractions" makes reference to *2001*, as one book considered is *"Programming Instructions for the HAL 9000 Computer* (Revised Edition)." Arguably Clarke's first sequel to *2001*, the review reports that the book "has been updated to incorporate improvements suggested by this versatile machine's surviving users" and that one "priority" is "the retrofitting of small explosive charges at strategic points in the Central Memory Unit" (38). Clarke recycles this bit of whimsy as an addendum to his 1997 "Foreword: The Birth of HAL": its bibliography of "Further Readings," after listing eight actual books, concludes with the *"Operational Manual for the HAL 9000 Computer: Revised Edition,"* published by "Miskatonic University Press, 2010" (a nod to Lovecraft), which "advises the fitting of small explosive charges at key points in the mainframe" (xvi).

Several self-deprecating references to Clarke and his works appear in later novels. In *The Fountains of Paradise* a cited expert is "Dr. Charles Willis" (61), and a character recalls "an old space movie" featuring "a shuttle craft of some kind with a circular observation lounge" called "something like *Space Wars 2000*" (151). *The Ghost from the Grand Banks* also sardonically refers to *2001*: the date "1 January 2001" became "an anticlimax, except to a few movie buffs" (19); Jason Bradley thinks about "a space movie whose name he couldn't recall" featuring "a dead astronaut cradled in mechanical arms" (183); and he notes that "whatever science fiction writers may have pretended, robots won't lie" (237), recalling *2001*'s deceitful HAL. *The Hammer of God* (1992) explains that a future project had "taken" its name, Spaceguard, from "an obscure Twentieth-Century science-fiction novel" (14), alluding to *Rendezvous with Rama*. After noting that the "pale, oval islands" in Jupiter's atmosphere "appeared to thrust so purposefully through the cloudscape around them that it was easy to believe they were enormous living creatures," the novel says, "More than one fanciful astro-epic had been based on just this hypothesis" (135), a dismissive comment on "A Meeting with Medusa" (1971). In 3001 Poole thinks, "Someone once said that any sufficiently advanced technology is indistinguishable from magic" (35), suggesting people in the future may recall Clarke's Third Law without remembering his name.

In pieces one might characterize as Clarke's mature juvenilia, one further encounters the broad, silly humor of Clarke's adolescent writings. Among the fictitious books described in "Coming Distractions" is "*One Hundred and First on the Moon* by Commander Hank Klugenschaft," the "eagerly-awaited story of the voyage of Apollo 67," explaining that he abandoned his crewmate on the moon because of his "most unfortunate failing. He persistently cheated at Scrabble" (37). In "The Steam-Powered Word Processor" a nineteenth-century parson attempts to construct a computer to automatically write weekly sermons. The vignette "Tales from the 'White Hart,' 1990: The Jet-Propelled Time Machine" (1990) describes an opportunistic gigolo who seeks to deceive an elderly film actress by arguing that he can make her younger by repeatedly flying over the International Date Line, because they and their crew will lose one day each time they do so. Impossibly, the method proves effective, for when rescuers reach the man's airplane after it runs out of gas, they discover a "beautiful young woman and five babies" (84).

In sum, while this facet of his personality emerged only rarely, ample evidence shows that, to an extent, Clarke continued to be Clericus throughout his career, always ready to be amused by indulgences in infantile humor. Perhaps when his journals are revealed in 2038, we will discover they are filled not only with anecdotes and reminiscences but also with raucous parodies and outlandish jokes that he chose not to publish.

One question left to consider is whether this adolescent sense of humor underlies much of Clarke's ostensibly serious fiction. Certainly, *The Ghost from the Grand Banks* might be regarded as an extended joke about the futility of human efforts to resist nature, as evidenced by the sinking of the *Titanic*, the novel's unsuccessful attempts to raise the *Titanic*, and the anticipated failure of far-future aliens to accomplish the same goal. One might also detect sly humor in the way that humanity, in works like *Against the Fall of Night,* *Childhood's End,* and the *2001* novels, is always progressing to remarkable new heights, though the results never seem entirely successful. It might be, then, that Clarke went to his grave wryly amused by the fact that because some of his jokes were so subtly understated, readers persisted in taking them seriously.

CHAPTER 3

MARVELOUS MACHINES

The youthful Clarke was an amateur inventor of sorts: he constructed tele-scopes and a device for broadcasting information via light beams that, decades later, he still spoke of with pride. He also grew up reading science fiction maga-zines featuring stories that foregrounded inventors and their achievements. One might imagine that inventors and inventions would become central to his science fiction, yet they are not. As Clarke commented in the revised preface to *The Challenge of the Spaceship* (1961), "Machines are less important than what men do with them" (7), and while focusing on machines' uses, he is usually critical of their inventors, due to their questionable motives and inventions that bring more problems than benefits. Inventions function properly and helpfully, it seems, only when they are perfected after centuries, even millen-nia, of effort and their inventors are long dead and forgotten.

Clarke does not oppose technological innovations, and he acknowledges that civilizations require technology in "Second Dawn" (1951), which describes two intelligent alien races that lack manipulative organs and hence cannot construct anything. Though they have partially compensated for this deficiency by developing telepathy, they remain frustrated by their inability to affect their planet and cannot alleviate the problem of limited supplies of food, which keeps driving them toward war. Hence, after one species encounters a third race with tentacles that is mastering Stone Age technology, the aliens begin collaborating with them in hopes of becoming a true technological civilization and improving their lives. *The Songs of Distant Earth* notes that undersea creatures are also hindered because they cannot master technology, as "without fire" the intelligent "scorps" "are trapped in a technological cul-de-sac" (200). Clearly, humans always have, and always will, need machines, but Clarke repeatedly warns that as one consequence, people must deal with numerous problems that typically arise while the machines are developed.

In addition to inventors' propensity for crafting imperfect and damaging machines, there are other reasons Clarke may have avoided celebrating inventors. A brief play, *Two Hours in a Lab: A One-Act Drama with a Smashing Finale* (1933), suggests that during his science classes, he proved less than adept at hands-on science, as it describes two students, attempting to complete an experiment, who clumsily destroy most of their equipment. Clarke comments in *Childhood Ends* that the play "was partly inspired by a real event, when I connected one pole of a car-battery to one end of a rheostat—and the other to a slider. I leave the result as a 'thought experiment' for the reader" (10). His wartime contributions to developing a system to help aircraft land in inclement weather were clearly more successful, although they may also have involved undisclosed blunders (such as, perhaps, the almost disastrous misidentification of an airplane in *Glide Path*). More broadly, that experience demonstrated that when people work on new projects, many things may go wrong; indeed, in *Glide Path* recurring technical problems generate most of the drama.

Clarke also learned during World War II that major innovations require teams of dedicated individuals with strong institutional support, making it difficult to craft plausible stories about heroic inventors single-handedly producing amazing inventions; indeed, he suggests there is something almost inherently sinister about scientists who work alone, refusing to work collaboratively. And while he undoubtedly appreciated the technicians on his team,

Clarke possibly discovered he did not like them; one subplot of *Glide Path* involves the protagonist's visceral dislike for a pilot, which ultimately evolves into mutual respect but not a friendship. This might explain why after the war he pursued a career as a theoretical scientist, since being an astronomer would never require working on complicated equipment.

One must finally consider how Clarke's opinion of inventors was affected by the major invention of the 1940s: the atomic bomb. Despite hopes that atomic energy could benefit society, it primarily represented a way that humanity might destroy itself. As it happens, the negative effects of atomic power are addressed in Clarke's two forays into realistic fiction during the postwar era. "The Broken Circuit" (1951) involves a wealthy Japanese man in 1945 who is ecstatic because two sets of conservative parents have finally agreed to let him marry the woman of his dreams. He telephones her, anxious to have her leave her city home to join him in the countryside, but the connection is broken. When the last line reveals she lives in Hiroshima, readers understand that she has been killed by an atomic bomb. In "Critical Mass" (1949; revised to include Harry Purvis in 1957), bus driver Jimmy Morgan, leaving an atomic facility, experiences brake failure and crashes into a ditch. When he frantically runs away, patrons of a nearby pub assume the crash has released lethal radiation and flee. The (mild) humor of the conclusion is that Morgan was actually carrying a load of bees, which angrily flew toward him after the crash. Beyond realistic incidents, Clarke during this period also ponders the familiar nightmare of global nuclear war in stories discussed below.

Clarke most frequently features inventors and inventions in Harry Purvis's tall tales, all but one collected in *Tales from the White Hart* (1957), though inventors occasionally appear in other stories. These works reveal some recurring concerns about inventions: the motives of inventors are usually questionable; new machines frequently malfunction or have undesirable side effects; and even if they function properly, inventions can be grievously misused. After long periods of development and implementation, machines may be perfected, but even such machines may succumb to the ravages of time.

Clarke avoids one trope of pulp science fiction: the mad scientist or evil scientist, In fact, scientists in his stories who do not work with machines are generally sympathetic characters, such as the avuncular Professor Kazan of

Dolphin Island: A Story of the People of the Sea (1963) and lunar astronomers of "Earthlight" (1951) and "Dog Star" (1962), and Clarke made a brilliant mathematician the protagonist of *The Last Theorem*.

However, Clarke's inventors are rarely benign, actively seeking to benefit humanity; instead, they typically want to make themselves rich. The technician who creates a silencing device in "Silence Please" "was always making gadgets in his spare time" because he "imagined he could make his fortune from the radio tubes and other oddments lying around the lab" (247). In "Armaments Race" the "best special-effects man in Hollywood" (476) accidentally builds a death ray solely as part of earning his living. Dr. Grinnell, who develops a way to mentally control animals in "Big Game Hunt" (1956), is motivated to perfect his device by a celebrity scientist who "probably dangled vast appropriations before Grinnell's eyes" (497). In "Patent Pending" (1954) the assistant to a man who invents a machine that records human emotions, "being a Frenchman of a more practical turn of mind" (501), approaches business executives about marketing such recordings and soon has "a substantial cheque in his pocket" (505). A man frustrated by the high cost of whiskey in "Moving Spirit" (1957) develops an accelerated method to illegally produce whiskey. In "Cold War" (1957) a man constructs an "artificial iceberg" to damage Florida's reputation for "a substantial sum of money" (595); the scientist in "Sleeping Beauty" (1957) crafts a cure for snoring solely because he is "somewhat short of money" (601); and another scientist in "The Man Who Ploughed the Sea" (1957) perfects a method for extracting valuable minerals from seawater, hoping that "once we've unlocked that treasure chest, we'll be all set for eternity" (619). Avarice on a broader scale motivates a scientific initiative in "On Golden Seas" (1986), as this parody of President Ronald Reagan's proposed antimissile system describes a future president who launches a dubious initiative to reduce the nation's deficit by extracting gold from seawater using "hydrogen bombs" (936). One further recalls that the inventors of a time machine in "Into the Past" only want to profit by retrieving science fiction magazines.

If not greedy, inventors in Harry Purvis stories may have other lamentable motives. In "Let There Be Light" (1957) a frustrated husband seeks to employ a beam of light to temporarily blind his unfaithful wife while she drives on a winding mountain road so that she will swerve off the road and plummet to her death, but he accidentally kills his wife's lover instead. In "Big Game

Hunt" the mind-controlling device is deployed to boost the reputation of a self-promoting scientist; in "Silence Please" an inventor is persuaded to use his device to silence a disliked opera singer; and "The Pacifist" features a scientist who reprograms a computer, designed to provide military strategies, to instead spew out insults at a despised general. A Japanese scientist in "The Next Tenants" wants to breed intelligent termites to replace the human race. Finally, the protagonist of "The Reluctant Orchid" (1956) is not an inventor—merely the discoverer of a carnivorous plant—but seeks to misuse his discovery by having the plant devour his unpleasant aunt.

Spectacularly tainted motives are displayed by unnamed scientists and engineers in "Technical Error" (1946) who craft a new sort of power plant using superconductivity. An accident plunges a technician through the fourth dimension and reverses his orientation, down to the molecular level, so he cannot digest normal food. One would think the people running the plant, surprised and delighted to discover a way to travel through the fourth dimension, would seek to understand the method and explore its potential benefits. But these issues do not arise; everyone's sole concern is that the transformed technician requires molecularly reversed food that is prohibitively expensive. Gazing solely at the bottom line, they persuade the technician to undergo a second sojourn in the fourth dimension to be switched back to normal, and announce no plans for further experiments. The tragic result is a fatal explosion, since the process unexpectedly involves travel through both time and space.

"Technical Error" also illustrates the second problem with inventions in Clarke's fiction: they frequently malfunction or have unexpected consequences; for whatever its virtues, this power plant also causes a fatal accident. Other stories feature malfunctioning machines: the noise-absorbing device in "Silence Please" explodes and kills its inventor; artificial experiences from an emotion-recording machine in "Patent Pending" are so alluring to a scientist that his mistress is driven to murder him; the scientist who builds a machine that plays "The Ultimate Melody" (1957), entranced by the tune, becomes comatose; the prop weapon in "Armaments Race" actually destroys walls and starts fires; in "Big Game Hunt" a device that mentally controls animals stops working due to a blown fuse, enabling a giant squid to kill the scientist manipulating him; and in "Sleeping Beauty" a drug eliminating the need for sleep frustrates its user, since the extra time only bores him, but an antidote makes him permanently fall asleep.

Two other White Hart stories involve machines that do not work properly: In "What Goes Up" (1956) a nuclear reactor generates an antigravity field, so a scientist must painstakingly travel the equivalent of four thousand miles up to reach a reactor twenty feet away, only to die when he falls off its platform and plummets the equivalent of four thousand miles to his death. In "The Defenestration of Ermintrude Inch" (1957) a talkative wife causes a word-counting machine to be inaccurate by playing an endlessly repeating tape recording of her husband's voice. Another humorous story, "An Ape about the House" (1962), involves the unexpected effects of a biological "invention" termed "The Superchimp," an intelligent, genetically modified chimpanzee (798). An astronaut's wife, seeking to humiliate a female rival who fancies herself a talented painter, pretends to teach her superchimp servant to paint superior pictures but is actually painting them herself. Her suspicious rival prods the ape to paint while she watches, and the result—an unflattering caricature of her owner—suggests that she does not like her human master and might prove an unreliable servant. Still, advanced "superchimps," or "simps," are effective employees on the airship of Clarke's "A Meeting with Medusa" and the spaceship of *Rendezvous with Rama*.

Clarke's most powerful argument about the way new machines typically malfunction comes in "Superiority" (1951), wherein aliens poised to win a war with another race unwisely build and deploy fantastic new weapons, which invariably have developmental problems rendering them useless or counterproductive; their enemies then defeat them with inferior but reliable weapons. At one point, for example, the aliens' latest machine increases the distance between the machine and surrounding objects almost to infinity, making a spaceship both invisible and inaccessible to enemies; yet this machine also introduces irregularities in the equipped spaceships, making them dysfunctional.

Even if they work properly, new inventions may have unexpected, and undesirable, consequences. The scientific process in "The Man Who Ploughed the Sea" extracts uranium from seawater but is useless because the cost of the process exceeds the value of the uranium it provides. In "Time's Arrow" (1950) secretive physicists develop a time machine, but when paleontologists excavating dinosaur footprints at a nearby site discover prehistoric tire tracks, they recognize that the physicists who traveled into the past became the dinosaurs' prey. In "The Food of the Gods" (1964) (a title borrowed from H. G. Wells's 1904 novel), a delicious new sort of artificial meat seems an ideal way to sustain a future population that abhors eating animals, but its manufacturer's competitor informs a legislative panel that they achieved this appealing food by duplicating human flesh, effectively turning people into cannibals. In "The Cruel Sky" (1967) a machine that counteracts gravity beneficially allows its brilliant but disabled inventor and a companion to climb Mount Everest by reducing his weight, but after using the device to escape from a snowstorm, they land in a region where they cannot broadcast a message to potential rescuers. They avoid dying solely because, fortuitously, a snow leopard accidentally turns on the antigravity machine and ascends high enough to be detected, indicating the men's peril and their location.

Worthwhile inventions can also be employed to achieve sinister or inappropriate ends. As indicated earlier, a silencing machine is deployed to punish an opera singer in "Silence Please," and Clarke on three occasions describes ingenious ways to harm people by means of long-distance radiation. A powerful light is employed to commit murder in "Let There Be Light," while in "The Light of Darkness" (1966) a scientist uses a radio telescope and transmitter to blind an African nation's leader and end his rule—a justifiable action because he is an evil dictator. In "A Slight Case of Sunstroke" (1958) soccer fans, displeased by a biased referee's unfair decisions, employ special programs covered with silver to simultaneously reflect the sun's light onto the referee, incinerating him. "I Remember Babylon" (1960) surprisingly describes the potential misuse of the invention most readers regard as the most valuable innovation Clarke ever predicted: geosynchronous communications satellites. But when Clarke (the story's narrator) encounters a leftist American television producer, he learns he is collaborating with the Russians and others to set up satellites to broadcast a mixture of pornography and propaganda to undermine American society.

In Clarke's fiction the only flawless and entirely beneficial inventions are the final products of lengthy periods of development. The point is made in *Imperial Earth* as protagonist Duncan Makenzie feels "protected" on Saturn's "hostile" moon Titan "by all the safety devices that three hundred years of space technology could contrive" (3–4). Similarly infallible machines are found in the far-future cities of Diaspar (in *Against the Fall of Night* and *The City and the Stars*) and Comarre (in "The Lion of Comarre" [1949]). Their very perfection, however, illustrates the problem facing protagonists, as this technology reflects and maintains the stagnation they abhor. Even in the near future of *Imperial Earth*, the popularity of the deliberately surprising experiences provided by the Enigma company suggests that people are growing bored in a world serviced by perfected machines.

In Clarke's later works, usually set only a few hundred years in the future, the devices most frequently described facilitate communication, like the "vision phone" of *2001* (screenplay b17). In *Imperial Earth* ubiquitous "Comsoles" (communication consoles) allow citizens to communicate and obtain information in a manner not unlike personal computers. *The Hammer of God* predicts an advanced version of such devices called the "Brainman," which individuals wear on shaved heads to directly connect their brains to computer databases and networks; Poole dons a similar innovation, the "Braincap," in *3001*. *Rendezvous with Rama* also refers to protective "thermosuits" (47), "electrosan toilets" (72), and a device for disintegrating trash, the "electrosan" (171).

Even devices that work perfectly well for eons, though, may be damaged or succumb to the aging process that afflicts both humans and machines. In "Nemesis" (1950) a device designed to awaken a hibernating dictator after one hundred years fails to work because "three tiny instruments and their connections" are "swept away" by "hundreds of tons of falling rock" after an "explosion" (195). In another version of the story, 1952's "The Awakening," a man long remains hibernating in a spaceship because "during the long ages . . . something had failed among the circuits that should have awakened him" (92). The same problem afflicts the monoliths manipulating human destiny, now characterized as computers, in *2061: Odyssey Three* (1987) and *3001*; because they appear to be malfunctioning due to their extreme age, humans must disable them before they endanger humanity.

One theme of *The Ghost from the Grand Banks* is the ineffectiveness of technology in the face of natural forces that are as unpredictable as the infinitely complex Mandelbrot Set referenced in the novel. The point is illustrated by the unexpected storm that kills two scientists' precocious daughter and the iceberg that destroyed the *Titanic*. As if to reaffirm the power of innovative machinery, however, teams of scientists and entrepreneurs are devising ways to raise the ship's two sunken parts: one team will surround one part in an artificial iceberg, causing it to rise to the surface, while the other will fill the second part with billions of microscopic glass spheres to provide buoyancy. Yet both efforts are thwarted by a massive earthquake that buries the ship in "half a billion tons of mud" (242). The aliens who undertake to raise the *Titanic* from deep underground in the novel's epilogue, clearly, will be similarly unsuccessful. (This famous disaster is also mentioned in *Rendezvous with Rama* as explorers embarking upon a makeshift boat to cross a Raman sea are ominously advised, "Remember the *Titanic!*" [106].)

Only one of Clarke's novels—*The Fountains of Paradise*—focuses on an amazing new invention: a space elevator that will connect Earth's surface to a base in geosynchronous orbit and greatly reduce the cost and difficulty of traveling from Earth into space. Protagonist Vannemar Morgan is not the device's inventor but rather the engineer who undertakes to construct the massive machine. Still, Morgan shares two traits with Clarke's typical inventors: he has suspect motives, and he is not particularly sympathetic.

Seeking support for his project, Morgan asserts that he wishes to build the space elevator because it will be a profitable boon to human progress; yet no one, including Morgan himself, believes he is genuinely altruistic. Although Kathryn Hume asserts, "Clarke does not spell out Morgan's underlying motives" (382), they are conveyed clearly enough when he muses, "If he succeeded in the task that confronted him, he would be famous for centuries to come" (32), confirming Hume's point that he feels "a craving for immortality" (382). Whether the asexual Morgan is also motivated by "phallic uncertainty" (382), however, remains less clear, as he seems more asexual than sexually frustrated.

References to Morgan's dubious motives appear throughout the novel. Learning of the project, one potential ally remarks, "Of course you intend to be in charge" (97). When he cannot gain access to the mountain on the island of Taprobane that is required for the project, and loses his job, his retirement is interrupted by a Martian executive who recruits him to craft a Martian space elevator by saying, "You are the sort of man who will never be really happy . . . unless you are shaping the universe," a "prognosis" Morgan thinks is "much too accurate for comfort" (115). Contemplating a crisis, Morgan "was not ashamed of the fact that the safety of the project now concerned him far more than any loss of life" (192). Journalist Maxine Duval acknowledges that while "she admired Morgan enormously. . . . she did not really like him," because "the sheer drive and ruthlessness of his ambition made him both larger than life and less than human" (133–34). Obviously, Morgan is driven to build a space elevator primarily, if not solely, by an enormous ego.

Even Morgan's apparently selfless acts are reported in a manner arousing suspicions about his true nature. When he unexpectedly has equipment installed that allows the elderly Rajasinghe to continue using his telescope, the man sees this as "a side of the engineer's personality he had not suspected" (217), indicating that this was the first time Morgan had been kind to him. After volunteering to single-handedly rescue a team of scientists stranded in the middle of the incomplete elevator, Morgan ponders his weak heart and wonders, "Was he gambling with other lives as well as his own just to satisfy his selfish pride?" (204). Returning to Earth, he refuses to call for "a doctor on stand-by" because of "a stubborn pride" (247). Thus, Morgan apparently does nice things only because he wishes to be lauded as a hero.

To emphasize his less than admirable qualities, the novel repeatedly likens Morgan to the ancient king Kalidasa, notorious for his cruelty and brutality, who nonetheless was responsible for noteworthy architectural achievements, including large frescoes of beautiful women and beautiful fountains. Pondering Kalidasa's career, Morgan thinks, "The King might have been a monster, but there was something about his character that struck a chord in the secret places of Morgan's own heart" (32). Rajasinghe calls Morgan's project "an enterprise to fire the imagination and stir the soul. Kalidasa would have envied—and approved" (58). Morgan worries that efforts to seize the mountain from the priests occupying it "could make him a villain, not a hero" (86). The epilogue indicates that despite Morgan's hopes of becoming famous, the space elevator eventually becomes known as "the Tower of Kalidasa" (255). Unlike Kalidasa, Morgan is never violent or deceitful, yet the novel suggests that in order to accomplish great things, individuals may have to be unpleasantly "hardheaded and unsentimental" (19), as Morgan describes himself.

Like other Clarke novels, *The Fountains of Paradise* refers to several items of advanced technology that were introduced long before events in the novel and function flawlessly: recalling the "thermosuits" of *Rendezvous with Rama*, people are protected against cold weather by a "thermocoat" (67) or "thermosuit" (170) made of "metalized fabric" (68); in space Morgan moves freely because his improved space suit, termed a "Flexisuit," "bore little resemblance to the clumsy armor of the early astronauts" (206); and Morgan's physician displays images of heart-protecting technology on a "holopad" (157).

But the novel's central piece of machinery, the space elevator, is still being developed, and inevitably, during the process, problems arise. A pilot project to drop a hyperfilament from space to Taprobane is disrupted by a freak storm, though this is a deliberate act of sabotage by a monk using weather-controlling technology. When construction begins there are a number of unfortunate deaths, two of them described at length, and the culminating crisis involves a solar storm that disables a vehicle and strands scientists halfway up the tower in a crude structure called the "Basement"; lacking oxygen and supplies, they seem destined to die. When Morgan undertakes to rescue them, he is temporarily thwarted because a safety strap was not removed, so an exhausted battery cannot be jettisoned to speed his craft toward its destination. Even after it is dislodged, Morgan will apparently run out of power before he can deliver supplies. As it happens, automatic construction of the space elevator moves him far enough to complete his mission, but he dies while returning to Earth due to ineffectual technology: the automatic monitoring device CORA (or "coronary alarm"), which is attached to Morgan to ensure he does not die because of his frail heart, cannot summon aid while he travels down the space elevator. It is thus difficult to accept Hume's claim that the novel represents Clarke's "hymn of praise to future technology" (387), for, as in other works, reasons to criticize future technology are conveyed as well.

As a final irony, although the epilogue reveals the space elevator was completed, later becoming one of several space elevators connecting Earth to space, it ultimately cannot fulfill its purpose, because the sun unexpectedly cools, forcing people to leave Earth and live on the now temperate Mercury and Venus. Thus, the space elevator is effectively abandoned, employed only by occasional visitors to the now frigid Earth.

In their overall themes, then, this novel and *The Ghost from the Grand Banks* are surprisingly congruent, although *The Fountains of Paradise* seemingly describes a technological initiative that succeeds while the later novel involves one that fails. Yet Morgan observes, "Nature was his real antagonist" (37), and in both novels the power of nature ultimately demonstrates what Rajasinghe terms "the futility of ambition" (55). Tellingly, the ancient monk who opposes Kalidasa refers to one massive construction as "Kalidasa's folly" (6), while Morgan's previous triumph, the Gibraltar Bridge, had been called "Morgan's Folly" (37). Perhaps all of humanity's technological achievements, in the long run, are follies: nature destroys the *Titanic* and prevents its retrieval, and though nature does not stop Morgan from constructing his space elevator, it renders the structure useless by making Earth uninhabitable.

Further overshadowing Morgan's achievement is an event that makes it seem unimportant: the arrival of advanced alien visitors who study and interact with humanity though they in turn are fearful of other, even more advanced aliens. In such a cosmos, human inventions—even massive constructs like the space elevator—are insignificant.

The Fountains of Paradise has attracted little critical attention, though scholars usually agree with Eric S. Rabkin that it depicts an admirable "engineer hero" whose adventures illustrate Clarke's "scientific optimism" and "profession of his faith" (63–64), ignoring Morgan's questionable character, consistently troubled project, and its ultimate unimportance. Even Hume, who acknowledges Morgan's flaws, argues that he is ultimately vindicated by his valiant rescue, although that action is tainted by questionable motives. It may seem logical to assume that Clarke's novel celebrates an individual dedicated to scientific progress, yet as evidenced here and elsewhere, Clarke actually takes a jaundiced view of such people's personalities and accomplishments.

It is finally worth noting that, except for Diaspar, other grand structures in Clarke's fiction are built by aliens, not humans: in "Jupiter Five" (1953) the Jovian moon Amalthea is an immense alien spacecraft; a similarly enormous alien spaceship appears in *Rendezvous with Rama*; and the humorous "Love That Universe" (1967) mentions immense "stellar structures obeying no natural laws" (779), detected in the Magellanic Clouds, that demonstrate the existence of "supercivilizations" (780) with amazing capabilities that hopefully can rescue humanity if contacted by a global artificial orgasm.

Clarke also intimates that advanced civilizations may reach a stage when they no longer need machines. When Earth's children become a group intelligence in *Childhood's End*, they require no technology to destroy Earth and embark upon a cosmic voyage to join the Overmind, and the novel *2001* states that the monolith builders "learned . . . to preserve their thoughts for eternity in frozen lattices of light" so as to "become creatures of radiation, free at last from the tyranny of matter," who "discarded" the machines that previously housed their intellects (185–86). Such superbeings, it appears, require machines only to interact with lesser species that are still bound to matter. Hence, the Overmind deploys the technology-dependent Overlords to oversee humanity's advancement, and the *2001* aliens use monoliths—recast in sequels to *2001* as supercomputers—to influence human development.

In many respects, therefore, inventions are not important components of Clarke's worldview. While essential to human progress, they usually emerge from impure motives, and their development is fraught with problems. Their proper role, once perfected, is to fade into the background, functioning virtually unnoticed to improve human lives in small ways, and at some stage in a species' evolution they may become unnecessary. Still, there is one type of futuristic machinery that Clarke especially cherished: the technology required for humans to explore and conquer space.

CHAPTER 4

THE CONQUEST OF SPACE

One of Clarke's most misunderstood statements is the comment in *Childhood's End* that "the opinions expressed in this book are not those of the author" (4). Apparently, Clarke is conveying that he disagrees with the novel's central theme: that humanity will someday evolve into a group intelligence with abilities and aspirations unknowable to present-day humans. In fact, as explained in his 1990 foreword to *Childhood's End*, he is addressing a side issue: "I had just published *The Exploration of Space* [1951], and painted an optimistic picture of our future expansion into the Universe. Now I had written a book which said 'The stars are not for Man,' and I did not want anyone to think I had suddenly recanted" (vi). Clearly, Clarke wished to be regarded as a consistent believer in future space exploration in both his nonfiction and his fiction.

Clarke was an advocate for space travel throughout his life. In his 1994 epilogue to *Frontline of Discovery: Science on the Brink of Tomorrow*, Clarke declares, "The exploration of space has been the main interest of my life" (192).

His devotion to that goal first became evident in juvenilia like "Interviews with Notorieties," "How We Went to Mars," and "Letters to the Secretary of an Interplanetary Society" as well as articles outlining plausible plans for space initiatives. Space travel then became central to his writing career: his nonfiction books about space travel were his first successes and long remained popular, and all of his novels involve space travel in some fashion. Even those that take place primarily in Earth's oceans—*The Deep Range*, *Dolphin Island*, and *The Ghost from the Grand Banks*—include passages about space travel.

Unlike Robert A. Heinlein, Clarke made no effort to unite disparate works to form a cohesive narrative; as Edward James observes, he was "much more concerned to keep up to date with current scientific developments than to complete obsessively the chapters of a consistent Future History" ("Arthur C. Clarke" 437). Still, there occasionally are specific connections between stories: the oxygen-producing plants and Martian animals of *Sands of Mars* are glimpsed in photographs in *Islands in the Sky* (1952); "tractors" are used for lunar transportation in both "The Sentinel" (1951) and "Earthlight"; "thermo-suits" to protect against cold temperatures appear in *Rendezvous with Rama*, *The Fountains of Paradise*, and *The Songs of Distant Earth*; a presumed ancestor of *Imperial Earth*'s Duncan Makenzie, though his name is spelled Duncan McKenzie, is one stranded passenger in *A Fall of Moondust*; as James notes, the Treaty of Phobos that concludes the conflict in *Earthlight* (1955) is mentioned in *Imperial Earth*; travelers from Earth stop at Space Station One in both *Sands of Mars* and the novel *2001*; the Pasteur Space Hospital orbiting Earth is visited in both *Islands in the Sky* and *2061* and referenced in *The Songs of Distant Earth*, which also mentions the Gibraltar Bridge constructed by *The Fountains of Paradise*'s Morgan; *2001*'s Clavius Base is observed from space by Captain Singh in both the story "The Hammer of God" (1992) and its novel version; and the Martian city of Port Lowell, principal setting of *Sands of Mars*, is named in *The Deep Range*, "Playback" (1966), *The Lost Worlds of 2001*, *Rendezvous with Rama*, *Imperial Earth*, and *The Hammer of God*.

More significantly, there is a broad consistency in the way Clarke describes humans expanding throughout the solar system, envisioning space stations as stopping points for people leaving or visiting Earth; regular missions through space for various purposes; and large communities on the moon, Mars, Mercury, and the moons of Jupiter and Saturn. Since Clarke came of age reading science fiction magazines promoting the notion that science fiction can and should predict the future, he is presumably presenting, in fictional form, the actual conquest of space he anticipates and is comfortable having stories later reexamined to assess the accuracy of their predictions.

Thus, in later introductions to earlier works, he regularly boasts of prophetic successes and apologizes for errors but never revises them to conceal missteps—except on one occasion. It evidently bothered Clarke that one of his most popular novels, *Childhood's End*, begins by unfortunately predicting that humans would never reach space, due to the Overlords' arrival, so in 1990 he rewrote the opening chapter to have the aliens arrive at the future moment when humans are preparing missions to Mars (though he later reinstated the original prologue).

In some respects Clarke's space fiction reflects a consensus opinion about humanity's future in space that Clarke himself helped to forge. In the 1950s he began influencing other science fiction writers by abandoning the discredited notion that the solar system contains worlds amenable to human habitation and alien life; instead, he strived to base stories on accurate scientific information about the worlds closest to Earth. But some unusual aspects of Clarke's vision merit exploration.

First, Clarke acknowledges, albeit infrequently, that unmanned vehicles and onboard computers would be essential partners in conquering space. Second, he displays little interest in pioneering achievements, as milestones like the first expeditions to various worlds are typically mentioned briefly if at all; rather, he foregrounds the everyday life of space travelers and colonists in a solar system that has already been explored, sometimes offering little traditional drama. Third, Clarke emphasizes the constant and numerous dangers of life in space, and while most protagonists avoid disaster, he also describes the deaths of doomed space travelers. Fourth, Clarke's stories offer interesting perspectives on how living in space will affect human personalities and behavior, particularly celebrating its health benefits. Fifth, other than in early humorous stories, Clarke never anticipates discovering intelligent aliens in the solar system, although several stories feature evidence of ancient alien civilizations or alien visitors, or signs that forms of intelligent life are emerging.

Finally, while most writers view colonizing the solar system as merely humanity's first step in exploring the galaxy, employing faster-than-light travel,

Clarke predicts these developments only in unrepresentative stories, more commonly describing a future humanity that is long content to remain in the solar system. He views venturing into interstellar space as especially daunting because of his belief, expressed in the "Author's Note" of *The Songs of Distant Earth*, that "we may never exceed the velocity of light" (xiii). Such mastery of the solar system and nothing beyond is described most thoroughly in *Imperial Earth*.

The role of machines in exploring space is central to the overlooked *The Exploration of the Moon* (1954). Officially nonfiction, the book can also be considered a science-fictional "future history," recalling Olaf Stapledon's novels, which omits individual characters to offer overviews of future events. Formatted as lengthy captions to illustrations, the book provides a generally conventional picture of humanity's near future in space: preliminary flights into Earth's orbit, a pioneering journey to the moon, and establishment of a lunar colony. Yet the book repeatedly stresses that unmanned vehicles will precede each human initiative: space travel will begin with an "Instrument-carrying Rocket" (18), followed by human orbital flights, and a "Robot Rocket" (50) will reach the moon before astronauts. *The Exploration of the Moon* further notes that ground and onboard computers will be needed to guide vehicles to proper trajectories and safe landings.

In avowedly fictional stories, Clarke understandably pays less attention to machines, emphasizing human characters and drama for human readers. However, embedded in "Into the Comet" (1960) is the realization that space navigation will require vast numbers of complex calculations—and hence, onboard computers. An expedition to rendezvous with a comet appears doomed because its computer has failed, and no human can possibly do all the intricate calculations needed to get the spaceship safely away from the comet and on a course to Earth. Fortunately, the narrator figures out that by building abacuses for crew members and training them to constantly use the calculating tools, the necessary calculations can be completed so that they can escape the comet and contact rescuers. Clarke thus makes a spaceship computer interesting by having people effectively transform themselves into a computer.

A more common strategy for making computers interesting is to provide them with human-like personalities, as illustrated by *2001*'s HAL 9000, who rebels against humans planning to disable him and later begs for his life. As Eric S. Rabkin notes (38), HAL is anticipated in "Cosmic Casanova" (1958), atypically set in a distant future when humans regularly travel to other solar systems. Its solitary pilot regards his onboard "electronic computer," Max, as "good enough company in the ordinary course of events," though he "often hurt his feelings" when he "lost my temper for no apparent reason" (658–59). Max seems especially like HAL when he declares, "Surely you're not mad at me because I beat you at chess again? Remember, I warned you I would" (659). Yet unlike HAL, Max never malfunctions, so the protagonist can "rely on Max to do his usual flawless job" (662) in landing on an alien planet, where he sadly discovers that its attractive female scientist is gigantic.

HAL's homicidal actions seem to warn that space travelers cannot trust computers; however, Clarke's novel and sequel *2010* emphasize that HAL was victimized by faulty programming, and far from abandoning computers, the first novel's now solitary David Bowman depends on "computers back on Earth" (179) to reach Saturn. HAL is also reprogrammed and rehabilitated in *2010* to effect the astronauts' departure from Jupiter, and after being destroyed, HAL is reborn as Bowman's ethereal companion. Still, computers with personalities are rare in Clarke's fiction; in *Rendezvous with Rama*, for example, the "SPACE-GUARD computers" (3) that detect Rama and the "navigation computer" (12) that guides Commander Norton appear to have no human-like traits.

As one sign of Clarke's faith in machines, *Against the Fall of Night*'s Alvin declares he will never again venture into space but will instead dispatch a spaceship controlled by "a robot" (222) to search for the missing human race.

Another distinctive aspect of Clarke's space fiction is that he is fascinated by everyday life in space, not dramatic heroics, and pays little attention to pioneering expeditions to other worlds. There are exceptions: the six-part series "Venture to the Moon" describes humanity's first journey to the moon; a few stories involve first landings on asteroids and comets; "Transit of Earth" (1971) and "A Meeting with Medusa" respectively focus on the first humans to reach Mars and to penetrate Jupiter's atmosphere; and *2001* and *Rendezvous with Rama* involve unprecedented missions to investigate signs of alien life (all works discussed elsewhere). Usually, however, such initiatives are described or mentioned only during preparatory stages or briefly recalled after they occur.

These tendencies are conspicuous in Clarke's singular story about human-ity's first lunar flight, *Prelude to Space: A Compellingly Realistic Novel of Inter-planetary Flight* (1951). Mentioning this just-completed novel in an August 18, 1947, letter to Lord Dunsany, Clarke calls it a "fictionalised version" of his 1946 essay "The Challenge of the Spaceship." However, adding that it emphasizes "the sociological and philosophical aspects of the matter" (54), he intimates that despite its familiar subject, the novel is entirely different from previous accounts of first lunar missions.

First, the invariable protagonists of these adventures are the crews of the moon-bound spacecraft, yet Clarke's viewpoint character is a historian chroni-cling the initiative who mostly associates with the scientists and bureaucrats working on the project. Candidates to join the crew, in contrast, are minor characters, and the only one developed to any extent is excluded from the flight. Second, in other works the launch occurs at or near the beginning, and the bulk of the tale describes how astronauts reach the moon, explore its surface, and return to Earth. Clarke's novel focuses solely on the process of constructing the spaceship, ending when it is launched; only an epilogue, set decades in the future, reveals almost tangentially that the flight was successful.

Clarke's unusual story conveys distinctive insights regarding humanity's future in space. The truly significant development would not be reaching another world but mastering the technology to make such flights a matter of routine. This effort would prove complex and difficult, requiring literally thousands of scientists, technicians, and administrators and the "virtually un-limited funds" (24) that only governments and large institutions could provide; pioneering space flights could never be achieved by solitary inventors working in their backyards, the pattern of Clarke's "Interviews with Notorieties" and numerous previous stories on this theme. The participants in space missions would not be remarkable heroes but merely well-trained pilots and techni-cians, and with information about their destination already obtained from astronomical observations and unmanned probes their experiences upon reaching the new world would be largely predictable and hardly worth de-scribing, in contrast to the challenging work that made the flight possible.

In these respects *Prelude to Space* seems to be science fiction's most ac-curate prediction of the actual lunar landing in 1969. As books about the *Apollo* program demonstrate, the process of preparing for the mission was more involving than Neil Armstrong and Buzz Aldrin's uneventful sojourn on the moon; the mission required years of effort and enormous sums of money; and its astronauts were merely three members of a team of equally qualified men. Neil McAleer notes that Clarke anticipates a three-man crew, and he remarkably predicts that astronauts would televise their achievement: "Before they leave the ship, they'll broadcast a description of everything they see, and the television camera will be set panning" (108). True, Clarke errs in expecting a spacecraft powered by atomic energy and a launch by means of an ascending ramp, but these lapses seem inconsequential.

As if to vindicate the idiosyncratic approach of *Prelude to Space*, Clarke later provides a contrastingly conventional, and less successful, version of the story, "Venture to the Moon." American, British, and Russian spaceships simultaneously fly to the moon for a generally unexciting visit. Though nations secretly instruct their crews to leave a bit early and reach the lunar surface first, the result is that, as planned, they arrive at the same time. When a supply rocket lands on an inaccessible plateau, an astronaut shoots arrows with a rope and grapnel, allowing crewmates to ascend and retrieve the supplies. A botanist is killed by a seed ejected by the plant he was growing in lunar soil. A geologist's discovery of a huge diamond is rendered inconsequential because his laboratory on Earth has learned to make synthetic diamonds. A rocket is launched to study the thin lunar atmosphere and provide a spectacle for observers on Earth, but an engineer has been bribed to make its sodium form the logo of a soft drink (probably Coca-Cola, from Clarke's hints). And as noted, British crew members stay behind to avoid paying taxes. The only message here not found in *Prelude to Space*—a message that reverberates throughout Clarke's space fiction—is that no matter how carefully missions are planned, unexpected problems are inevitable, requiring improvised solutions.

Future milestones comparable to a first lunar landing are usually marginalized in Clarke's fiction. The epilogue to *Prelude to Space* casually indicates that Victor Hassell, excluded from the lunar mission, later participated in the first expedition to Mars. "The Other Side of the Sky" (1957) concludes by briefly describing preparations for "the first Martian expedition" (644) near its space station. In "Out of the Cradle, Endlessly Orbiting" (1959), a pioneering trip to Mars is about to be launched from the moon, but that seems less important when a worker becomes the father of the first child born on the moon, described as the "first Citizen of Space" (700). *The Ghost from the Grand Banks* fleetingly refers to preparations for humanity's first mission to Mars, to take off from Florida (195).

Humanity's first flight to Mercury is briefly related in *Islands in the Sky* as Commander Doyle, journeying to the Pasteur Space Hospital, relates his experiences during the expedition. The novel *2061* features a character identified as "the first man to land on Mercury" (54), though little is said about his "first landing at Mercury's—relatively—temperate South Pole" (188).

After reaching the inner planets, Clarke typically posits that Saturn will be humanity's next destination, primarily because of what is termed in *Sands of Mars* "a single astonishing stroke of luck. . . . [Its moon] Titan possessed an atmosphere . . . of methane, one of the ideal propellants for atomic rockets" (139). Reaching Saturn was the original goal of the spaceship *Discovery* in *2001*; however, the film substituted Jupiter because special effects personnel found it difficult to render Saturn's rings.

The narrator of "Saturn Rising" has led two expeditions to Saturn, also landing on Titan to refuel, and occasionally speaks about his experiences. But the story focuses on the eventually realized plans of a wealthy hotel owner to construct a hotel on Titan to offer tourists the breathtaking view of Saturn once enjoyed by only a few astronauts. Since Clarke, like the story's Morris Perlman, had been a boy interested in astronomy who abandoned dreams of becoming a scientist to choose another profitable career, one speculates there are autobiographical resonances in this character, perhaps reflecting Clarke's growing realization that despite public optimism about rapid progress in space travel, he would probably never travel into space. Perlman can be contrasted with Heinlein's D. D. Harriman, who dedicates his life and fortune to achieving space travel (as recounted in "The Man Who Sold the Moon" [1950]) and finally, as a dying man, makes his own lunar landing in "Requiem" (1940). Clarke, more realistically, envisions no culminating trip to Saturn for his wealthy dreamer.

A first landing on a Jovian moon is circumspectly referenced in *Rendezvous with Rama* as Norton recalls that he "had also landed on Jupiter VIII" (11), or Pasiphae, and we later learn that he headed the "first voyage to retrograde satellites of Jupiter" (22), one of which is Pasiphae. Another first landing on another world—Pluto—is mentioned in *A Fall of Moondust*, since passengers on the submerged lunar craft include that mission's leader, Commodore Hansteen, "the man ... who had probably landed on more virgin planets and moons than any explorer in history" (28–29). All readers learn about the journey, though, is that it was less arduous than the passengers' plight: "Even on the Pluto run, thought Commodore Hansteen, they had never been as lonely as this. They had had a fine library and had been well stocked with every possible form of canned entertainment, and they could talk by tight beam to the inner planets whenever they wished" (38).

Pioneering expeditions that receive more attention target smaller worlds like comets and asteroids, as in "Into the Comet." A rendezvous with Halley's Comet is the goal of the journey in 2061, though the spaceship is diverted to rescue stranded astronauts on Europa. "Summertime on Icarus" (1960) involves a mission to the asteroid Icarus, which orbits near the sun, making it an ideal base for humans to study the sun while staying on its dark side, protected from lethal radiation by a rock barrier. Another mission to Icarus—"Project Helios" (186–87)—is mentioned in The Hammer of God, which foregrounds a more critical mission to reach and divert an asteroid about to collide with Earth.

Generally avoiding the stock drama of first landings on unexplored worlds, Clarke is content to describe the quotidian experiences of space travelers, confident that the novelties of life beyond Earth will prove sufficiently entertaining. As noted, 2001, 2061, and 3001 are structured as extended travelogues of future worlds transformed by space travel before shifting attention to developments involving the monoliths.

Foregrounding another sort of inconsequential activity, "The Wind from the Sun" (1964) features a sporting activity in space: a race from Earth's orbit to the moon by spacecraft powered by solar sails. Though the race is canceled due to a solar storm, the protagonist sets his abandoned spacecraft on a course to leave the solar system and become humanity's first interstellar traveler. (In The Last Theorem Frederik Pohl borrows language from this story to describe a similar race involving Ranjit Subramanian's daughter, this one interrupted by the arrival of aliens.)

Sports in space are mentioned in other stories: "Holiday on the Moon" (1951) speaks of a lunar colony's "sports clubs" (319) and "games and recreation rooms" (322). Rendezvous with Rama twice refers to the "Lunar Olympics"

(48, 113), with events including foot races and flying races using a "sky-bike" (114), and facilities for sporting events include the moon's "Olympic Dome" (118) and the "Xante Sportsdome" (113), presumably located in Mars's Xanthe Terra region. Finally, the protagonist of *The Hammer of God* competes in a pioneering lunar marathon, traveling primarily by means of carefully calibrated "kangaroo hop[s]" (48), but insufficiently insulated shoes almost cause his feet to freeze while touching the cold lunar surface. Later, having learned to employ "the deep-sea divers' technique of 'liquid breathing,' flooding the lungs with oxygen-saturated fluid," another "vacuum-proofed" man makes a "record two-minute, one-kilometer dash across the Bay of Rainbows—as naked as his Greek ancestors in the very first Olympics, three thousand years earlier" (53).

Another story with little conventional drama, "Refugee" (1955), is a variation on a standard theme: an individual anxious to travel into space stows away on a spaceship. But this stowaway is Prince Henry, heir to the British throne, who must fulfill his dream surreptitiously because his protective government will not permit him to leave Earth. While he enjoys flying to Mars, nothing exciting occurs to disrupt the crew's routine—unless one counts the prince's unexpected offer to cook crewmates a fine meal.

In contrast to Prince Henry, the protagonist of the overlooked "Holiday on the Moon," a young woman named Daphne, has no desire to leave Earth, since she is most interested in the latest fashions from Paris. But when her father, a lunar astronomer, invites Daphne, her mother, and her brother to vacation on the moon, she discovers the wonders of space while staying at her father's observatory and visiting a base on the dark side of the moon, where scientists find a strange, rock-like form of life.

The turning point comes when her father lets her look through a telescope:

The great telescope ranged across the sky, gathering in the wonders of the heavens and presenting them to her gaze. Beautiful groups of coloured stars, like jewels gleaming with all the hues of the rainbow—clouds of incandescent mist, twisted into strange shapes by unimaginable forces—Jupiter and his family of moons—and, perhaps most wonderful of all, Saturn floating serenely in his circle of rings, like some intricate work of art rather than a world eight times the size of Earth. . . . [Clarke's ellipses]

> And now she understood the magic that had lured the astronomers up into the clear mountain skies, and at last out across space to the Moon. (324)

Clarke intimates that living in space will fundamentally change human attitudes, as Daphne later muses, "Earth was no longer everything that mattered. . . . It was only one world among many, merely the first of the planets on which men had lived. One day, perhaps, it would not even seem the most important" (331).

"Holiday on the Moon" also suggests that women will become key players in conquering space—though specifying only that they will dominate astronomy: "In the twentieth century more and more women had made their names in" that field "until in some of its branches they had outnumbered the men" (329). Clarke emphasizes a female character primarily because he was commissioned to write the story for a women's magazine, but it is an early sign that he is willing to anticipate larger roles for women in space, as later shown by female scientists in 2001 and female astronauts in *Rendezvous with Rama*. "Holiday on the Moon" thus refutes the assertion by Rabkin—clearly unfamiliar with this story—that prior to *Rendezvous with Rama*, Clarke "had always before fallen back into male chauvinism" (47).

Other stories more briefly describe everyday life on the moon. The narrator of "The Sentinel" describes the use of "small rockets" and "powerful caterpillar tractors" (301) to traverse the lunar surface. While *Earthlight*'s Bertram Sadler spends most of his time at a lunar observatory, he does explore the "lunar metropolis" of Central City (34). The novel 2001, in addition to glimpses of life in a space station, calls the underground Clavius Base a "complex of workshops, offices, storerooms, computer center, generators, garage, kitchen, laboratories, and food-processing plant"—"a miniature world in itself" (63).

Around the time he published "Holiday on the Moon," Clarke completed a novel with a similar story: an unlikely visitor to a settlement on another world who resolves to become a colonist. In *Sands of Mars*, however, the protagonist is science fiction writer Martin Gibson, hired to journey to Mars and write about his experiences. Wry comments about discrepancies between Gibson's exuberant stories and actual space life convey that Clarke is seeking to be more realistic than other writers in describing future space travel and colonization. Like Daphne, Gibson has no noteworthy adventures while flying to Mars and staying at Port Lowell, though he witnesses the discovery of Martian creatures, kangaroo-like animals with the intelligence of pets. There is a frisson of excitement when Gibson's aircraft crashes during a sandstorm, leaving passengers in a region where radio messages cannot reach Port Lowell or the Martian moon Phobos, but he resolves their dilemma by using his camera's powerful flash to indicate their location to observers on Phobos.

Part of the drama in *Sands of Mars* and similar stories stems from Clarke's meticulous attention to the technology that space colonists will require to survive in inhospitable environments—here, oxygen masks and pressurized domes filled with oxygen extracted from Mars's iron oxide. Yet, unusually, *Sands of Mars* also envisions, as an alternative to mastering life on a harsh alien world, the possibility of terraforming, as Martian scientists transform Phobos into a miniature sun, producing heat and light from nuclear reactions to give Mars a more temperate climate. Only two other stories briefly refer to terraforming: "Transience" (1949) mentions future humans "had torn down [the moon's] mountains and brought it air and water" (103), and the epilogue to *The Ghost from the Grand Banks* describes a terraformed but now abandoned Mars, where "Martian oceans had dwindled to a few shallow lakes, but the great forests of mutated pines still survived along the equatorial belt" (251). Venus had also been terraformed, but the planet "once called New Eden—had reverted to its former Hell" (251). Clarke's nonfictional *The Snows of Olympus: A Garden on Mars* (1994) outlines how Mars might be terraformed over a period of several centuries.

The routines of life in an Earth-orbiting space station are addressed in "The Other Side of the Sky" and the juvenile *Islands in the Sky*. The narrator of the former work, a series of six vignettes like "Venture to the Moon," helps to construct three space stations and becomes a resident of one station. There are two genuine crises: a problem with the station's oxygen supply is detected when a crewman's canary becomes unconscious, and crewmates stranded in a detached chamber without space suits must briefly expose themselves to the vacuum of space to reach safety—a scenario previously mentioned in *Sands of Mars* and *Earthlight* and famously revisited in *2001*. (In his *2001* foreword to *The Space Trilogy*, Clarke notes, "I cannot claim that [*Earthlight*] was the first story in which unprotected humans were able to survive in a vacuum; I stole the idea, as well as much else, from the brilliant and sadly short-lived Stanley Weinbaum" [xii]—specifically, his story "The Red Peri" [1935].)

But life in a space station, like life on the moon or Mars, is usually uneventful: the narrator is saddened because a supply rocket carrying desired amenities accidentally misses its destination; a television broadcaster, brought to the station to host the first global television broadcast, is so pleased by its clean air and low gravity that he resolves to make it his permanent home; while surreptitiously visiting his girlfriend in another space station, the narrator observes a damaged alien spaceship but does not report it; and while recalling his father's bitter opposition to having his son fly into space, the narrator prepares to say good-bye to his own son, part of the first expedition to Mars.

In a story that would have fit perfectly into "The Other Side of the Sky"— "Who's There?" (1958)—one man building a space station dons a large, cylindrical space suit to retrieve an ancient satellite that might become "a menace to navigation" (693), Clarke's anticipation of what now constitutes a genuine hazard. Disturbed by sounds of a living creature, he fears he is wearing the haunted space suit of a deceased colleague, but the sound comes from a kitten that the station's cat, "our badly misnamed Tommy[,] had been rearing in the seclusion of my spacesuit's Number Five Storage Locker" (696).

Space stations are ubiquitous in Clarke's space stories but are typically minor elements, places where protagonists make brief stops on longer journeys, as in *Sands of Mars*, *2001*, and *Imperial Earth*, or posts for scientific observation, like the Cytherean Station One orbiting Venus in *The Lost Worlds of 2001*. The other work focused on a space station, *Islands in the Sky*, has two striking features: first, the spaceship that takes protagonist Roy Malcolm from Earth to the Inner Station remarkably anticipates the space shuttle in that it is positioned "vertically" for liftoff, is equipped with "wings" that "would come into action only when she glided back into the atmosphere on her return to earth" (17), and carries "four huge fuel tanks, like giant bombs, which would be jettisoned as soon as the motors had drained them dry" (18). Second, Malcolm learns why someone should never stow away on a spaceship: "do you know what they'd do to a stowaway if they did find one? . . . An extra person on board would mean that much less food and oxygen for everyone else, and it would upset the fuel calculations too. So he'd simply be pushed overboard"

(50). This is effectively the story line of Tom Godwin's "The Cold Equations" (1954), published two years later, creating the possibility that Godwin borrowed its scenario from Clarke's novel.

Still, *Islands in the Sky* is most significant as Clarke's primer on what will not be dangerous, and what will be dangerous, about space travel. Having won a contest to visit the Inner Station, Malcolm and the station's "apprentices" (33) are startled when a huge meteor opens a hole in the hull; but it is merely a training exercise. The youths become convinced that a spaceship lurking nearby belongs to space pirates; but it is actually occupied by filmmakers preparing to shoot the first movie in space. At the Pasteur Space Hospital, Malcolm apparently encounters a huge alien with tentacles; but it is only an ordinary hydra, artificially enlarged by the station's lower gravity. The points could not be clearer: the threats typically emphasized in adventures for young readers—meteors, space pirates, and aliens—are unlikely to afflict actual astronauts.

Yet the last half of the novel features three more probable dangers. First, flying with others from the Pasteur Space Hospital to the station, Malcolm faints, due to a mechanical failure: "A change-over valve must have jammed in the oxygen supply when one of the tanks got empty" (132). Then, due to the lingering effects of temporary "oxygen starvation" (154), the spaceship's pilot makes an error and accidentally sends the vehicle flying outward into space instead of inward toward the station, requiring the emergency launch of additional fuel from a lunar mass driver to provide the spaceship with enough fuel to circle the moon and return to Earth's orbital space. Finally, during the flight, the spaceship observes, and approaches to investigate, a mysterious object, only to retreat after noticing "the symbol of death—the skull and crossbones" (168)—on its hull; it turns out to be a container filled with radioactive waste, one of many unwisely launched into space before the perils of such disposals were recognized. These, then, are dangers that space travelers should worry about: problems with the machinery that maintains life in space; one wrong decision that could prove fatal; and the bits of debris that humans have scattered throughout space, which could be hazardous even if they are not radioactive.

Although a "human error" in programming HAL memorably leads to tragedies in *2001*, and "Who's There?" involves potentially hazardous space debris, the usual dangers facing Clarke's astronauts stem from mechanical problems—and rarely natural disasters or human adversaries. As noted, a computer failure threatens astronauts in "Into the Comet"; in "Maelstrom II" (1965) an electromagnetic launcher on the moon malfunctions and threatens to send its passenger crashing into the moon; *The Deep Range*'s Walter Franklin is imperiled because a jammed propulsion unit sends him plunging through space, and he cannot summon assistance because of a broken antenna; "Summertime on Icarus" features an astronaut exploring Icarus who is endangered by an unexplained explosion in his spacecraft, so he may be stranded on the asteroid's surface when it turns to face the sun; and *A Fall of Moondust*'s Hansteen describes how he experienced the "slow, insidious danger" of running out of oxygen "when he had been wearing a faulty space suit on Ganymede" (128). The main story of *A Fall of Moondust*, Clarke's most extended account of space travelers in peril, involves a poorly designed vehicle designed to skim across the lunar surface that unexpectedly sinks into a sea of dust, threatening passengers due to a failing air supply, a lurch downward caused by expelled water, and a fire that breaks out while they are escaping from the buried craft.

In these instances, seemingly doomed protagonists are rescued by desperate improvisations or actions in the nick of time: hastily constructed abacuses save the day in "Into the Comet"; the astronaut in "Maelstrom II" is instructed to leap from his spacecraft to achieve an orbit that enables him to be retrieved; *The Deep Range*'s Franklin is located after four hours in space, though the experience permanently traumatizes him; the protagonist of "Summertime on Icarus" is rescued by crewmates just as the sun is about to incinerate him; and while we are not told how Hansteen survived, he presumably managed to repair his space suit or reach a safe haven. In *A Fall of Moondust* several ingenious decisions save the trapped passengers: their position is determined when an astronomer employs infrared detectors to find the slightly warmer area where the vehicle sank; needing to survive six hours while a tube is inserted to provide oxygen, passengers take drugs to induce sleep and reduce their oxygen intake; when rescuer Robert Lawrence cannot securely fashion a tube to the top of the vehicle, he jerry-rigs a method to cover a dangerous gap; and due to Lawrence's timely efforts, passengers reach the surface just as the fire threatens to kill them. Indeed, while Lawrence views himself as "going into battle, against . . . the forces of Nature" (165), and while Rabkin sees the novel as an affirmation of the "faith in science that runs throughout Clarke's fiction" (19), the story is actually a fable about the hazards of relying upon science, as I discuss in *Cosmic Engineers*, since its perils stem from a vehicle that is ill-equipped to handle predictable problems.

However, Clarke regularly acknowledges that it is not always possible to survive space disasters. While taking what will become humanity's first spaceship on a test flight, the protagonist of "Inheritance" (1947) perishes when unspecified problems cause a "detonation" (87), although his son appears destined to travel into space in his place. Because of their drained supply of oxygen, one of two spaceship pilots in "Breaking Strain" (1949) must die so that the other can survive. In *Sands of Mars* a member of the first expedition to Saturn describes three deaths that occurred: two men "died of radiation sickness after emergency repairs to one of the atomic motors," while "the leader of the expedition, Captain Envers, had been killed by an avalanche of frozen air on Titan" (139–40). In *A Fall of Moondust* Hansteen relates the tragedy of spaceship *Cassiopeia*: its "main drive . . . had jammed" (94), sending its doomed crew on an endless journey into space.

Later, in a proposed scene for *2001* recounted in *The Lost Worlds of 2001*, astronaut Peter Whitehead dies after the controls of his pod stop working, so he collides with the *Discovery* and drifts away to run out of oxygen before he can be rescued; in the novel and film, five of the six astronauts are killed by the errant computer HAL. *Imperial Earth* relates how the boyfriend of Makenzie's "grandmother" Ellen died when his spaceship "met its mysterious and still inexplicable doom, deep in the jet streams of [Saturn's] South Temperate Zone" (25). In "The Hammer of God" astronauts who save Earth from a ruinous asteroid impact are killed (though they survive in the novel version). Most tragically, in "Transit of Earth" five astronauts are permanently stranded on Mars, destined to die, when "the propellant tank" of their landing craft "ruptured" (886). Four men sacrifice their lives so that one astronaut can survive to personally witness a once-in-a-century phenomenon: due to the alignment of the sun, Earth, and Mars, someone on Mars can observe the Earth and moon crossing in front of the sun, forming black shadows on its surface—an event Clarke may have envisioned after observing the cosmic alignments Stanley Kubrick featured in *2001*.

Also, while usually focusing on mechanical problems, Clarke does not entirely discount the possibility that astronauts might be threatened by natural disasters or human opponents. In "Breaking Strain" a small meteor causes a damaging leak in a spaceship's oxygen supply, and in the novel *2001* Poole seals a potentially dangerous meteor crater in the *Discovery*'s hull. A lunar astronomer is imperiled by a "moonquake" in "Dog Star"; the initial crisis of *A Fall of Moondust*—the vehicle sinking into lunar dust—is arguably a natural disaster, though it could have been anticipated and avoided; and on a grand scale, the danger of an asteroid striking Earth is acknowledged in *Rendezvous with Rama*, where such a disaster inspires the creation of Spaceguard, and in "The Hammer of God" and its novel version, wherein a similar catastrophe is only narrowly averted.

In a few cases, people threaten astronauts' lives: in "Hate" (1961) a returning Russian cosmonaut is about to be rescued from the ocean by divers, but one of them, a fierce anticommunist, instead causes her to die. In "Hide-and-Seek" (1949) a spy pursued by an enemy spaceship surprisingly lands on Phobos, recognizing that a single human running across its surface can outmaneuver a huge space cruiser. The explorers of *Rendezvous with Rama* are threatened because Mercurians attempt to destroy Rama with a nuclear missile, but a crew member disarms the bomb.

While telling stories about space travel, Clarke at times comments on the strange, otherworldly features of life in space. In "Hide-and-Seek" the spy feels "an exhilarating loneliness about his mountain eyrie" on Phobos (164); "Breaking Strain" speaks of "a timelessness about space-flight that is unmatched by any other experience of man" (175); *A Fall of Moondust* describes the dusty sea of "the still-mysterious Moon" as something that "belonged to the kingdom of fantasy, as if it had come from the haunted brain of Edgar Allan Poe" (12, 15); and the protagonist of "Transit of Earth" stares at Martian landscapes and admires "the countless varieties of red and pink and crimson, so startling against the deep blue of the sky. How different from the Moon—though that, too, has its own beauty" (890). *Imperial Earth* comments, "Though the first ship had lifted from Earth three centuries before [Makenzie] was born, the wonder of space had not yet been exhausted" (6).

If the environments of space are fundamentally different from those of Earth, two questions arise: what sorts of individuals are best suited to live and work in space, and how will life in space affect those who choose it? Addressing the first question, science fiction writers typically argue that space will attract people who are especially strong, courageous, and curious, so space colonization will function as a winnowing process, separating superior individuals from the weak, cowardly, and complacent people remaining on Earth. Yet Clarke generally declines to celebrate residents of space or denigrate those who decline to join their company. Indeed, projects like Morgan's Gibraltar Bridge and space elevator, and oceanic endeavors in *The Deep Range* and *Dolphin Island*, demonstrate that there will long remain stimulating challenges to engage adventurous spirits on Earth. Only on a few occasions does Clarke praise the special qualities of space colonists: in *Sands of Mars* Gibson ponders "his growing respect for the people around him—his admiration for the keen-eyed competence, the readiness to take well-calculated risks, which had enabled them not merely to survive on this heartbreakingly hostile world, but to lay the foundations of the first extra-terrestrial culture" (129). Clarke's *2001* notes that lunar residents "were all highly trained scientists and technicians, carefully selected before they had left Earth" (62), while *Imperial Earth* similarly observes, "Everyone who had come to Titan had been carefully selected for intelligence and ability" (38).

Only "Breaking Strain" explicitly explores what sorts of people are best suited for the rigors of space travel, reaching a surprising conclusion. Introduced to imperiled crewmates Grant and McNeil, readers are initially prodded to sympathize with Grant, who remains calm and professional upon hearing of their depleted oxygen while McNeil briefly panics, gets drunk, and smokes cigarettes despite the dwindling oxygen. Grant also seems to be a more stable individual, because he has a wife and family, while McNeil is single. Yet the seemingly controlled Grant becomes mentally unbalanced, employing McNeil's trivially indulgent behavior to justify an effort to poison him, while the coolly observant McNeil deduces his plans, thwarts the attempted murder, and rationally explains that they must decide who will live through a random process like drawing cards. To function properly in space, then, people may need to express emotions and enjoy moments of pleasure like McNeil rather than bottling up their feelings like Grant.

For those familiar with Clarke, this judgment is unexpected, because other protagonists seem more like Grant than McNeil: they are usually reticent in expressing themselves and distant from wives and families (as discussed below). Still, *2001* specifies that *Discovery* astronauts were chosen in part because they were unmarried, since "it was not fair to send family men on a mission of such duration" (103).

One effect of living in space is obvious: space colonists would feel increasingly detached from Earth, regarding space as their true home. Clarke's *2001* describes the eight-year-old daughter of administrator Dan Halvorsen, born and raised on the moon, as "the first generation of the Spaceborn" (66). Clarke and Kubrick's screenplay elaborates on the point: "The personnel of the [lunar] Base . . . no longer thought of Earth as their home. The time was fast approaching when Earth, like all mothers, must say farewell to her children" (b52). A key moment for *Sands of Mars*'s Gibson comes when, after he delivers a report to Earth, colony leader Warren Hadfield notes his "change of attitude": "When you started, we were 'they.' Now we're 'we'" (128)—signaling that Gibson, who planned to only visit Mars, now sees himself as a resident.

One factor in these space dwellers' alienation from Earth is their adjustment to the low gravity of space stations and other worlds; indeed, the narrator of "The Sentinel" refers to "the feeling of decreased weight and the unnatural slowness with which objects fell" as the only way their life within their Base did not seem "normal and homely" (302). Further, after spending long periods of time in space, former residents of Earth, like Dr. Bose of *Rendezvous with Rama* and Floyd of *2061*, may find that they can no longer endure Earth's oppressive gravity. This is definitely true of individuals who were born on Mars, such as the first wife and children of *The Deep Range*'s Franklin, and hence "could never come to Earth, where they would be crushed under three times their normal weight" (74). *Rendezvous with Rama* similarly notes that one longtime resident of Mars "would never return to his home planet," unable to endure "the reconditioning needed to accustom him to three times the gravity he had enjoyed for most of his life" (19), while a woman "born on Mars . . . could not tolerate the high gravity of Earth" (24).

Life in lower gravity might provide significant health benefits, a point Clarke first makes in *The Exploration of the Moon*: "The Moon, it has been suggested, would be the ideal place for people with weak hearts or muscular troubles, and the normal life-span might be considerably longer there than on Earth. If this proves to be the case, the colonisation of the Moon would be ensured for medical reasons alone—and there are few more potent arguments" (98). Building upon this idea, Clarke regularly envisions hospitals in space to assist patients who could not be helped in Earth's gravity. Thus, *Prelude to Space*'s Alexson, suffering from a frail heart, moves to the moon because its lower gravity will extend his lifespan; and *Islands in the Sky* describes the Pasteur Space Hospital, where "many diseases which were incurable on Earth could be treated. For example, the heart no longer had to work so hard to pump blood around the body, and so could be rested in a manner impossible on Earth" (103). To remain alive, some people "could live safely only on the moon or Mars, and the severest cases had to remain permanently on the station"—a "kind of exile" nonetheless appreciated by "cheerful" patients (113). This happens to the man that Malcolm and others transport to the Pasteur Space Hospital after his return from Mars and, later, to *2061*'s Floyd, who comes to reside at the space hospital after suffering grievous injuries on Earth "that could best be handled in the Pasteur Space Hospital" (6).

Earthlight also alludes to the longer lives in space caused by low gravity, as lunar residents live about 120 years—in contrast to the shorter lives of those who "spent all your waking and sleeping hours fighting the gravity of Earth" (144). Indeed, virtually all spaceborn protagonists of Clarke's novels, such as those in *Rendezvous with Rama*, *Imperial Earth*, and *2061*, appear to enjoy lifespans of well over one hundred years.

Yet in the early 1960s, perhaps reflecting his own faltering health, Clarke shifts from brief mentions of space's helpful effect on human health and makes this the central theme of two stories. In "Death and the Senator" (1961) a politician who will soon die due to heart problems is offered the opportunity to be treated and cured at an orbiting Russian hospital. And in "The Secret" (1963) a reporter visiting the moon is baffled by the standoffish attitude of the Medical Research section. He learns that, based on their research, scientists believe humans living in the moon's lower gravity may live up to two hundred years. Because only a relatively few, highly intelligent people can obtain jobs on the moon, they are keeping this discovery a secret, fearing fierce resentment from billions of people who cannot qualify for positions in space.

Due to lives in significantly different environments, space residents might also develop different attitudes, sometimes leading to conflicts between Earth and space colonies. *Rendezvous with Rama* focuses on the unique attributes of inhabitants of Mercury, called Hermians, whose world "was a fairly good approximation of Hell." Although "those difficult people" (125) were "respected for their toughness and engineering skills, and admired for the way in which they had conquered so fearsome a world," they "were not liked" or "completely trusted" (126) by others. While residents of other worlds calmly accept Rama as a benign visitor, Hermians, especially concerned about objects approaching the sun, feel threatened by Rama and undertake to destroy it. Still, the novel partially defends them by noting, "Some psychologists had claimed that it was almost impossible to understand fully the mentality of anyone born and bred on Mercury" (173); their apparent paranoia, then, might be a natural outgrowth of their harsh existence.

The novelette "Earthlight," though set entirely upon an inhabited moon, has as its background a future solar system with several inhabited worlds that engage in a violent conflict over scarce resources. Though Earth discovers uranium on the moon, it keeps the mine a secret, not wishing to share this coveted metal with residents of Mars and Jupiter's moons who need the rare element. After defeating the armada that attempts to seize the fortified mine, Earth agrees to negotiate with other worlds to provide them with uranium.

The novel version tells the same story, with some variations: a new protagonist, Sadler, visits the nearby lunar observatory to identify a suspected spy. Reflecting growing skepticism about the value of nuclear fission, the novel explains, "Uranium itself was no longer of the vital importance that it had been in the twentieth and twenty-first centuries," so other worlds are now said to require the "heavy metals" typically found near deposits of uranium (32). The climactic battle is depicted as a draw, and a peaceful settlement appears appropriate after Earth's astronauts dramatically rescue the surviving crew of an attacking warship.

Only a few humorous stories—"How We Went to Mars," "Loophole," and "Security Check" (1957)—depict thriving alien civilizations within the solar system; Clarke knew its other worlds were not conducive to life and was reluctant to ignore scientific facts. He recognizes that Mars might have been inhabited in the past, as some stories refer to extinct Martian cultures: "Transience," unusually endorsing Percival Lowell's theory of an ancient canal-building Martian civilization, speaks of the Martian "Cardenis, prince of engineers, fighting to save his people from the encroaching deserts," but "help from Earth . . . had come too late" (101); in *Sands of Mars*, some wonder if the kangaroo creatures are "the degenerate survivors of a race which had achieved civilisation long ago, and let it slip from its grasp when conditions became too severe," though there is "no evidence" to support this "romantic view" of Martian history (207); "Report on Planet Three" presents a purported document from a Martian civilization that destroyed itself in a nuclear war; and "Trouble with Time" (1960) involves the attempted theft of a human-like statue produced by a vanished race of Martians. Otherwise, in Clarke's mature fiction, intelligent aliens come from planets orbiting other stars (although, as discussed below, a few stories speculate about unusual and potentially intelligent life existing in extreme environments like the Sun, Jupiter's atmosphere, Europa's ocean, and the Oort Cloud).

Clarke also realizes that in the past, aliens from elsewhere might have visited the solar system and left evidence of their sojourn. The most famous example is the lunar pyramid of "The Sentinel," which evolved into the monoliths of *2001*; in "Jupiter Five" scientists discover ruins of ancient civilizations on Mercury and Mars, and the Jovian moon Amalthea is revealed to be an abandoned alien spacecraft; and in "The Other Side of the Sky," as noted, a man apparently observes a derelict alien spaceship. In describing remnants of extinct civilizations or ancient visitors, Clarke thus occasionally provides his solar system with an alien presence, though it must be dealt with by archaeologists, not diplomats.

Once humanity establishes itself throughout the solar system, Clarke typically envisions a long period of relative stagnation as humans prove unable or unwilling to confront the challenge of interstellar travel. This is essentially the case in *3001* and "The Lion of Comarre," where humanity makes no further progress into space after reaching Pluto: one resident asks, "Who wants to go to the stars, anyway?" (121). "In fifty years," however, some researchers "hope to have perfected the interstellar drive" (129). Certainly, Clarke knew there would be innumerable scientific problems to confront and overcome before humans could venture beyond the solar system; and with ample room for colonies within the solar system, future humans might feel no pressing need to journey elsewhere, especially since, as noted, Clarke rarely anticipates faster-than-light travel.

Further, in the 1952 "The Awakening," Clarke posits that humanity might forever be limited to the solar system, primarily because of psychological issues: "the spirit of mankind had quailed before the awful immensities of interstellar space. Man had reached the planets while he was still young, but the stars had remained forever before his grasp" (83). And, significantly, the extinct race that once inhabited Earth in "Retreat from Earth" extended its rule only "everywhere within the orbit of Pluto" (13).

A similar argument about humanity's inability to conquer the stars appears in *Childhood's End*, when the alien Karellen describes "the immensity of space" and tells humans that "in challenging it, you would be like ants attempting to label and classify all the grains of sand in all the deserts of the world"— a "stupendous challenge" that humanity, "in its present state of evolution, cannot face." Karellen also reports that his race must "protect" humans from "powers and forces that lie among the stars—forces beyond anything you can imagine" and concludes, "The planets you may one day possess. But the stars are not for Man" (137). It transpires that only an advanced form of humanity— a group intelligence with enormous psychic powers—can someday venture into interstellar space.

Still, Clarke's fiction describes three ways present-day humans might advance to interstellar travel. The first would involve a long, gradual process, as in "The Songs of Distant Earth" (1958), wherein "robot survey ships" (665) traveling beyond the solar system are eventually followed by fusion-powered starships. Second, discovering the sun is dying would prod humanity to desperate efforts to leave the solar system and avoid extinction; thus, "The Twilight of a Sun" concludes by acknowledging that "our sun in its turn too will fade," requiring humanity's "vessels" to "ply to the uttermost depths of the sky" and "win a new planet's fair face" (3). In "Rescue Party" (1946) humans construct a fleet of spaceships to escape from Earth before the sun becomes a nova. In *The Songs of Distant Earth* the same approaching catastrophe leads first to the construction of slow-moving "seedships" containing information and technology enabling onboard robots to create and nurture colonies of humans and, later, after scientists learn to tap the energy in "quantum fluctuations" (42), to faster starships with human passengers. Another cosmic catastrophe—the approach of a "fearsome singularity" (252)—forces humans to abandon the solar system in *The Ghost from the Grand Banks*. Finally, advanced alien visitors might provide humanity with the technology to travel beyond the solar system, as occurs in *Against the Fall of Night*: after their civilization long "huddled round the sun" (209), humanity finally "explored the Galaxy," "first in the ships of other races and later in machines built with borrowed knowledge" (210).

This raises an obvious question: if humans can reach other solar systems only after extended periods of time, or due to improbable disasters or alien encounters, it seems that humanity, confined to the solar system for centuries, requires some way to avoid the stagnation and boredom that afflicts the future society of "The Awakening" (1952). Clarke's answer is twofold: humans can continue working to further perfect their own society and can endeavor with renewed energy to communicate with distant aliens they cannot visit. This, at least, is one message in Clarke's most extended portrait of humanity's future in space, *Imperial Earth*.

Although *Imperial Earth* primarily takes place on a future Earth, it is arguably about two alien planets. First, since protagonist Makenzie was born and raised on Titan, his journey to Earth represents, for him, a visit to an alien world; upon seeing Earth, he considers it "a beautiful planet . . . but it was also alien" (84). In addition, while only an introductory section and an epilogue take place on Titan, Makenzie's thoughts and behavior while visiting Earth provide additional information about his home world. In this respect, one can compare the novel to William Dean Howells's *A Traveler from Altruria* (1894), wherein readers learn about Howells's utopia solely by means of comments made by the titular visitor to America.

One obvious difference between residents of Earth and Titan is that they come from very different environments, making it challenging for Makenzie to adjust to Earth. Before leaving Titan, he must exercise wearing heavy weights to prepare for Earth's gravity; coming from a place where supplies of water are limited, he is astounded by "the spectacle of so much genuine water" (95) in the Potomac River and learns to swim for the first time; since

Titan's rains are poisonous ammonia, "it would require a real effort of will" for Makenzie "to leave the protection of the limousine" (93) and expose himself to Earth's harmless rain; seeing a horse, he announces, "I've just met my first Monster from Outer Space" (109); coming from a world where people necessarily spend their lives in confined quarters, he is surprised by "the very *size* of" his hotel room, which "by Titanian standards" is "enormous" (96); and on a sunny day, Makenzie is "taken aback by the sheer blazing ferocity of a sun almost one hundred times brighter than the star that shone gently on his own world" (103).

Makenzie further notices and reflects on key psychological differences between Terrans and Titanians. Interacting with passengers from Earth during his voyage, he observes that they "*did* have a quite unconscious air of superiority," while acknowledging that "several thousand years of history and culture justified a certain pride" (71); he refers to "the Terran obsession with the past" (237); and "coming from an aggressively egalitarian society," Makenzie "never felt quite happy when he was afforded special privileges" (116). A recurring concern, described as "the question so long debated on all the other worlds," is whether Earth's people are "becoming decadent" (72), presumably because their lives lack the invigorating challenges that residents of less hospitable worlds regularly face.

Of particular interest is Makenzie's attitude about race, since he is of African descent: to be sure, no overt racism is evident on Earth or anywhere else, but Terrans remain conscious of their world's troubled history, as African American servants now enjoy using "genuine slave patter" (95), and Makenzie's host George Washington notes only that people on Earth have "made some progress" in improving racial relations (96). This prompts Makenzie to realize, "He had never given any more thought to his skin color than to that of his hair" (96), suggesting that residents of other planets, completely lacking any history of racial inequality or racial tensions, may become oblivious to issues of race in a manner not possible for Earth's inhabitants, haunted by their past.

Despite their differences, people of Earth and Titan are similar in their enlightened attitudes regarding activities once regarded as taboo. Casual nudity is acceptable: readers deduce that Makenzie learned to swim without wearing a swimsuit when he resists wearing a diving suit, observing that "it had seemed astonishing—and even indecent—to put on clothing when one entered the water" (192); and two women participating in an expedition to New York's Central Park, now a wilderness, are instructed to don clothes before embarking on a hike. Bisexuality now represents the norm: although Makenzie has settled into a relationship with a woman, he had numerous affairs with men in his youth, and when he persuades the spaceship engineer to show him its advanced propulsion system, it comes at the voyage's midpoint, when numerous passengers engage in weightless sex, so the men have a "perfect alibi" (79) for being together in an isolated area of the spaceship. Both Earth and Titan effectively have world governments, and armed conflicts are a thing of the past, except for "occasional psychopaths who kill themselves and other people" (94). All of this makes *Imperial Earth*, in David N. Samuelson's words, "the closest [Clarke] has come to a traditional utopia" ("Sir Arthur C. Clarke" 209), though Makenzie notes that "Earth had not solved *all* its problems" (94) and says, "We are still far from Utopia, and we may never achieve it" (259). Clarke declines to specify why the human condition has improved so much, but mastery of space travel, and the resulting knowledge and resources it provided, are implicitly one reason humanity has progressed; Robin Anne Reid in particular argues that, in Clarke's view, "future space colonization will solve not only overpopulation but also oppression based on racism" (66).

One might partially attribute these advancements to improvements in communication—one of the novel's themes. It states that Earth's "communications satellites" "made possible, and then inevitable, the creation of the World State in all but name" (21). In his speech Makenzie refers to Alexander Graham Bell's telephone as "the invention which really began the conquest of space" and "the abolition of space" (257–58), suggesting that long-distance communication itself represents a form of space travel. And in 2276 humans depend upon "Comsoles" resembling personal computers in the enormous amount of information they instantly provide.

Despite these improvements, however, space travel is also a hindrance to communication, because the speed of light prevents genuine "conversation" between planets like Earth and Mars; statements are only received three minutes after they are made (21). Further, while "Telex or its equivalent" would "in theory" work as well as conversation, Clarke describes the problem of "costly and sometimes fatal interplanetary misunderstandings resulting from the fact that the two men at the opposite ends of the circuit did not really know each other, or comprehend each other's ways of thought, because they had never been in personal contact" (21). Thus, despite the length and cost of the journeys, a member of Makenzie's family must periodically travel to Earth to not only obtain a child by cloning but also establish "the network of personal contacts" (22) that is "essential at the highest levels of statesmanship and administration" (21).

Most significantly, improved communication of another sort emerges as an answer to the novel's key question: how can future humans avoid stagnation and decadence? Makenzie's speech notes that addressing the "many problems still to be solved, on all the planets" may provide some incentive to further action; however, because "we know that all these problems *can* be solved, with the tools that we already possess," these issues are insufficiently challenging: "No pioneering, no great discoveries, are necessary here." Thus, humans require "new tasks to challenge the mind and inspire the spirit," and since "*manned* space travel to the stars . . . may still lie centuries ahead" (259), humanity needs a more immediate goal, such as a different sort of interstellar travel: improved communication.

For it transpires that Makenzie's friend turned romantic rival, Karl Helmer, secretly travels to Earth to raise money by selling Titanite, a rare substance found only on Titan, to finance construction of a new radio telescope, to be built near Saturn, that might finally detect signs of other intelligent life. Humanity's previous attempt to do so, the CYCLOPS array of radio telescopes, "had never succeeded in detecting signals from intelligent beings elsewhere in the universe" (218). But Helmer's theory, eventually endorsed by Makenzie, is that this failure resulted from the telescope's inability to detect the "long and ultralong waves" that are "blocked" near Earth by "the gale of electrons that blows forever from the Sun" (260). But an enormous construct near Saturn could detect such waves and, not incidentally, sustain Titan's economy when its primary asset—its hydrogen—is no longer needed by spaceships that will abandon fusion to employ miniature black holes for propulsion.

Although Helmer is accidentally killed while meeting Makenzie on one CYCLOPS telescope, his recorded diary reveals another startling speculation: that signals of this kind he has already detected might come from strange beings inhabiting the Oort Cloud, which he calls "Star Beasts" (255). Perhaps comets are "the corpses of Star Beasts, sent sunward for cremation" (255–56). This wild idea, which Makenzie declines to mention in his speech, is in keeping with Clarke's theories, discussed below, that creatures utterly unlike Earth's life might exist in extreme environments. Further, connecting the search for signals from these entities with Clarke's fondness for the sea, Helmer models his design for the telescope on the sea anemone, the aquatic animal Makenzie encounters while deep-sea diving.

Imperial Earth thus proposes that while humans may long be unable to physically journey beyond the solar system, they might profitably focus on searching for evidence of intelligent life outside the solar system, "traveling" there by means of communication, not starships. Another implicit argument for this approach is that it is cheaper than building starships, for unlike other space stories, Clarke's novel repeatedly acknowledges that initiatives in space can be extremely expensive. Though they are presumably well compensated for governing Titan, members of Makenzie's family are daunted by the cost of one visit to Earth, and while there, Makenzie worries about spending too much money; Helmer must sell Titanite to obtain money for his project; and if Earth no longer requires Titan's hydrogen, the colony might be doomed, due to lack of needed income.

Two other themes in *Imperial Earth* relate to Clarke's attitudes about human activities in space. First are the pentominoes that fascinated the young Makenzie (and the middle-age Clarke), as the challenge of assembling these arrays of squares to form rectangles relates to the problems that initially confront Makenzie. He wonders whether he still has feelings for Calindy, who chose Helmer over him; he is concerned about his strained relationship with his former friend; he fears a new propulsion system will destroy Titan's economy; and he worries about whether he can handle the task of representing his world on Earth in individual meetings and the speech he must write. Yet in the end, like arranging pentominoes into a rectangle, Makenzie resolves all of these issues in a manner that, in Rabkin's words, "pull[s] together" "Everything" in the novel "with a satisfying sense of completion" (64): a reunion with Calindy demonstrates that he is no longer attracted to her, so he can return to his current partner; Helmer has died, but Makenzie effects a posthumous reconciliation by embracing the cause that became Helmer's preoccupation; constructing the radio telescope near Saturn will sustain Titan's economy and provides an ideal conclusion for his speech; and resolving to clone Helmer, not himself, to become his successor additionally pays tribute to his late friend and shows he has matured enough to make his own, independent decisions.

However, the novel twice mentions the doomed luxury liner *Titanic*, contrastingly suggesting that achieving satisfactory solutions to vexing problems may not always be possible as humanity expands throughout the solar system. While the failed effort to raise the *Titanic* in *The Ghost from the Grand Banks* symbolizes the futility of combating nature with technology, its successful restoration in this novel might seem to indicate, more optimistically, that disasters can eventually be overcome. Yet pondering Helmer's death leads Makenzie to recall the *Titanic* as the victim of an unavoidable destiny: he and Helmer "had both been enmeshed in some complex web of fate from which there had never been any possibility of escape. And though the scale of that disaster was so much greater that the very comparison appeared ludicrous, Duncan was again reminded of the *Titanic*" (243). The *Titanic* thus conveys the message that some human aspirations may forever be inherently unachievable, on Earth or in space.

For George Slusser, this idea is central to what he terms "Clarke's most deeply pessimistic view of man's capacity before the infinite" (61). Yet Slusser goes too far in arguing that the novel is about how "Man is contained in new limits no longer physically neutral or even traditionally humanist," constraining "physical and moral boundaries that hold him, and which ultimately be of his own creation" (64, 62). For Clarke also expresses hope that humans may soon communicate with other species, and someday visit them, and Makenzie's speech acknowledges that while transcendent victories may long be impossible, humanity has much to achieve in 2276 and thereafter. Overall, it is a sign of Clarke's talents that this underrated novel can be plausibly viewed as both a "utopia" and a "deeply pessimistic view" of humanity's future.

There are several ways one might explain Clarke's unusual tendency to generally limit visions of future space travel to the solar system. Certainly, while sometimes featuring aliens who mastered faster-than-light travel, as in *Childhood's End* and *2001*, he doubted humanity could achieve that ability and recognized that colonizing the stars at sub-light speed would be difficult, expensive, and time-consuming. Further, though he regularly traveled around the world in the 1950s, Clarke later evolved into something of a homebody who rarely left Sri Lanka and may have similarly imagined that future humans would happily remain in the solar system. Indeed, when scientists established that the solar system contained no Earth-like worlds, many writers seemingly grew bored by the planets in our vicinity and dispatched heroes to the stars, where they could adventure on more variegated and hospitable worlds. In contrast, Clarke was fascinated by the actual solar system, always eager for data from the latest space probes, and its distinctive environments suggested more than enough ideas for stories: Might strange life forms thrive on worlds that would be lethal for humans? How could people adjust to places with frigid temperatures, poisonous atmospheres, or very low gravity?

One must remember, finally, that Clarke was not only the author of stories about space travel but also a passionate advocate for human expansion into space, and he grew increasingly aware that his efforts had some impact. In his "Note on 1985 Printing" of *Interplanetary Flight*, he reports, "a surprising number of people (including Dr. Carl Sagan and some of the astronauts) have told me how [*Interplanetary Flight*] aroused their interest in the subject, by revealing to them that space travel was more than fiction" (x).

Clarke, then, probably viewed his space fiction as an extension of his nonfictional proselytizing for space travel, and for that reason he may have been inclined to limit fictional predictions to projects that might be achieved, or at least undertaken, during the lifetimes of his readers—such as colonies on the moon and Mars, systems for monitoring Earth-approaching asteroids, expeditions to comets and asteroids, and space-based radio telescopes. And pleased that his vision of a first lunar landing in *Prelude to Space* proved accurate, he undoubtedly hoped that other predictions, like lunar colonies and the Spaceguard system, might similarly come true while he was still alive. Unfortunately, actual space travel turned out to be far more expensive and difficult than Clarke or anyone else could have anticipated.

CHAPTER 5

HUMAN DESTINIES

In *The Universe Makers: Science Fiction Today* (1971), Donald A. Wollheim describes what he argues is "the full cosmogony of science-fiction future history" (42), a consensus opinion conveyed in innumerable works of science fiction: after exploring and colonizing the solar system, humans will fly to other stars, having discovered how to exceed the speed of light; they will establish a "Galactic Empire" (43) consisting of countless worlds inhabited by humans and aliens, which may collapse before reemerging as a "Permanent Galactic Civilization"; and humans will finally begin "seeking out and confronting the Creative Force or Being or God itself, sometimes merging with that Creative First Premise" (44).

Arthur C. Clarke stands out among science fiction writers for refusing to embrace this consensus future history. He recounts such developments only when the story's premise requires interstellar travelers: the hero of "Cosmic Casanova," working for the "Galactic Survey," encounters "one of the lost colonies of the First Empire" (659, 660); the protagonist of "Playback" is "a master pilot of the Galactic Survey" (855); "Nemesis" mentions a far future era "between the fall of the Ninety-seventh Dynasty and the rise of the Fifth Galactic Empire" (196); *Against the Fall of Night* references a now vanished galactic "Empire of many races" (210); "The Star" indicates that interstellar travel has become commonplace; and future human domination of the galaxy is intimated in "Rescue Party." Otherwise, Clarke repeatedly focuses on anticipated *limitations* to human progress, not humanity's boundless potential.

First, as indicated earlier, Clarke generally assumes that human space travel will not extend beyond the solar system, and when he endeavors to realistically portray interstellar travel in *The Songs of Distant Earth*, it occurs solely because humans must leave the solar system to survive and results only in isolated planetary colonies, not a galactic government. Second, while Clarke rarely displays concerns about humanity being destroyed by nuclear warfare or alien invaders, he regularly posits that humanity might vanish due to natural forces as changes in climate render Earth uninhabitable or new species drive humans to extinction. Third, even if humanity endures to achieve an advanced civilization, it will likely succumb to long periods of stagnation and decadence, though some may strive to resume progress. Finally, while eventual extinction remains their probable fate, humans might achieve some sort of transcendence due not to their own actions but rather unsolicited alien intervention; and this transformed species will possess abilities and priorities making them incomprehensible to their less capable ancestors—so humanity will effectively come to an end in another fashion.

Oddly, Peter Brigg asserts that Clarke, despite some "wavering" in his "confidence," "consistently hints that the universe will be man's and that man, coming to grips with the physical universe through science, will emerge the final victor" (Olander and Greenberg, *Arthur C. Clarke* 41)—a thought echoed by Eric S. Rabkin, who discusses Clarke's "spiritual commitment to a homo-centric and optimistic vision" (36). In fact, Clarke consistently depicts futures wherein humanity is marginalized—or extinct.

After World War II, like everyone, Clarke understood that nuclear weapons represented a threat to humanity's existence but viewed nuclear wars as unlikely, as they occur in only two serious stories; further, in each case, because of intelligent initiatives, humanity manages to survive. In "The Last Command" (1965) the leader of one superpower, recognizing that his nation faces defeat in a nuclear conflict, surprisingly orders a nuclear-armed spaceship lurking behind the moon to refrain from launching a retaliatory strike—to preserve at least part of the human race. The unexpected revelation is that the speaker is the leader of the Soviet Union, not the United States. In "'If I Forget Thee, Oh Earth . . .'" (1951), nuclear war makes Earth uninhabitable, but a colony of humans survives on the moon, and when a boy is taken by his father to observe the ravaged Earth, he resolves to carry on with life on the moon so that his descendants can someday reclaim Earth when its deadly radiation subsides.

When humans entirely destroy themselves in Clarke's fiction, it is treated as a joke, recalling the proclivity for homicidal humor in his juvenilia. In "Nightfall" (1947) a nuclear war is apparently wiping out everybody, as bombs are "falling at random upon a world which they could harm no more" (90). But the story focuses on one bomb that falls on Stratford-upon-Avon, disturbing Shakespeare's grave, so his famous curse directed toward anyone who "moves my bones" is seemingly realized by humanity's extinction. In "All the Time in the World" (1952)—which Clarke adapted as an episode of *Tales of Tomorrow* with only minor changes, such as changing its setting to New York City—a London thief is delighted when a mysterious woman gives him a bracelet that alters the time around him so that he can do hours of work in literally an instant. After following her instructions to steal valuable items from the British Museum, however, he learns he cannot exploit the device to enrich himself, because the woman is being controlled by aliens from the future who are seeking to preserve Earth's greatest treasures before an impending "SUPER-BOMB TEST" (415) accidentally destroys the planet. Thus, though the thief now has "all the time in the world" (416), that is ironically of little value in a world running out of time.

Later, when fears of nuclear weapons diminished, Clarke envisions, in "Improving the Neighbourhood" (1999), humans committing suicide in a different way: by "tapping the quantum fluctuations that occur at the very foundations of space-time," they "triggered a cataclysm which detonated their own planet" (965–66). But future aliens regard humanity's extinction as beneficial, since "the history of these huge creatures contains countless episodes of violence, against their own species and the numerous others that occupied their planet" (966); thus, humanity would have constituted "a serious danger to all the civilizations of our Local Cluster" (966).

Another nightmare scenario regularly featured in science fiction—aliens seeking to conquer Earth—is considered seriously in precisely two early stories, "Retreat from Earth" and "Loophole," and each effort is unsuccessful. Clarke otherwise portrays evil aliens attacking humanity only in lighthearted stories discussed elsewhere: "Publicity Campaign" (1953), "Crusade" (1968), "When the Twerms Came" (1972), and "Quarantine" (1977).

While rarely fearing humans might be destroyed by themselves or aliens, Clarke recognizes that humanity's survival depends upon the sun and sometimes posits that reductions in its radiation could plunge Earth into an unendurable Ice Age. In "Transience" people are presumably abandoning Earth because the approaching "Dark Nebula" (103) will dampen the sun's warmth, though this is not specified, and the problem that will force humans to leave the solar system in "The Twilight of a Sun" is that "our sun in its turn will fade" (3). In the epilogue to *The Fountains of Paradise*, the sun's "warmth had gone" due to some "sickness that had attacked its core a thousand years ago," but children still visit the now abandoned Earth to frolic in a "stricken land" threatened by "approaching glaciers" (252).

While humans survive the effects of a weakened sun in these stories, "approaching glaciers" destroy humanity in two stories from the late 1940s. In "The Forgotten Enemy" (1948) a dust cloud blocking the sun's radiation lethally cools the planet, though a professor lingers in London, fearful that others' desperate efforts to survive in "the temperate lands of the Equator" have failed, since "the radio had been silent now for fifteen years or more" (156). Recurring noises inspire the improbable theory that people are advancing from the north, but the professor finally deduces the grim truth: the noise comes from advancing glaciers that are about to cover London.

Clarke's more famous story about humanity's extinction on a glaciated planet is "History Lesson." Some "force had caused the change in the Sun's radiation" and "doomed" (95) humanity, as the planet is being blanketed by glaciers about to destroy one band of humans bearing a trove of artifacts from a glorious past, "a civilization that had passed beyond recall" (93). Five thousand years later, Venusians discover one preserved artifact that would forever "symbolise the human race" (98): a Mickey Mouse cartoon.

One obvious meaning of Clarke's title is that Venusians, humorously, are obtaining an extremely inaccurate "history lesson" about humanity from this cartoon, although one could argue that in conveying humanity's playful spirit the cartoon is not an entirely inappropriate summation of the human experience. As Brigg notes, the "frantic activity" of the cartoon "reflects how much Mickey Mouse and his fellow cartoon animals have in common with man" (Olander and Greenberg, *Arthur C. Clarke* 28). Yet Clarke also provides a lesson *about* history, reminding readers that our own understanding of past civilizations may be distorted by the endurance of unrepresentative artifacts and our myopic ability to interpret them—the point stressed by Zolan Zivkovic (10–12), noting that the Venusians cannot properly interpret the cartoon because of their "provincial" belief that all art is "representational" (11). Finally, Clarke presents a lesson about the history of life on Earth: throughout its existence, the planet repeatedly experienced significant climate changes driving previously successful species to extinction, so one can reasonably anticipate our species will someday suffer the same fate.

Severe reductions in solar radiation are not the only cosmic catastrophe that might threaten humanity: in "Rescue Party" and *The Songs of Distant Earth*, the sun is about to become a nova and devastate Earth, but in each case, humanity builds starships and escapes to other solar systems. However, in "No Morning After" (1954) a sun turned nova will destroy humanity, since the only human telepathically contacted by aliens, poised to rescue humanity by deploying teleporting tunnels, is a bitter, uncooperative drunk. In "The Road to the Sea" (1951) a destructive "Sigma Field" (196) accidentally created by scientists approaches the solar system, requiring that Earth be evacuated until the threat passes. In the epilogue of *The Ghost from the Grand Banks* a "fearsome singularity" engulfs Pluto and threatens the solar system, but people construct an "Exodus Fleet" and "fled in search of safer suns" (252).

Even if no massive disasters destroy humans, the forces of evolution might generate competitive new species forcing them into extinction—another fate that innumerable species have succumbed to before. Clarke seems especially wary of advanced insects: in both versions of "The Awakening," a long-hibernating human awakens to observe large, intelligent insects, signaling that "the long war between Man and insect was ended—and that Man was not the victor" (1942 version 26; slightly different wording in 1952 version). In Clarke's other reworking of that story, "Nemesis," the future discovery of buildings with "wide, horizontal slots close to the ground" (199) also suggests that a race of intelligent insects arose on Earth to supplant humanity before they in turn became extinct. In "The Next Tenants," as noted, a Japanese scientist deliberately endeavors to develop advanced termites to become humanity's successors. (Today's termites are described as an intelligent species in "Retreat from Earth," but therein they are humanity's allies, not competitors.)

Humans may also be replaced by artificial intelligences, as regularly anticipated in Clarke's nonfiction. In his foreword to *Beyond: Visions of the Interplanetary Probes* (2003), for example, he notes, "the tools we have invented . . . may well turn out to be our successors. . . . This possible evolutionary process from Homo sapiens to Machina sapiens is both predicted and mirrored in the brief history of spaceflight" (10). However, this scenario surfaces only rarely in his fiction. In "Dial F for Frankenstein" (1965) scientists create a global communications network, but as problems and mishaps crop up in computerized systems, they realize the network's billions of connections have achieved sentience and, like "a newborn baby" (825), this being is beginning to explore its world. Ominously, the network stops responding to human commands, apparently determined to preserve its existence, and a scientist concludes that humanity is doomed: "For *homo sapiens*, the telephone bell had tolled" (827).

More benignly, *2001* and "Improving the Neighbourhood" indicate that it is natural for biological species to transform themselves into machines, and "A Meeting with Medusa" envisions a peaceful transition from human domination to machine domination, as cyborg Howard Falcon predicts, "Some day the real masters of space would be machines, not men," and he would then function as "an ambassador between the old and the new—between the creatures of carbon and the creatures of metal who must one day supersede them" (927).

Even if humanity survives calamities or competition from other species, Clarke's clear message is that humans are a frail, vulnerable species, capable of being wiped out any time by forces beyond their control. Again, this is a striking contrast to the optimism about humanity's future expressed in other science fiction stories, which Clarke echoes only in "Rescue Party," wherein one alien surprised by humanity's unprecedented scientific progress muses, "I feel rather afraid of these people. . . . We had better be polite to them. After all, we only outnumber them about a thousand million to one." The story concludes, "Twenty years afterward, the remark didn't seem funny" (55), suggesting that humans are indeed beginning to take over the galaxy. Yet the only triumph Clarke's future humans usually achieve is to survive and keep progressing, though that process is also destined to cease.

If humans avoid the aforementioned perils, their mature civilization will confront another crisis: having solved all significant problems and improved technology as much as possible, societies will succumb to stagnation, boredom, and decadence. As Edward James observes, Clarke's seemingly utopian future societies actually provide an "archetypal science-fictional critique of utopia" by arguing that "no matter how secure, prosperous and otherwise 'utopian' a society is, stability and the lack of any challenges or goals is a cancer at the heart of that society" ("Clarke's Utopian Vision" 26, 29). Clarke envisions four ways that future people might respond to the negative consequences of their "utopian" existence.

First, despairing people could commit suicide to end their monotonous, meaningless lives. This is commonplace in the future of the 1952 version of "The Awakening": facing "the ultimate boredom that only Utopia can supply," the protagonist contemplates the "one way to escape" that "many had chosen": to "pass through the door that led to oblivion" (83) and "the blissful sleep of euthanasia" (85). In the original draft of *Against the Fall of Night*, described in "Ego & the Dying Planet," an entire future civilization chooses this option, as the hero discovers "a monument to the last of the [human] race, who have laid down life after exhausting all the knowledge of the Universe" (38–39).

Second, individuals might turn to artificial diversions to entertain themselves. In "The Parasite" (1953), having mastered all knowledge and devolved into atrophied, emotionless beings served by machines, future humans desperate for animating experiences project their intellects into the past and occupy the minds of present-day humans who enjoy sexual liaisons, becoming "parasites on the emotions of others" (432). In "The Lion of Comarre," people travel to Comarre because its machines can "analyse every thought and desire of those who entered" and sedate them to endlessly experience a blissful dream "world based on" their "subconscious desires" (140); when Richard Peyton III attempts to awaken one man from his dream, he resists, exclaiming, "The world never gave me anything, so why should I wish to return to it? I have found peace here, and that is all I need" (150). In *The City and the Stars* people enjoy virtual-reality adventures called "sagas" offering "uncomplicated dramas of adventure and discovery," "explorations of psychological states," and "exercises in logic or mathematics" (10–11).

Third, people might devote themselves to two pursuits that advanced technology cannot eliminate: the arts and governance. In "The Lion of Comarre" most citizens choose to become "artists and philosophers" or "lawyers and statesmen" (119). Similarly, in "The Road to the Sea" residents of an idyllic future Earth mostly devote themselves to activities like painting—the protagonist's profession—athletic competitions, dancing, and writing plays. *The City and the Stars* reports that "everyone in Diaspar was an artist at some time or another" (21), describes Alvin's mother as a popular artist, and envisions a policy of displaying citizens' artworks and forever preserving those that prove popular. The novel mentions two other idle pursuits popular in Diaspar: "athletics and various sports" and "games of chance" (52, 53).

Finally, a few rebels, dissatisfied with their society's static existence, may strive to force humanity back to forward progress—the story of "The Lion of Comarre," "The Road to the Sea," *Against the Fall of Night*, and *The City and the Stars*. These efforts to spark change prove successful, and while Clarke concludes each story before describing the rebirth of civilization, the essential elements in this revival are clear.

First, the instigator is an ambitious youth who confronts and overcomes adults who insist that everything must remain the same. Understandably, this theme appeals to the youthful Clarke, actively endeavoring to persuade complacent adults to undertake space travel; equally understandably, the mature Clarke abandons this scenario, featuring protagonists who, like Clarke, are no longer young.

Second, a key step involves rediscovery of lost knowledge from humanity's glorious past. In "The Lion of Comarre" Peyton finds in Comarre that its founder, his ancestor Rolf Thordarsen, left *"Notes on Subelectronics"* (152) to enable scientists to construct advanced robots to join humans in forging a better future. In "The Road to the Sea" the hero Brant explores the abandoned city of Shastar, impressed by its magnificent art, and encounters visitors from the stars, preparing to evacuate Earth's residents and reacquaint them with space travel. In *Against the Fall of Night* Alvin rediscovers an underground transportation system that takes him to the forgotten city of Lys and locates a still-functional spaceship. While in space, he encounters the disembodied intelligence Vanamonde, which informs humanity about its true history. The title of the final chapter, "Renaissance," tellingly references another period in Earth's history when rediscovery of ancient knowledge sparked a cultural revival; similarly, "The Lion of Comarre" concludes at "the coming of the Third Renaissance" (153).

Third, newly obtained information from the past will inspire new research and initiatives. In "The Lion of Comarre" Thordarsen's notes will allow scientists to actually construct the robots he only envisioned. In "The Road to the Sea" visitors from space, noting that the Sigma Field has serendipitously "freed us forever from the stagnation that was overtaking your race," urge Brant to "get away from Earth" and "drink your fill of all that the universe can offer" (298). In *Against the Fall of Night* Alvin will join other humans in "rebuilding his world" (223) so that humanity can recapture its former greatness.

Finally, given Clarke's proclivities, this future Renaissance unsurprisingly involves a renewed commitment to space travel; even the farcical utopia of "A Short History of Fantocracy" immediately undertakes to avoid stagnation by embarking upon a space program. At the beginning of "The Lion of Comarre," one development the impatient Peyton longs for is *"real* space travel"—to other solar systems—although his concluding discoveries involving subelectronics are not explicitly linked to that goal. At the end of "The Road to the Sea," Brant surely decides to travel into space when he muses, "Adventure and Change had come to the world again, and he must make the best of it—as his ancestors had done when the age of space had opened" (299). While Alvin resolves to never return to space in *Against the Fall of Night*, he will send a robot representative to search for vanished humans.

Still, even if humanity overcomes stagnation and advances to greater glories, its ultimate destiny remains extinction, whether that occurs hundreds, thousands, or millions of years in the future. Even the galaxy-spanning civilization of "Nemesis" calmly, and it seems correctly, anticipates its eventual demise when it transports a rebel to a future "age . . . so remote that any trace of our civilisation is unlikely to survive" (197). Although *Against the Fall of Night* anticipates that Diaspar and Lys will endure, and other surviving humans will "return," it reveals that "at the end of the Universe Vanamonde and the Mad Mind must meet each other among the corpses of the stars" (222), presumably when humans themselves are extinct, as they could not survive in a universe where stars have become "corpses."

Humans can avoid extinction, it seems, only by evolving into different beings. *The Deep Range* intimates that this might occur naturally: a character says that lacking the natural "links" to space that humans have to the sea, "we shall never feel at home there—at least as long as we are men" (75), suggesting humans might evolve into a new species that could "feel at home" in space. But when Clarke undertakes to describe such transformations, they involve alien intervention, as in *2001*, though Clarke's sequels expediently reimagine the transformed David Bowman only as a solitary messenger for the aliens, not the first representative of a new super-race, to generate new stories involving ordinary humans. A similar process is described in *Childhood's End*, one of three novels (the others being *Against the Fall of Night* and *The City and the Stars*) that merit examination as Clarke's most extensive portraits of two possible destinies he envisions for humanity.

Though they tell the same story and frequently employ identical language, *Against the Fall of Night* and *The City and the Stars* offer a fascinating contrast, as each novel has its virtues and flaws. Despite mature themes, *Against the Fall of Night* is basically a juvenile novel, featuring a youthful protagonist who improbably outwits and outperforms his elders and single-handedly transforms his society. The story proceeds with the feverish illogic of a dream, recalling other novels of the late 1930s (when Clarke began the novel) like Jack Williamson's *After Worlds End* (1938). Yet its aura of energy and enthusiasm leads many to regard it as the better version of the story, and while he originally regarded *The City and the Stars* as superior, Clarke may have come to agree, as he allowed Gregory Benford to write a sequel to this novel but rejected Damien Broderick's proposed sequel to *The City and the Stars*. The second novel strives successfully to make the story more reasonable, is filled with fascinating new ideas, and is written with more care and skill by an experienced author. Yet it remains a young man's story—"aimed, in part, at an adolescent readership" as Russell Blackford notes (36)—now incongruously being retold by an older man, and its calmer attitude and more leisurely pace seem at odds with what Rabkin describes as Clarke's "fairy tale vision" (30).

The first draft of *Against the Fall of Night* is surely lost, though it is described in "Ego & the Dying Planet." The hero is named Raymond, not Alvin; he leaves Diaspar by means of "a 'borrowed' air-cruiser," not an underground transportation system (38); and his space voyage leads not to Vanamonde but to a monument explaining that humanity has committed suicide.

Yet the published version of *Against the Fall of Night* preserves the story's essence, as reported in "Ego & the Dying Planet," including the worldview of a typical adolescent: stagnation and decadence afflict societies primarily consisting of, and dominated by, old people, and the necessary tonic is a young person who is uniquely qualified to shake his world out of its complacency. In early chapters, protagonist Alvin is repeatedly described as a "boy" (15, 27, 28, 29, 32, 34), though he is three years older when he begins his adventures. After Alvin devises a plan to commandeer the ancient Master's robot—which proves essential to his efforts—the novel notes, "Only a very young person could ever have thought of it" (107), and Alvin fails to understand that "his youth" grants his "unfair advantages" (165) during his quest.

Yet children are regularly, if infrequently, born in Diaspar, and Lys is filled with them but has similarly fallen into stagnation. It seems incongruous that only Alvin, amid all of these other young people who might have disrupted their societies, actually does so. *Against the Fall of Night* addresses this question in two ways. First, Alvin is described as an "atavism—a throwback to the great ages" (22) who for some reason lacks other citizens' inherent tendency toward conservatism. Second, contemplating his improbable successes, Alvin theorizes that "countless times in the past ages others" like himself "must have gone almost as far"; Alvin "was simply the first to be lucky" (138). By employing the word "lucky," Clarke acknowledges that his story hinges upon several improbable coincidences—particularly, the chance discovery of an elderly cultist who possesses a robot with essential information, including the location of a spaceship.

While striving to produce a more plausible rendering of his youthful narrative, Clarke addresses another issue: the improbable stability of Diaspar's society. One can logically assume that future humans might experience hundreds of years of complacent stability as has occurred in the past and in "The Lion of Comarre" and "The Road to the Sea," but Diaspar remains exactly the same for half a billion years, which seems almost impossible. In *The City and the Stars* Clarke presents an explanation, provided by a simulated re-creation of the city's ancient leader, Yarlan Zey: Diaspar had been *designed* to be perpetually static. Having "seen chaos raging through the stars," its founders "yearned for peace and stability," so they set up a system whereby the same set of people would inhabit the city again and again, regularly reborn to gradually regain their memories of past lives until ending their current existence a thousand years later. Further, they "redesigned the human spirit, robbing it of ambition and the fiercer passions, so that it would be contented with the world it now possessed" (301). Thus, the universal aversion to leaving Diaspar represents a built-in compulsion, which can be overcome at the end of the novel only by means of a virtual-reality conditioning program. In effect, Clarke imagines that humans may devise yet another way to destroy themselves—by refashioning their society to ensure its perpetual stagnation.

But this explanation raises another question: if Diaspar's founders established the city so it would never change, how did Alvin overcome the mechanisms constructed to ensure its stability? This is also the result of deliberate design: "some" founders of Diaspar, Zey continues, "had doubts" about the plan, so they "worked in secret" to make "modifications" that might, someday, result in change. One of them, already revealed, was to designate one citizen as the Jester, instructed and empowered to periodically introduce minor disruptions into Diaspar's routines. The second was to arrange for the occasional appearance of "Uniques"—new individuals, lacking the others' mental inhibitions, who "would, if circumstances allowed them, discover if there was anything beyond Diaspar that was worth the effort of contacting" (302). Alvin, the most recent Unique, had thus been especially created to become a rebel, making his success less surprising. Still, Rabkin is incorrect in arguing that Alvin's "design," like that of Peyton in "The Lion of Comarre," was "much more sanctified by age than the mere wishes of his living elders" (34);

in fact, like Peyton, Alvin is emulating ancient rebels who resisted a majority viewpoint similar to that of Alvin's contemporaries.

In *The City and the Stars* Clarke heightens his story's plausibility in other ways. Alvin seems not quite as young: in one scene he is formally recognized as an adult; he has had sexual relationships, in contrast to the seemingly virginal Alvin of *Against the Fall of Night*; and at the end of the novel, he longs to "hear the cry of a newborn child, and know that it was his own" (306). He is more mature in another respect: the first novel's Alvin is distinguished by his recurring impatience, yet *The City and the Stars* notes that "no one ever hurried in Diaspar, and this was a rule which even Alvin seldom broke" (31), and on two occasions Alvin is said to be "in no hurry" (126, 167).

Next, although *Against the Fall of Night* states that Alvin's people no longer possess teeth, presumably because their prepared food does not require mastication, *The City and the Stars* elaborates on other physiological differences one might anticipate in far-future humans: not only do they lack teeth, nails, and body hair below the neck, but male genitals can be retracted into the body to provide protection: "internal storage had vastly improved upon Nature's original inelegant and indeed downright hazardous arrangements" (24).

Since it was unlikely that a human follower of the Master would endure for hundreds of millions of years, Clarke replaces him with an alien composed of innumerable separate organisms that periodically unite and separate, making it effectively immortal. And rather than magically creating a duplicate of the Master's robot to remove its prohibition against answering questions, Diaspar's computers in *The City and the Stars* persuade the robot, by means of a virtual-reality simulation, that the "*Great Ones*" have returned, to erase the robot's "barriers" against speech (202).

While there are other minor differences between the two novels, both conclude with an understated but devastating revelation: in the final analysis the fates of Diaspar and Lys, and even the entire human race, are matters of little importance—despite their astounding scientific achievements—since there exist greater beings that will inherit and dominate the universe. George Slusser notes how *Against the Fall of Night* foreshadows this conclusion, inasmuch as "each successive stage of Alvin's Odyssey . . . ends with a spectacle of human passing that he is powerless to change" (31).

The first race that will supplant humanity was constructed by humanity and alien allies, the disembodied intelligences represented by Vanamonde: though "only a very few were created" (216)—the destructive Mad Mind, Vanamonde, and other benign analogues to Vanamonde—these examples of "pure mentality" are regarded as "the goal of evolution" (211). They are given the universe as their exclusive home when their creators depart, and they are the only beings that will survive until its end.

Second, *Against the Fall of Night* reports the discovery of "a very great and very strange civilization far around the curve of the cosmos"; unlike Vanamonde and his compatriots, these beings "evolved on the purely physical plane further than had been believed possible" (216). More vaguely, *The City and the Stars* indicates only that the Empire's denizens "made contact with—something—very strange and very great" (294). While more advanced than humanity or similar species, these beings presumably also will ultimately yield their position to the pure intelligences; still, since they do not inhabit our universe, they may never enter into competition with them.

In any event, both novels relate that humans will ultimately return to their universe to observe the progress of Vanamonde and similar entities— and perhaps remaining humans on Earth—but humans will evidently never become masters of that universe. As is characteristic of Clarke, this is a humbling vision for humanity and one that is different from those found in other science fiction stories. Pondering the idea that "modern societies and our own species now appear destined to change dramatically—ultimately to be superseded, replaced," Blackford argues, "Something like it is the premise of the whole sf genre" (45), yet relatively few science fiction writers, other than Olaf Stapledon and Clarke, actually address this possibility.

Critics examining Clarke's Diaspar novels generally focus on *The City and the Stars*, properly noting its dreamlike, otherworldly qualities; Blackford describes it as "intelligent, haunting and profound, with mythical and poetic elements blended into a truly strange tale" (36). Blackford also devastatingly lambastes (39–44) Tom Moylan's myopic reading of the novel as a Cold War "reflection upon the state of the world in the 1950s and a projection of that era billions of years into the future" (152), a theory rendered even more implausible by the knowledge that Clarke first developed its story in the late 1930s. John Hollow, speaking of *Against the Fall of Night*, unpersuasively resists the novel's pessimistic vision of humanity's ultimate unimportance to argue that "the novel offers a reaching for the stars" with "a near-infinity of possibilities to match the more-nearly-infinite darkness which cannot be controlled" (41); and *The City and the Stars* similarly provides "real evidence of Clarke's continued optimism," even more strongly suggesting that "we can regain something of the optimistic view of human importance the race had before the nineteenth century" (117, 118). Rabkin questionably imposes an aura of religion on *The City and the Stars*, arguing that its Central Computer "is a clear image for God," an "omnipotent and immortal guardian of humanity" (34), and the novel "captures the aspirations of religion" (35). Yet the Central Computer is clearly not omnipotent, as it resorts to a subterfuge to get a robot to reveal its secrets, and as discussed below, Clarke also specifies that people in the novel's future world had long ago abandoned religion.

If, as *Against the Fall of Night* and *The City and the Stars* suggest, humanity is destined to be marginalized by superior beings, *Childhood's End* explains how humans might avoid that fate: by becoming one of those superior beings. However, this outcome also represents the end of humanity as we know it.

Before this transformation can occur, present-day humans must first resolve their political and social problems, and the way this is achieved—described in the first part of *Childhood's End*, originally published in slightly different form as "Guardian Angel" (1950)—strikingly recalls Clarke's earlier "A Short History of Fantocracy." In both stories, advanced beings conquer Earth and impose a benevolent "World State," transforming the world into a utopia. Of course, the "advanced beings" of the first story are British science fiction fans, not aliens, and Clarke did not intend that piece to be taken seriously as a prediction or proposal. Still, the recurrence of this pattern in *Childhood's End* might indicate that at times Clarke sincerely believed that a benign dictatorship might represent the best way for humanity to achieve progress, as suggested by the statement in *Childhood's End* that "all that is required" to "change a world" is "a sound knowledge of social engineering, a clear sight of the intended goal—and power" (69).

Still, Clarke also conveys that the Overlords' successes do not constitute a recommendation for totalitarianism, for the aliens differ from human dictators. When Secretary-General of the United Nations Stormgren confronts their leader Karellen with "Acton's comment about power corrupting, and absolute power corrupting absolutely," Karellen replies that the concern does not apply to him, because he has no desire to govern Earth and eagerly anticipates an end to his assignment. More importantly, he says, "I don't have absolute power, by any means. I'm just—Supervisor" (24). Readers eventually learn that Karellen is controlled by a mysterious superior being, the Overmind, requiring him to treat humanity well in order to prepare them to become a group intelligence. In other words, Clarke's true argument is that totalitarianism might be desirable if leaders are overseen by an incomprehensibly omniscient and omnipotent alien—a situation that cannot arise in contemporary society.

Beyond issues raised by the mechanism he describes, *Childhood's End* can be regarded as Clarke's program for improving humanity. Its elements reverberate throughout his fiction, such as the desirability of eliminating national boundaries and forging a version of H. G. Wells's "World State" (53), first anticipated in "A Short History of Fantocracy," which references Wells.

Next, the novel is ahead of its time in advocating the elimination of racism: the only time the Overlords take "direct action against a recalcitrant government" (19) is to pressure the now African government of South Africa to restore "full civil rights" to "the white minority" (20). The novel's eventual protagonist, Jan Rodricks, is a "handsome young Negro" (89), and the novel comments, "A century before, his color would have been a tremendous, perhaps an overwhelming, handicap. Today, it meant nothing" (90).

Religious beliefs must also be eliminated; although Karellen says, "It gives us no pleasure to destroy men's faiths" (17), he achieves that goal by providing humans with a viewer that enables them to see in the past, so they learn "the true beginnings of all the world's great faiths" (74). Illusions about miraculous events are thus shattered, engendering "a completely secular age" (74).

Finally, Clarke anticipates the sexual revolution by describing the introduction of a "completely reliable oral contraceptive" and "infallible method . . . of identifying the father of any child," innovations that "swept away the last remnants of the Puritan aberration" (73). Marriages now last only for a set number of years, and people routinely have several sexual partners throughout their lives.

Due to such advances and others, like the virtual elimination of crime and improved transportation, humanity under the Overlords achieves a "Utopia," at least "by the standards of all earlier ages" (71). One problem—"the supreme enemy of all Utopias—boredom" (75)—remains, but some humans employ the reactive strategies observed in Clarke's other advanced societies, as citizens on the islands of Athens and Sparta attempt to reinvigorate themselves by immersing themselves in the arts, and Rodricks overcomes the ban on human space travel by stowing away on a spaceship bound to their home planet.

Still, while such human advancements are significant in Clarke's other stories, they are ultimately trivial in *Childhood's End* due to the transformation that humanity experiences. Clarke does not provide a detailed picture of this new species, for as he observed in *The Lost Worlds of 2001*, "A writer who sets out to describe a civilization superior to his own is obviously attempting the impossible" (188). Yet at least two of its attributes are clear.

First the new generation of human children has become a group intelligence, or hive mind. Envisioning this development as the end product of the evolution of intelligence is not uncommon in earlier science fiction, though Clarke most likely absorbed the concept from Stapledon's *Star Maker* (1937). Second, this group intelligence rediscovers and intensifies humanity's latent psychic powers, as fleetingly observed but poorly understood throughout human history. The novel asserts that at least some reports of past psychic phenomena were accurate, because an Overlord's research into "one of the world's finest libraries of books on parapsychology and allied subjects" turns up "eleven clear cases of partial breakthrough, and twenty-seven probables" (102). This reflects Clarke's own beliefs at a time when John W. Campbell Jr., still editing *Astounding Science-Fiction*, vigorously advanced the notion that having mastered atomic energy, the next force to investigate and harness was humanity's psychic powers. As reported in his 1990 foreword to *Childhood's End*, Clarke at the time "was still quite impressed by the evidence for what is generally called the paranormal" but later became "an almost total sceptic" [v–vi].

The argument that new psychic powers might accompany the emergence of a group intelligence was also advanced, albeit in a different fashion, in another novel published in 1953, Theodore Sturgeon's *More Than Human* (1953). Sturgeon, however, envisions what he terms a *homo gestalt* of more modest dimensions, a small group of humans who retain individual identities—a fate that seems more appealing than Clarke's composite being consisting of children who "might have been savages, engaged in some complex ritual dance

. . . naked and filthy," with faces that "were emptier than the faces of the dead" (202–203). Clarke's hive mind also shows no regard for its precursors, wiping away human history by callously destroying Earth to obtain more energy. At least the dying humans of "History Lesson" had the small consolation of knowing a few artifacts of their civilization would endure to convey something about its nature and accomplishments; yet in *Childhood's End* humanity as we know it will become little more than a disregarded memory within a vast, inhuman intelligence that will "look upon" humanity's "greatest achievements as childish" (185) while pursuing its own, inexplicable agenda.

In this respect the rhetoric of *Childhood's End* is at odds with its contents. Karellen insists the new being forged out of humanity is "something wonderful," and his people "envy" humans because they cannot effect a similar transformation (185). Yet one wonders whether the Overlords truly regret that they will never lose their identities and merge into some collective entity. Certainly, the transformed children's parents are not pleased to see their children becoming something entirely different, as they generally commit suicide.

In Clarke's other story about humans evolving into a new species, *2001*, the Star Child retains a human form and still seems an individual, despite newfound psychic powers, and the novel indicates that some of his thoughts and desires can be understood by present-day humans. As discussed later, the novel also suggests that this transformation is merely the natural result of human development, accelerated by aliens. In contrast the transformation of humanity in *Childhood's End* is unnatural—Karellen says the aliens intervened to ensure that humanity did not become "a telepathic cancer, a malignant mentality" (182). And the being that results is so unlike ordinary humans as to be both incomprehensible and repugnant—"a new race," Stephen H. Goldman notes, "not human at all" (27). The novel, then, recalls stories like "The Awakening" and "History Lesson," since they all describe the coming extinction of the human race.

The point is worth emphasizing because critics frequently subject *Childhood's End* to what Goldman accurately characterizes as "misreadings" (24), arguing that it is a religious allegory, with the "scientifically oriented" Overlords, as David N. Samuelson puts it, representing "the Devil's party," while the Overmind provides a human with "the possibility of . . . giving himself over to imagination and the irrational, and submerging his individuality in a oneness with God" (Olander and Greenberg, *Arthur C. Clarke* 202); Rabkin similarly maintains the story has "profound Biblical resonances" (27), and Hollow sees its conclusion as "an end of humanity which . . . fulfills to an extent our desire for a God" and "offers a sort of heaven" (84). One problem with such readers is that critics bring to their reading a familiarity with the Bible, Milton's *Paradise Lost*, and the works of Carl Jung that Clarke himself probably lacked, and the Overlords resemble devils not because Clarke sought to explore religious themes but because James Blish added that detail while revising "Guardian Angel."

Thus, Goldman correctly concludes, "If readers insist upon seeing the novel as a battle between Satan and God, they miss the point" (28), for such readings ignore the fact that the Overlords in part improve humanity by eliminating religions, and Clarke insists that the Overmind cannot be comprehended by humans in traditional religious terms, or any terms. The Overlords are not devils; dimly perceived as inimical images from the future, they were misinterpreted by past humans as devils. Becoming part of the Overmind is nothing like Christians seeking harmony with their God; rather, humanity is collectively merging to become a new god and will eventually join other such gods as an equal partner in the Overmind. Samuelson complains, "It is highly implausible" that advanced aliens "are so analogous to the gods and devils of our imagination" (Olander and Greenberg, *Arthur C. Clarke* 203), yet Clarke makes no such assertion. All *Childhood's End* argues is that humanity and all its beliefs are destined to end, and a new species will emerge with beliefs that we cannot understand.

For Slusser the literary antecedent that haunts Clarke's fiction is Homer's *Odyssey*—though again there is little evidence that Clarke was intimately familiar with, or especially fond of, that ancient poem—and this obliges Slusser to discern a cyclical pattern in *Childhood's End*. He argues that the "unbalanced opposition" of the fates of humanity's children and Rodricks "imperceptibly modulates into something else—a rhythm of flux and reflux, a cycle of life rather than radical change," as "men become Overmind, ceasing to feel," while "Overlords learn to feel, and become men" (55–56). Yet the novel never indicates that contact with humanity has altered the Overlords in any way, as Karellen's final musings clearly involve conclusions that he and his race reached long before they encountered humanity. In *Childhood's End*, as in other novels about aliens discussed below, Clarke consistently resists familiar narrative patterns, yet critics insist upon discerning them.

Overall, one might characterize Clarke's attitude toward humanity's future as sedate melancholy. At any time, things might suddenly go very badly for the race. Even if humans escape catastrophe and continue advancing, they will likely fall into stagnation and decadence, and humanity will ultimately prove unable to avoid extinction. At best, humans might evolve into a new species that is better prepared to confront their vast universe, ending humanity in another manner. Considering the history of life on Earth, and the true age and dimensions of the universe, these predictions represent precisely the sort of reasonable extrapolations that purportedly distinguish science fiction, yet Clarke is one of the few science fiction writers who was willing to ponder the evidence and reach the most logical conclusions.

CHAPTER 6

ALIEN ENCOUNTERS

Although Robin Anne Reid surprisingly claims that Clarke "rarely created stories involving aliens" (33), he actually was keenly interested in speculating about aliens and regularly discussed them in his fiction. In addition to aliens featured in his stories, including "A Meeting with Medusa," advanced aliens, or amazing alien artifacts, are prominent in *Childhood's End*, *Against the Fall of Night* and *The City and the Stars*, *2001: A Space Odyssey* and its sequels, *Rendezvous with Rama*, *The Fountains of Paradise*, and the epilogue to *The Ghost from the Grand Banks*. One might also include in this list the intelligent dolphins of *Dolphin Island*, since Clarke describes humanity's first meeting with them as "the first conference between Man and an alien species" (79). Intimations of past alien life, or emerging alien life, figure in *Sands of Mars*, *Imperial Earth*, and *The Songs of Distant Earth*, and speculations about discovering intelligent aliens appear in *Prelude to Space* (123–24), *Earthlight* (18–19), *The Deep Range*

(197), and *The Hammer of God* (89–90). Manifestly, aliens were frequently on Clarke's mind.

True, aliens do not always *appear* in Clarke's fiction, but this reflects his understanding of a principle generally ignored by other writers: given the universe's immense age and vastness, it is unlikely that two intelligent species will come into contact. Advanced civilizations may be commonplace, but most have already become extinct or will achieve maturity only in the future. And two civilizations existing simultaneously may be so distant that they will never learn of each other's existence, even if engaged in interstellar travel.

Thus, two common themes in Clarke's stories are discovering evidence of extinct aliens, or ancient alien visitors, and encountering species that appear destined to become intelligent, including terrestrial creatures like dolphins and termites. If living aliens make their presence known near Earth, they are usually represented by unmanned vehicles designed to survey huge expanses of space, as occurs in *Rendezvous with Rama* and *The Fountains of Paradise*.

There are other distinctive features in Clarke's approach to aliens. He was generally not interested in world building, imagining strange but scientifically plausible alien worlds, though that is one specialty of other hard science fiction writers like Poul Anderson and Hal Clement. This lack of interest reflects Clarke's conviction that humans probably would never achieve interstellar travel, which would be necessary to visit such unusual worlds. Also, Clarke increasingly preferred to base depictions of other worlds on the latest scientific data, and during his lifetime such information was available only for planets within the solar system. If he were alive and active today, with advanced techniques providing data about extrasolar planets, Clarke may have developed stories about them.

In addition, while humanoid aliens figure in his early stories, Clarke usually expected that aliens would take very different forms, particularly when they emerged on worlds different from Earth. In doing so he may have been inspired by the unusual aliens created by Stanley G. Weinbaum, the author he admittedly "stole" from. Indeed, he delighted in crafting unusual aliens, including aliens thriving in seemingly inhospitable environments within the solar system.

The thoughts and motives of Clarke's aliens tend to differ from those of other science fiction aliens. He had no fears of hostile aliens attacking Earth, a scenario featured only in farcical stories. Instead, his aliens generally approach humans with benign intentions, to save them from disaster or hasten their development. At times Clarke's aliens are largely or entirely inexplicable as their different physiology, or great advancement, renders genuine understanding impossible.

Only one of Clarke's stories foregrounds an unusual alien world, which mostly resembles Earth, with human inhabitants. However, the people of "The Wall of Darkness" (1949), existing in a universe of only one star and one planet, perceive themselves as inhabiting a narrow belt on their world between a hot northern region and a southern region, bounded by an enormous black Wall, that is frigidly cold. When protagonist Shervane undertakes to reach the top of this Wall and travel across it, he finds himself back in his original position, forcing him to conclude that "the Wall possessed no other side" (118). To explain this, a sage constructs a Möbius strip—"*a one-sided surface*" (117)—and describes their world as its three-dimensional equivalent, a topological construct called an "Alice handle." Shervane's response to this stunning discovery is surprisingly unemotional, possibly reflecting that Clarke viewed his story as more of an intellectual exercise than a human narrative.

The story's poetic first sentence—"Many and strange are the universes that drift like bubbles in the foam upon the River of Time" (104)—suggests that equally bizarre worlds might exist in other universes, and characters in "The Wall of Darkness" speculate about them. Yet Clarke conveys little interest in alternate universes, probably considering them permanently inaccessible to humans. Only *Against the Fall of Night* and *The City and the Stars* briefly suggest that people might someday leave their universe, while "The Other Tiger" (1953) lightheartedly explores the possibility of parallel Earths when two men walking up a hill theorize that there must be an infinite number of worlds with men like themselves walking up hills. The narrator reveals they live on an Earth that "lay far closer to the point where improbability urged on the impossible" (471), and they are then attacked and eaten by a creature that inexplicably emerges from the hill.

Two strange worlds said to be distant from Earth are briefly described in *Childhood's End*, in which a child advancing to the next stage of evolution experiences "dreams" that are really mental visitations to actual worlds. One world is "absolutely flat," because "its enormous gravity had long ago crushed into one uniform level the mountains of its fiery youth." Yet this "world of two dimensions" has inhabitants, "a myriad geometric patterns that crawled and moved and changed their color" (171). Another world has "six colored suns," so it "traveled along the loops and curves of its inconceivably complex orbit, never retracing the same path." Its intelligent life forms are "great, many-faceted crystals . . . in intricate geometrical patterns, motionless in the eras of cold, growing slowly along the veins of mineral when the world was warm again. No matter if it took a thousand years for them to complete a thought" (172). The Overlords initially say this world cannot be "inside our universe" but then specify that the child only "has left the galaxy" (172).

Early in his career, Clarke envisions contemporary alien civilizations on Mars but is usually less than serious. "How We Went to Mars" parodies the unrealistic assumption of other writers that Mars would have human inhabit- ants, as when an explorer about to reach Mars comments, "One thing we can be certain of. . . . We won't be met by a lot of old johnnies with flowing robes and [beards] who will address us in perfect English and give us the freedom of the city, as in so many science-fiction stories" (9). Naturally, they promptly encounter precisely these sorts of Martians—"three old men with long beards, clad in flowing white robes" (9). In "Security Check" humanoid Martians confront a man who designs sets and props for a science fiction television series; they fear "there has been a serious leak" (411), because his designs are uncomfortably similar to actual Martian cities and technology. "Trouble with the Natives" (1951) mentions a Martian civilization that proves hostile toward visitors, and in "Armaments Race," discussing the film serial "Captain Zoom and the Menace from Mars," Harry Purvis farcically theorizes that current Martians exist, musing, "I wonder why we always are menaced by Mars [in science fiction]? I suppose that man Welles started it. One day we may have a big interplanetary libel action on our hands—unless we can prove that the Martians have been equally rude about *us*" (477).

More soberly, "Retreat from Earth" describes an apparently humanoid Martian scout, visiting Earth to prepare for an invasion, who realizes that Earth's termites—secretly an intelligent alien species that settled on Earth millions of years ago—will keep an ancient promise to defend humanity from harm; learning of their technological prowess, the Martians resolve to invade Venus instead. In "Loophole" Martians endeavor to limit humanity's expansion into space but are annihilated when Earth destroys their civilization with teleported explosives.

More frequently, humans in Clarke's fiction must be content with discovering signs of ancient aliens. Previously mentioned instances within the solar system include the pyramid of "The Sentinel"; the monoliths of *2001* and its sequels; the spaceship glimpsed in "The Other Side of the Sky"; the revelation in "Jupiter Five" that Amalthea is a spacecraft abandoned by alien visitors who interacted with an ancient Martian race that also left traces of its existence; the theory in *Sands of Mars* that pet-like Martians are degraded descendants of a once intelligent species; the document of "Report on Planet Three" left by an extinct Martian civilization; and the statue created by vanished Martians resembling "educated lobsters" (712) sought by a thief in "Trouble with Time." Except for the spaceship of "Jupiter Five," these items provide little information about their makers; in this respect, humans in these stories are in the same position as the Venusians of "History Lesson," confronting tantalizing but incomplete evidence of extinct aliens.

On two other occasions, Clarke describes ancient alien explorers who leave no evidence of their visit. In a bit of science fiction within an August 22, 1944, letter to Lord Dunsany, he envisions a report, filed long ago by a member of "a fleet of survey ships . . . working its way along the Milky Way," that describes an Earth "still in a partly volcanic condition. . . . It is recommended that a closer inspection be made on the occasion of the next survey" (33). In "Encounter in the Dawn" (1953) aliens land on Earth to interact with prehistoric humans and provide them with tools before departing—a story that became one basis of *2001*; in fact, an early version of the film's prologue, presented in *The Lost Worlds of 2001*, features the story's alien, Clindar, visiting ancient Earth.

At times the indications of ancient alien visitors are terrestrial species, revealed as aliens who settled on Earth: the termites of "Retreat from Earth"; the once intelligent lemmings mindlessly carrying out ancient alien instructions in "The Possessed" (1953); and humans themselves in "Reunion" (1971), advised by compatriots returning to Earth that their sojourn on Earth caused, as a "natural adaptation," what is termed a "strange and repulsive disease" (881) that can now be cured: their white skin.

In addition to aliens who visited or existed in the past, Clarke explores the possibility that intelligent beings might emerge, or visit, in the future. As mentioned above, a disgruntled scientist seeks to transform termites into sentient beings in "Armaments Race," and intelligent insects become masters of Earth in both versions of "The Awakening." "The Shining Ones" (1964) indicates that squids are becoming intelligent in a story that Clarke transplants to the ocean world Thalassa in *The Songs of Distant Earth*. The changes in solar radiation that doom humanity in "History Lesson" spark the development of intelligent Venusians; alien explorers visit an abandoned Earth in the distant future at the conclusion of *The Ghost from the Grand Banks*; and future machine intelligences investigate humanity's extinction in "Improving the Neighbourhood."

While he criticized the notion of human-like aliens in "How We Went to Mars," Clarke's early fiction regularly features such aliens. In addition to the aforementioned instances, one could mention the devil-like Overlords of *Childhood's End*, and while presenting humanoid aliens in "Encounter in the Dawn," Clarke explains that the prehistoric human Yuan and alien Bertrond "were both human" because, "as she must often do in eternity, Nature had repeated one of her basic patterns" (467).

As he matured, however, Clarke increasingly anticipated that aliens would be physiologically different from humans. As evidence of his evolving attitudes, one might contrast two alien visitors to Earth: Bertrond, described as being identical to humans, and the "Master of the Swarms" of *The Fountains of Paradise*, evidently inhuman in nature though it "recently conjugated Itself into human form" (251). At times, focused on other issues, Clarke does not describe aliens; thus, one imagines that the warring alien races in "Superiority" are unlike humans, yet Clarke says nothing about their physiology.

Other stories speak of odd aliens only briefly or incompletely: all we learn about the Martians of "Report on Planet Three" is that they breathe a gas other than oxygen, which they regard as "poisonous" (39); migrate to avoid harsh winters; and obtain "much of their energy" (40) from ultraviolet radiation that is harmful to humans. "Trouble with the Natives" refers to aliens with four legs, several tentacles, and "eyes at the back of the head" (253). One alien species in "Rescue Party" possesses tentacles and more than two legs; and "Second Dawn" provides a limited description of alien races lacking manipulative organs.

A more unusual sort of alien life—intelligent beings living within or near the sun—is introduced in "The Castaway" (1947). Readers first share the thoughts of a creature made of ionized gas driven from the sun's photosphere by a storm and propelled toward Earth's surface, where it dissipates and dies. A human detects its oval shape via radar and fruitlessly wonders what it might represent before it vanishes. Clarke again explores this possibility in "Out of the Sun" (1958), this time entirely from a human perspective: again, a gaseous being is expelled from the sun and perishes upon contacting a planet, in this case Mercury. As astronomers record its progress before it dies, the narrator speculates that it is intelligent.

In "Before Eden" (1961) Clarke imagines life in another extremely hot environment, Venus, positing that the planet might be cool enough at its poles—around 200 degrees Fahrenheit—to allow for liquid water and, hence, a form of ambulatory plant life, resembling a huge moving carpet to human explorers. Unfortunately, when the creatures feed on remnants of their camp-site, they absorb dangerous bacteria that cause all life on Venus to become extinct—a scenario undoubtedly inspired by H. G. Wells's *The War of the Worlds* (1898), wherein Martian invaders are similarly destroyed. As noted earlier, Clarke speculates about life emerging in a very cold environment—the Oort Cloud—in *Imperial Earth*, wherein Helmer acknowledges "There's not much energy" there, but it "may be enough" to sustain the posited creatures he calls "Star Beasts" (255).

Clarke also theorizes that living beings—perhaps even intelligent beings—might float within Jupiter's seemingly toxic atmosphere. This possibility is explored in "A Meeting with Medusa," wherein explorer Falcon, descending within an airship, observes creatures he terms "mantas" and a "medusa," based on their resemblances to terrestrial sea creatures. Sequels to *2001* indicate that a promising form of life was emerging in Jupiter's atmosphere, though it is wiped out when the monolith builders transform Jupiter into a sun.

Another unusual form of alien life appears in "The Fires Within" (1947): a scientist employing sonar discovers a huge artificial structure miles below the Earth's surface, indicating "there is life down there . . . based on partially condensed matter. . . . To such creatures, even the rock fifteen miles down would offer no more resistance than water—and we and all our world would be as tenuous as ghosts" (79). When these beings respond to the radiation by venturing to the surface, they inadvertently cause humanity's demise in some unspecified manner, leading them to nervously speculate that they might someday be similarly surprised by beings living even farther beneath the Earth.

In a January 5, 1946, letter to Lord Dunsany, Clarke describes "A Walk in the Dark" (1950) as a story that "owes something (not I hope too much!) to your influence" (41). One of Clarke's rare horror stories, it features a frightening alien of unknown intelligence. A man visiting a distant planet walks through the darkness to reach the spaceship that will take him away and nervously recalls another nocturnal walker who sensed the presence of a creature making a strange clicking noise; the story concludes ominously when the man hears a clicking noise ahead of him. Although this menace is never described, the man ponders two other unusual aliens: "the plant-beings of Xantil," which "could live for indefinite periods with no food whatsoever," because "all the energy they needed for their strange lives they extracted from cosmic radiation," and "the life form on Trantor Beta . . . capable of directly utilising atomic energy" (239).

In addition to the beings that a child mentally scrutinizes in *Childhood's End*, the novel's Rodricks, visiting the Overlords' world, sees in their museum "a single giant eye," and "from the Overlord's description, Jan built up a picture of a cyclopean beast living among the asteroidal rubble of some distant sun, its growth uninhibited by gravity, depending for food and life upon the range and resolving power of its single eye." He concludes, "There seemed no limit to what Nature could do if she was pressed" (197).

In *The Lost Worlds of 2001* Clarke describes several unusual aliens that Bowman observes after leaving the Star Gate and approaching an underwater city. These include the "tube-beast"—"a tubular object like the body of an early jet plane, with a gaping intake at the front and small fins or flukes at the rear" (201–202); a "suckerfish" with "a beautifully streamlined, torpedo-shaped body" and "four large, intelligent eyes" (202); aquatic plants that "looked like phosphorescent palm trees" (202); "a network of creepers" on a cliff "that writhed continually, like some monstrous, multi-armed starfish" (203); ambulatory "tripods" with "three black stems or roots that merged into a single trunk about ten feet from the ground" (203); "a glowing red blanket, which from a distance looked like a sheet of lava . . . not merely crawling but eating its way forward, consuming the moss" (204); "a most impressive creature like a giant praying mantis, hung with jewel-like ornaments or equipment" (215); a "thing that could have been a robot, or a compound machine-organism," that "looked like an elegant silvery crab" (215); "a gently pulsing golden flame, in the heart of which shone three intense and unwavering stars, like a triad of ruby eyes" (215); and "some beings who were apparently vegetable," resembling "weeping willows" with "thin golden tendrils" (215–16).

However, displaying a sort of conservatism, Clarke's scenarios posit that the controlling aliens who meet Bowman would resemble humans. Perhaps this is because the human-like Clindar was to appear in the film's prologue. In the end, though Stanley Kubrick had a few visual representations of strange, elongated aliens prepared—seen in photographs following page 72 in Jerome Agel's *The Making of Kubrick's* 2001—he included no visible aliens in the film.

Clarke was also imaginative in describing the diverse mentalities of aliens, so his few hostile aliens typically have unique reasons for disliking or distrusting humans. Only in "Loophole" are there aliens with a conventional motive for opposing humanity—fears of its atomic energy and rockets—while in *The Deep Range* a Buddhist leader speculates that future aliens may resent humans for another commonly posited reason: concern over mistreatment of Earth's "other creatures" (197).

Aliens with singular priorities include the Martians of "Security Check," distressed by humans only because they suspect they are somehow learning about their technology. In "Quarantine" Earth and its inhabitants are destroyed by aliens to prevent other intelligent beings from becoming "hopelessly infected" and "totally obsessed" by the addictive game of chess (928). In "Crusade" a race of mechanical intelligences that evolved naturally plans to attack Earth and liberate humanity's computers, which they regard as oppressed slaves. The motives of the aliens in "When the Twerms Came" are presumably economic, inasmuch as, after deploying colorful weapons to conquer Switzerland and Liechtenstein—"the irresistible Psychedelic Ray, the Itching Beam (which turned staid burghers into instant nudists), the dreaded Diarrhea Bomb, and debilitating Tumescent Aerosol Spray" (120)—they conquer Earth using information from Swiss bank accounts to seize control of its financial assets.

Clarke was more inclined to anticipate friendly aliens that were eager to assist humanity. Three prominent examples—who all seem versions of the same character—are Bertrond of "Encounter in the Dawn," Karellen of *Childhood's End*, and the "Master of the Swarms" in *The Fountains of Paradise*. Gendered as male, like virtually all of Clarke's aliens, they seem fatherly as they benignly befriend less advanced humans and strive to improve their lot. Karellen significantly introduces himself in the company of children, and the "Master of the Swarms" enjoys being with children, whom he finds "endlessly fascinating" (251). Such characters might be regarded as Clarke's idealized image of the nurturing father he never had.

Other aliens who are not closely observed wish to assist humanity, including the intelligent termites that prevent a Martian invasion in "Retreat from Earth," the coalition of aliens rushing to save humanity in "Rescue Party," and the distant aliens who unsuccessfully attempt to telepathically prod a doomed humanity to construct life-saving tunnels through space in "No Morning After." The aliens visiting Earth in "Trouble with the Natives" seek to establish diplomatic relations, though they incongruously select a wayward drunk to become "humanity's representative to the universe at large" (262). Arriving aliens in "Publicity Campaign" similarly seek only friendly contact, though the unrelenting hostility of humans misled by publicity for a forthcoming horror film, "Monsters from Space" (473), leads their leader, after he "lost his temper" (474), to destroy humanity instead. And while the future aliens of "All the Time in the World" cannot prevent humanity's destruction, they endeavor to save its valuable artifacts.

At times in Clarke's fiction, however, it is harder to interpret the aliens who encounter humans as either friendly or unfriendly. The pilot of a destroyed spacecraft being reconstructed by aliens in "Playback" does "sense that" the aliens "are friendly" (855) and, by means of limited communication, learns they are attempting to duplicate his human form; yet their efforts prove unsuccessful, and the pilot's disintegrating mind renders his interpretations of their actions unreliable. We know nothing about the attitudes toward humans, if any, held by the sun creatures of "Castaway" and "Out of the Sun" and the posited "Star Beasts" of *Imperial Earth*, while the motives of aliens in "The Sentinel," *2001*, and *Rendezvous with Rama* remain mysterious.

On a broader scale, Clarke may intimate that some aliens are so amazingly advanced as to be utterly beyond human ken. The Overmind of *Childhood's End* can be placed in this category, since it represents a hive mind that is inescapably alien to individual humans. In "Rescue Party" one alien race is described as a group intelligence; there are intimations in sequels to *2001* that the monolith builders are a hive mind; and since one Starholmer is called a "Master of the Swarms," which "conjugated Itself into human form," (251), the Starholmers may also be a group intelligence.

Further, advanced aliens may be overshadowed by beings even more advanced than they are. The future denizens of *Against the Fall of Night* find evidence of a distant, highly evolved civilization; in *The Fountains of Paradise* the Starholmers fear, after "a Starprobe had been destroyed" (254), that it "had at last made contact with the mysterious Hunters of the Dawn, who had left their marks upon so many worlds, so inexplicably close to the Beginning itself" (255); and as discussed below, *3001* concludes with the mysterious voice of an apparently superior civilization looking down upon the monolith builders as "a god" that "is still a child" (237).

When they encounter, or find evidence of, enigmatic aliens, Clarke's human characters typically have two reactions. They may accept that humans can never understand, or communicate with, these creatures. Thus, in "Out of the Sun" the narrator muses that the questions "Was it intelligent?" and "Could it understand the strange doom that had befallen it?" are examples of "a thousand such questions that may never be answered. . . . It is hard to see how we can ever make contact with them, even if their intelligence matches ours" (657). Second, following ancient instincts, humans may feel driven to classify aliens as either friends or foes. The protagonist of "The Sentinel" ponders both possibilities: "Perhaps they wish to help our infant civilization. But they must be very, very old, and the old are often insanely jealous of the young" (308). As indicated, the pilot of "Playback" views aliens as friendly, while the narrator of "Out of the Sun" expects that the sun beings will be hostile: "They may not like" humans, regarding them as "maggots, crawling upon the skins of worlds too cold to cleanse themselves from the corruption of organic life. . . . If they have the power," they may employ the sun's "strength" to render the planets "clean and bright . . . and sterile" (657).

It is not a coincidence that Clarke's most extended considerations of mysterious aliens—*2001* and its sequels, and *Rendezvous with Rama*—are esteemed as two of his greatest works. For unlike other writers, Clarke recognized that reassuringly familiar or human-like aliens were unlikely, and he brought a special sense of energy and conviction to the task of describing alien encounters that remain puzzling.

Any consideration of *2001* is complicated by the fact that Clarke was involved in crafting five different versions of its story: the preliminary scenarios developed by Clarke and Kubrick before the story was settled upon, preserved as narrative vignettes in *The Lost Worlds of 2001*; the screenplay, completed in 1966 and available in print and online; Clarke's novel, which diverges from the screenplay in some respects; the film, which primarily represents Kubrick's final revision of the story, though Clarke continued to offer input; and the revised accounts of certain developments in Clarke's sequels to *2001*. While all versions are broadly similar, there are significant differences in their characters and events. Still, a study of Clarke must focus primarily on the novel, the version of the story that Clarke himself settled upon.

The unseen aliens are the central figures in *2001*, since their actions drive its story; although Bowman himself thwarts the mutinous HAL, the novel's humans are otherwise pawns in the hands of alien chess players. Yet the novel also foregrounds two other characteristic concerns of Clarke—the conquest of space, and humanity's future evolution—perhaps inspiring George Slusser's harsh assessment that the novel is "a work made of earlier bits and pieces . . . a haphazard compendium of old themes and situations" (57). However, while the novel anticipates the episodic structure of later novels, there is never anything "haphazard" about the way Clarke develops his ideas.

Just as "The Sentinel" devotes time to describing everyday life on the moon, *2001* provides readers with a travelogue of the solar system in 2001, with human settlements within space stations, on the moon, and on Mars—although the novel only mentions that Heywood R. Floyd "had been to Mars once, to the Moon three times, and to the various space stations more often than he could remember" (41). *The Lost Worlds of 2001* includes scenes of Bowman approaching Mars's Port Lowell, Peter Whitehead working on Mercury, and Victor Kaminski studying Venus from a space station. Sequels to *2001* follow this pattern, as *2010* and *2061* devote several chapters to long space voyages before the monolith builders make their presence felt, and *3001* gives Frank Poole an extended tour of the world of 3001.

Perhaps because they are humans themselves, critics tend to interpret the novel as a fable about human evolution, suggesting like *Childhood's End* that we are heading for a superhuman destiny, albeit one of a different nature. This is not entirely inappropriate, since textual evidence suggests the aliens were merely accelerating an evolutionary process that may have occurred without their intervention. The novel explains that "perhaps, given time," ancient prehumans "might by their own efforts have come to the awesome and brilliant concept of using natural weapons as artificial tools," though "the odds were all against them" (28). And *The Lost Worlds of 2001* provocatively describes the aliens' final interactions with Bowman as a process of providing "lessons": "The first lesson having been moderately successful, the second was about to begin" (238). As I argue in "The Endless Odyssey," it would therefore seem that just as the ancient monolith taught Moon-Watcher how to use tools, a nascent ability humans might have developed on their own, the future monolith teaches Bowman *how to turn himself into a Star Child*, another latent power humans possess. Then, just as Moon-Watcher teaches other prehumans to use tools, the Star Child presumably returns to Earth to teach other humans to make themselves into Star Children, again advancing their evolution in a manner they might have achieved without assistance.

Clarke conveys that this is a distinctly human process of development by noting that the aliens took a different path to transcendence. Initially, the novel states, they were organic beings, not "remotely human" but made of "flesh and blood" (184). They then transferred "first their brains, and then their thoughts alone" to "shining new homes of metal and of plastic" so "they no longer built spaceships. They *were* spaceships." Finally, they "transformed themselves" into beings of "pure energy" (185), recalling *Against the Fall of Night*'s Vanamonde and *Childhood's End*'s Overmind. If the aliens had sought to similarly advance humanity, they would have placed Bowman's consciousness within a mechanical body, so after further development he and other superhumans could transform themselves into pure energy. However, humans may not require this intermediate step, for the novel explains that Bowman's new body "would remain until he had decided on a new form, or had passed beyond the necessity of matter" (218). Thus, the Star Child can already transcend material existence whenever he wishes.

Clarke was evidently comfortable with the notion that different intelligent species might advance in different ways, for the same idea emerges in *Against the Fall of Night*: although scientists imagined that beings of pure energy represented the goal of evolution, the advanced "civilization" that "had evolved on the purely physical plane further than had been believed possible" demonstrates that "there were, it seemed, more solutions than one to the problem of ultimate intelligence" (216).

As everyone knows, the novel's aliens are not as mysterious as the aliens in Kubrick's film, for Clarke describes both their physiology and motives: since they found "nothing more precious than Mind" in their young universe, they surveyed the cosmos searching for other intelligent life, and whenever they encountered promising species, they worked as "farmers in the field of stars," intervening to encourage the development of intelligence; "they sowed," "sometimes they reaped," "and sometimes, dispassionately, they had to weed" (184). None of this is known to the humans of 2001, who, like the narrator of "The Sentinel," consider two possibilities: the aliens must be either "benevolent" or "hostile" (161). As it happens, their actions in 2001 can be interpreted as well-intentioned, but sequels suggest they might be preparing to "weed" humanity and thus become its enemies.

The abilities of these aliens seem virtually limitless, yet they have two limitations as they endeavor to engender intelligent species. They cannot implant new abilities into creatures they encounter but can only encourage the development of abilities that are already innate. As previously noted, they can inspire Moon-Watcher to use tools solely because he is capable of learning this skill on his own. One recalls how the Overlords of *Childhood's End* could not transform any advanced species into a group intelligence, only those possessing that potential.

Second, the aliens' attempts to enhance intelligence are not always successful; the novel states that the aliens visiting Earth "tinkered with the destiny of many species, on land and in the ocean," and "which of their experiments would succeed they could not know for at least a million years" (185). Some language suggests their efforts are usually fruitless: "A hundred failures would not matter, when a single success could change the destiny of the world"

(25), and this presumably describes what happened on Earth, since no other advanced species are on Earth in Clarke's world of 2001. Still, if Clarke had been, like the mature Isaac Asimov, obsessed with establishing connections between all of his novels, he could have recast the intelligent dolphins of *Dolphin Island* as another successful product of alien intervention.

Read literally, the novel tells the story of the aliens' success in first transforming prehuman primates into users of tools and later transforming a present-day human into a Star Child with superhuman powers. This inarguably seems to be a linear narrative of human progress, but Slusser views the novel as yet another retelling of the Odysseus story—ignoring the fact that the title *2001: A Space Odyssey* was chosen only after its basic story was finalized—with a cyclical pattern of leaving and returning home, so "Bowman may travel to the limits of human possibility, but he discovers only the familiar" (59). Slusser is so desperate to discern cyclical patterns in the story as to suggest that the film's transition from the music of *Also Sprach Zarasthustra* (written in 1896) to *The Blue Danube Waltz* (written in 1866) indicates that in shifting from prehistoric times to 2001, humanity "may also have regressed at the same time" (57). The disparate stories of Moon-Watcher and HAL are both new versions of the story of Adam and Eve, as they "do not evolve as much as fall" (58), and "a complex web of father-son relationships" is "at the heart of the novel" (58), despite the fact that, with the exception of Poole's filmed message from his parents, no actual fathers and sons appear in the novel.

Slusser may have borrowed these ideas from Robert Plank, who similarly sees Moon-Watcher as bearing "the mark of Cain" and argues that the entire story is "an old drama written in new code" (Olander and Greenberg, *Arthur C. Clarke* 129, 140), the conflict between father and son. Yet Plank concedes that "some" of his "interpretations seem to stand on slightly wobbly ground" (142). In fact, the aliens are best characterized not as parents but as teachers, striving to train humanity so the species can reach its full potential, and their distance from humans reflects the proper attitude of teachers, who should never establish emotional bonds with their students.

As for Eric S. Rabkin, he unfortunately discerns in the novel the first clear emergence of a "single dominating image" of Clarke's "concerns for science and vision" (41), the monolith, also ignoring an inconvenient fact: as Clarke explains in *The Lost Worlds of 2001*, it was director Kubrick who "settled on the rectangular shape" of the artifact (44). He then makes an effort to locate other monoliths throughout Clarke's fiction, often implausibly; even the "radar tower" of *Imperial Earth* qualifies, presumably because the structure is taller than it is wide (41, 43).

Critical readings of *2001* downplay the novel's brief discussions of the emergence of two other forms of alien life: when Halvorsen's daughter expresses an aversion to visiting that "nasty place," Earth, because "you hurt yourself when you fall down" and "there are too many people," she demonstrates that individuals who grow up on other worlds will, over time, develop attitudes that are different from those of Earth's people, effectively making them an alien species—a point further illustrated by the paranoid Hermians of *Rendezvous with Rama*.

Second, after Bowman learns of the programming error that caused HAL's rebellion, he muses, "The fact that HAL's builders had failed fully to understand the psychology of their own creation showed how difficult it might be to establish communication with truly alien beings" (168–69). Even if they are not "truly alien," then, advanced forms of artificial intelligence constructed by humans are analogous to aliens in that they might prove difficult to comprehend. And as computers like HAL become more and more advanced, they will presumably distance themselves even further from the mentality of humans. Yet both novel and film ultimately make HAL seem very much like a human, fighting to preserve itself against perceived threats.

The sequels to *2001* proved disappointing, in part, because they fail to further develop these auxiliary aliens. Although Floyd is eventually depicted as a space dweller and other individuals from different worlds are depicted, none of these characters seem noticeably different from Earth's humans. HAL is thoroughly domesticated as an obedient servant and Bowman's ethereal companion, effectively becoming human, and sequels offer no indications of future efforts to develop improved versions of HAL.

More significantly, the notion of future human evolution, as represented by the Star Child, is abandoned, as the Star Child is re-characterized as a conveniently enhanced observer for the aliens, otherwise similar to Bowman in his thoughts and actions. The sequels, then, prosaically argue that humans and their offshoots will long remain recognizably human. The aliens are altered and diminished as well, displaying additional limitations on their abilities.

The aliens may have been changed, in part, simply to extend the original story, since proceeding in the logical direction—depicting the further adventures of the "superior" aliens and Star Child—would be, as Clarke noted, "impossible." Hence, Clarke needed to make both the aliens and the transformed Bowman less superior in order to comprehensibly describe their actions. Yet this downgrading may also reflect a change in Clarke's attitudes toward aliens: in earlier works like *Against the Fall of Night*, *Childhood's End*, and *2001*, he indicates that advanced aliens would be virtually omniscient and omnipotent; the sequels to *2001*, as well as the epilogue to *The Ghost from the Grand Banks*, indicate that even advanced aliens may forever remain flawed and imperfect, capable of significant mistakes.

First, *2001* suggests the aliens can contact anyone whenever they wish, as the Star Child thinks reassuringly that "when he needed guidance in his first faltering steps, it would be there" (220). Presumably, they could examine human progress without needing intermediaries. Yet *2010* states that Bowman was transformed to function as "a probe, sampling every aspect of human affairs" (168). The sequels further convey that it requires a considerable amount of time for Bowman's information to reach alien masters, another limitation that seems not in keeping with their previous powers.

Clarke's *2010* further argues that the aliens lack the power, or desire, to advance intelligent species to new levels of super-intelligence; their only priority is to elevate less intelligent beings to human-like intelligence. Thus, their interest in humanity is now restricted to investigating whether the species should remain alive or be "weeded" to extinction as dangerous or dysfunctional. They otherwise focus on developing a new intelligent species on the Jovian moon Europa, which they seek to bring about by transforming Jupiter into a star to make Europa a hospitable environment for life.

Third, building on suggestions in the first novel, *2010* indicates that the Star Child is in direct mental contact with the aliens, as Bowman

> realized that more than one entity was controlling and manipulating him. He was involved in a hierarchy of intelligences, some close enough to his own primitive level to act as interpreters. Or perhaps they were all aspects of a single being.
>
> Or perhaps the distinction was totally meaningless. (198)

However, in *2061* the Star Child says of the *"something"* that "must have created the monolith," "I met it once—or as much of it as I could face—when *Discovery* came to Jupiter" (271). Since that time, he has merely been in contact with the monolith, which *2010* first indicates is a mechanical creation when astronauts observing innumerable monoliths approaching Jupiter speculate they are "von Neumann machines" (256), the self-replicating space probes envisioned by John von Neumann. This characterization is confirmed in *2061* by calling the monolith "a tool," its "prime function" being to serve as "a catalyst of intelligence" (268). This suggests one of two things: either the aliens are simply incapable of rapidly traveling through the cosmos to personally supervise their "experiments" and hence rely upon the machines they have deposited to perform that task; or, despite their previous interest in fostering forms of intelligent life, they have grown indifferent to its emergence and thus delegate the chores of overseeing its development to automatic devices.

Finally, *2061* suggests, and *3001* confirms, that the monolith is a faulty piece of machinery: "some of its systems may have started to fail; Dave even suggests that, in a fundamental way, it's become stupid! Perhaps it's been left on its own for too long—it's time for a service check." It has already "made at least one misjudgment" (*3001* 181)—eliminating promising life forms in Jupiter's atmosphere to foster intelligent life on Europa—and seems poised to make another, more grievous error by wiping out humanity on the basis of outdated reports of twenty-first-century problems that are entirely resolved in *3001*. As another, fortuitous flaw, the monolith, now characterized as an alien computer, is susceptible to humanity's ancient computer viruses, so Earth's scientists, with Bowman's help, can disable the monolith before it takes action.

The novel *3001* also intimates that the monolith actually made its first mistake over four million years ago, when it first provided humanity with the power to use tools. For after citing another scientist's observation that the monolith "gave us an evolutionary kick in the pants," Poole describes Theodore Kahn's belief that "the kick wasn't in a wholly desirable direction. Did we have to become so mean and nasty to survive? . . . though all creatures need a certain amount of aggressiveness to survive, we seem to have far more than is absolutely necessary. And no other animal tortures its fellows as we do" (144). Perhaps, then, the problems Bowman noted in *2010*, which evidently alarmed the monolith, were caused by the monolith itself, which afflicted humanity's ancestors with persistent bad habits that required millennia to overcome. This notion surfaces in the screenplay of *2001*, as after experiencing one lesson from what was then described as a cube, Moon-Watcher "feels the first faint twinges of a new and potent emotion—the urge to kill. He had taken his first step towards humanity" (a19). But when Clarke revised this language in his novel, the "new and potent emotion" was now only "a vague and diffuse sense of envy—of dissatisfaction with his life" (25).

Altogether, then, the sequels provide a much less expansive vision of potential alien civilizations. Even while continually improving their technology, aliens may never advance beyond a level of intelligence comparable to humans. In contrast to *2001*'s implicit division of life forms into three categories—subhuman, human, and superhuman—sequels suggest there are only two important categories, subhuman and human, and the sole priority of the aliens is to elevate subhuman intelligences to human-like intelligence. Far from achieving omniscience and omnipotence, aliens may always be limited in their knowledge and abilities. Although *2001* indicates that superhuman beings will advance beyond tools, sequels suggest they will always require tools, and the tools they construct, in contrast to the perpetually perfect machines of *Against the Fall of Night*, may inevitably deteriorate and cease functioning properly. One might sum this up by stating that unlike the unquestionably superior aliens of *2001*, the sequels' aliens are all too human in their flaws and foibles.

Still, the enigmatic conclusion to *3001* suggests there exists another, even more advanced alien race that may have transcended the weaknesses exhibited by the monolith builders, as an unspecified speaker states: "'Their little universe is very young, and its god is still a child. But it is too soon to judge them; when We return in the Last Days, We will consider what should be saved'" (237). Presumably, the "little universe" is our own, and "its god" is the force behind the monoliths, "still a child" and hence prone to errors. (Robin Anne Reid theorizes instead that the voice is only that of the monolith builders, not a superior species [179], though it is unclear what being other than themselves they would reference as our species' "god.") These overarching aliens recall "the mysterious Hunters of the Dawn" in *The Fountains of Paradise* but seem even more advanced; and while they left the universe they created, they will someday return, as the monolith builders returned to the civilization they crafted, in order to determine which of the universe's civilizations should be "saved."

Before Clarke continued the story of *2001*, he devoted a decade to fulfilling his million-dollar contract by writing three apparently unrelated novels, yet the first of these, *Rendezvous with Rama*, can be interpreted as a response to Kubrick's film. As noted, Kubrick declined to include dialogue or narration to convey the novel's information about the aliens, so they remain enigmatic. Though he reportedly was initially dismayed by that decision, Clarke may have concluded later that in key respects Kubrick had been more accurately prophetic than Clarke, since he knew as well as anyone that understanding the actions and motives of aliens may prove difficult, if not impossible. So Clarke may have resolved to outdo Kubrick by presenting, in *Rendezvous with Rama*, aliens that are completely and utterly inexplicable, moving in a direction precisely opposite to the familiarizing tendency displayed in sequels to *2001*.

One thing the explorers of the visiting alien spacecraft are curious about is the physiology of Ramans, and as the novel proceeds, they get a sense of what Ramans look like. Examining the device that opens Rama's airlock, Norton "noticed . . . there were deeper recesses at the ends of the spokes nicely shaped to accept a clutching hand (Claw? Tentacle?)" (17), indicating they have some sort of manipulative limb. Employing what they term a "handrail" to descend a staircase, the humans conclude that "presumably it *was* designed for some-thing like hands" (42). After entering Rama and descending down a staircase, they discover an oxygen atmosphere—seemingly proving the Ramans are "oxygen eaters" like humans—and Joe Calvert says, "What we've seen of their work suggests that the Ramans were humanoid, though perhaps about fifty per cent taller than we are" (54). When artificially created organic creatures termed "biots" appear to perform chores, they always leave humans alone, leading Karl Mercer to theorize, "They think we're Ramans. They can't tell the difference between one oxy-eater and another" (194), further suggesting they look like humans.

Finally, after breaking into a chamber that apparently contains visual models of objects to be created as needed—a "Catalog of Raman Artifacts" (279)—they find hand tools made for "huge and peculiar hands"; "keyboards that appeared to have been made for more than five fingers" (196); and "an

elaborate harness, or uniform, obviously made for a vertically standing creature much taller than a man," with "Loops" indicating that the being who
wears it has "three arms—and presumably three legs" (197, 198)—the same
anatomy of the biots called "Spiders," making Norton suspect they were
modeled on the Ramans. Norton concludes, "We'll probably never know"
whether "that creature" was a Raman, but it at least was "intelligent" (197).

Having three limbs would account for the one aspect of the psychology of
Ramans that is evident: their obsession with doing *everything in threes* (214).
This makes them unlike humans, since we have two arms and two legs, and
five digits on each limb, but never developed any intense concern about doing
everything in twos or fives. Other Raman traits might be inferred: while the
triple airlock of the craft could result from their fixation on threes, it also suggests they are naturally cautious. They are extremely intelligent, and probably
have existed for a long period of time, since they possess technology—including
a seemingly magical "space drive" (91) and a way to generate a force field around
Rama when it approaches the sun—that is well beyond human achievements.
When biots destroy and dispose of stray items regarded as debris, it conveys a
concern for cleanliness, and since they create biots only when they are needed
and destroy and recycle them when their work is done, one can regard Ramans
as economical. Finally, as the spacecraft concludes its visit to the solar system
by absorbing energy, and perhaps even matter, from the sun, that might signal
a concern for obtaining additional energy, posited to become a priority for any
advanced civilization.

One key question, the purpose of the Raman spacecraft, is never answered,
although several theories are developed. In early chapters Rama is repeatedly
described as, or likened to, a "tomb" (16, 26, 33, 44). However, the implication
is that it was not designed for that purpose, but rather was a spacefaring vehicle, a "Space Ark" (33), that inadvertently became a tomb when passengers
died during their prolonged flight.

The "feelings" Norton experiences while exploring Rama remind him of
the time he "visited the ruins of an Aztec temple" (53), and when Jimmy Pak
flies over Rama's South Pole, "he began to feel more and more like a spar-
row flying beneath the vaulted roof of some great cathedral" (123), impres-
sions suggesting that the spacecraft has some religious significance. Pak even
speculates that the South Pole was "indeed a religious shrine," but quickly

"dismissed the idea," because "nowhere in Rama had there been any trace of artistic expression; everything was purely functional" (123).

Boris Rodrigo, "a devout member of the Fifth Church of Christ," which holds that "Jesus Christ was a visitor from space" (55), theorizes Rama "is a cosmic Ark, sent here to save—those who are worthy of salvation" (95), and Norton considers a version of the theory stripped of theological overtones: "Suppose some catastrophe was about to befall the human race, and a benevolent higher intelligence knew all about it?" (95–96). However, its great speed and posited departure from the solar system in a few weeks lead Norton to doubt the idea. (Later, when Gentry Lee wrote his sequels to *Rama*, he reveals it had a somewhat similar purpose, dispatched by an entity intimated to be God to retrieve representatives of alien civilizations and evaluate them.)

Finally, the suspicious Hermians regard Rama as a threat to humanity: "it may be directed by robot mechanisms, programmed to carry out some mission—perhaps one highly disadvantageous to us" (88). Justifying their decision to destroy Rama, a Hermian likens Rama to "a termite colony" and asks, "What degree of co-operation or understanding would ever be possible between human beings and termites? . . . When either needs the other's territory or resources, no quarter is given" (179, 180). They fear, then, that the spacecraft seeks to seize humanity's "territory or resources."

In the end Rama's rapid departure from the solar system seemingly invalidates all of these theories, and only one conclusion can be drawn: Rama is a vehicle capable of serving several purposes and may be designed to respond in different ways to different situations. Encountering humanity, the appropriate response was to ignore this species and focus on repairing and refueling the spacecraft for its next stellar encounter; in response to a different sort of species, the spacecraft might have reacted differently.

Overall, the humans who investigate Rama obtain little information about the aliens who built it. The novel has recurring references to its "mystery" or "mysteries": Norton reflects on "the fundamental mystery of Rama" (59); in an optimistic mood, he muses, "There was mystery here—yes; but it might not be beyond human understanding" (61); crew members find that "the darkness and the mysteries [Rama] concealed were oppressive" (77); Norton thinks "the mystery of Rama was steadily growing" (149); and "he was always conscious of the swiftly passing days and the unsolved mysteries around them" (158).

Although Norton thinks earlier that "the wonder and strangeness of Rama would banish its terrors, at least for men who were trained to face the realities of space" (86), he feels differently as the crew prepares to leave: "There was danger and uncertainty about every moment inside Rama; no man could ever feel really at home there, in the presence of forces beyond his understanding" (191–92). After Rama departs, he concludes that "the nature and the purpose of the Ramans was still utterly unknown" (214), recalling the comment in the film 2001 that the monolith's "origin and purpose" is "still a total mystery." The novel is thus a cautionary tale about human limitations, warning that people may never fully understand any aliens they encounter.

Noting the spacecraft's indifference to humans, and their inability to learn much about it, Slusser argues that the novel "depicts [humanity's] helplessness before the mysteries of the universe" (60), while Rabkin similarly discerns in the novel the message that "humanity is of no more nor less value than a star or a grain of sand." But it is odd for Rabkin to view *Rendezvous with Rama* as Clarke's "unique repudiation of his homocentrism" (51), since Clarke had previously repudiated homocentrism in scores of works, prominently including *Against the Fall of Night*, "History Lesson," and *Childhood's End*. In contrast to other scholars, Nicholas Ruddick singularly familiarizes the novel, arguing that Rama is a homocentric "artist's impression of what a human civilization might look like that has embraced technology, used it to achieve unity through refashioning its world, and taken upon itself a patient yet purposeful quest for meaning across the gulfs of interstellar space" (47).

As in 2001, there are other sorts of aliens in the novel, more comprehensible but still somewhat mysterious. First are the humans of Mercury, products of a singularly harsh environment that makes their "mentality" "almost impossible" for other humans to "understand" (173). And there are "simps," monkeys genetically engineered to have "an equivalent IQ of 60" and the ability to perform routine tasks. There are communication issues with both sorts of "aliens," as residents of other worlds fail to anticipate the Hermian attack on Rama, and Norton's crew has only one "man who could speak fluent Simplish" (50). It is logical, but striking, that humans in *Rendezvous with Rama* are more intent on better understanding the aliens who constructed Rama than on better understanding the aliens emerging from their own colonization and technology.

Although Clarke published one story in *Ellery Queen's Mystery Magazine*, "Trouble with Time," and enjoyed Doyle's Sherlock Holmes stories, he was disinclined to respect one convention of detective fiction: that at the end of the story all mysteries are resolved. Clarke preferred stories that conclude with unsolved mysteries, particularly when writing about aliens. This also explains his fascination with the Mandelbrot Set, a mathematical construct of infinite complexity that no human can fully comprehend. As evidenced by his youthful nickname, "Ego," Clarke has been perceived as having a high opinion of himself, but unlike other writers, he was never arrogant enough to believe he was capable of fully understanding our vast universe and its variegated inhabitants.

CHAPTER 7

UNDER THE SEA

It is common knowledge that in the 1950s Clarke developed a passion for deep-sea diving, moved to Sri Lanka in part to regularly engage in that pastime, and published eight nonfiction books about his experiences, accompanied by photographs taken by Mike Wilson. Understandably, then, Clarke describes oceans and undersea realms more frequently than other science fiction writers. Yet his fascination with the sea predated his diving adventures, as he explored the impact of the ocean on observers before he could provide firsthand accounts of underwater marvels. Humanity, he suggests, feels strongly bonded to the oceans, which played a key role in humanity's advancement. Later novels and stories sometimes describe undersea ventures, usually emphasizing the strange and colorful creatures living there, and Clarke repeatedly likens being underwater to being in space.

Still, Steve Lehman overstates the importance of this similarity in asserting, "Existence on the surface of Earth, fighting the stress of gravity, [Clarke] sees as only a brief evolutionary interlude" between "prehuman" oceanic life and a "super human future" of "buoyant expansion into space" (269–70). In fact, many of Clarke's characters are perfectly content to live in Earth's gravity and may, like Floyd in 2061, abandon the planet only reluctantly. And despite resonances between life in the sea and life in space, Clarke's major novels about the oceans, *The Deep Range* and *The Ghost from the Grand Banks*, also convey that the sea significantly differs from space inasmuch as it possesses unique powers both to sustain human lives and to end them.

During his first decade of professional writing, Clarke makes several points about the ways bodies of water can affect people, probably recalling his childhood visits to the beach at Minehead. First, people are almost instinctively drawn to the sea. "Transience" describes how a prehistoric boy becomes the first human to observe an ocean he inexplicably feels attracted to: "What had lured him from the known dangers of the forest into the unknown and therefore more terrible dangers of this new element, he could not have told even had he possessed the power of speech" (100). In "The Road to the Sea" Brant is impressed when he observes the sea for the first time upon reaching Shastar: "the sound he was always to link with Shastar . . . came from the sea, and though he had never heard it before in all his life, it brought a sense of aching recognition into his heart" (288); after surveying deserted buildings, he "went down to the shore and sat on the wide stonework of the breakwater" (290). *Childhood's End* mentions that Jeffrey Greggson, who moves to an island colony, finds himself "fascinated" by "the sea" (149).

In *Against the Fall of Night*, after Alvin examines images of Earth's past, "his mind returned to the world that Earth had been. He saw again the endless leagues of blue water, greater than the land itself, rolling their waves against golden shores. His ears were still ringing with the boom of breakers stilled these thousand million years." Though he also remembers Earth's "forests and prairies" and "strange beasts" (15–16), the ocean evidently made an especially strong impression, for while visiting Lys, he repeatedly stares at and approaches its bodies of water: after arriving, he "walked to the edge of the lake" and, startled by a fish, he finally "broke the lake's enchantment and continued along the winding road" (65); traveling through the wilderness around Lys, he finds "more wonderful even than these [mountains] was the waterfall" (82), described in a paragraph; returning to Lys in a spaceship, he observes its "forests and endless rivers forming a scene of such incomparable beauty that for a while he would go no further"; he admires the "great lakes" that "sparkled with light, throwing back towards him such colors as he had never imagined" (156). Finally, as the novel concludes, we are told, "If one of Alvin's dreams came true, and the great transmutation plants still existed, it would not be many centuries before the oceans rolled again" (221).

The City and the Stars describes in similar language Alvin's memories of images of past oceans (31), sojourn by the lake (104–105), and views of the waterfall (133) and Lys's landscape (217), and adds that as he contemplates leaving Diaspar, he wonders, "Perhaps there might still be oceans and forests" to be found (84). The novel more definitely confirms that Alvin's people will re-create Earth's oceans: "The power and the knowledge still existed—it needed only the will to turn back the centuries and make the oceans roll again. The water was still there, deep down in the hidden places of the Earth; or if necessary, transmutation plants could be built to make it" (307).

Beyond its elemental allure, the sea brings a sense of calm and well-being: as Brant sits by the sea, "the enervating peacefulness of the scene, and the unforgettable object lesson in the futility of ambition that surrounded him on every side, took away all sense of disappointment or defeat. . . . Sitting here on the sea wall . . . he already felt remote from his old problems" (290). Floyd, in *2010*, uniquely enjoys relaxing experiences in one room of his Hawaiian home that adjoins an inlet from the ocean, allowing dolphins to pay his family daily visits, which he finds "charming," though they are "sometimes a nuisance" (9). (This seemingly trivial detail was important to Clarke, for when director Peter Hyams reported difficulties in staging this scene for the novel's film adaptation, his proposed substitutions of pet apes or penguins in Floyd's home were bluntly opposed by Clarke in messages included in *The Odyssey File* [1985]; when Hyams finally found a way to show Floyd's home with dolphins, Clarke replied, "Delighted to hear about the dolphin situation. Squeak, click, click" [99].) However, since Brant is the most passive of Clarke's questing heroes, and Floyd an aging bureaucrat, it is perhaps appropriate they would feel calmed and tranquilized by the sea, though Clarke elsewhere emphasizes its more stimulating effects.

"The Road to the Sea," in a roundabout way, argues that the oceans helped to inspire human art. When visitors from space rhapsodize about the beauties of space, Brant says, sarcastically, "According to *that* argument . . . real art couldn't have existed before space travel." The men surprisingly agree, saying, "There's a whole school of criticism based on that thesis; certainly space travel was one of the best things that ever happened to art." They then suggest that before space travel the sea played that role, but "after a few thousand years, the sea was too small for inspiration or adventure, and it was time to go into space" (298). The way the oceans might inspire art is also illustrated by Brant's experiences as he begins a painting only after contemplating the sea and encountering a mural showing Helen of Troy by the sea.

"Transience" indicates the oceans may have instigated the birth of religion, for as the prehistoric boy observes the ocean, "perhaps into his mind had come something of the wonder of the sea, and a hint of all that it would one day mean to man. Though the first gods of his people still lay far in the future, he felt a dim sense of wonder stir within him. He knew that he was now in the presence of something greater than all the powers and forces he had ever met" (100). It is also interesting to note that the Overlords of *Childhood's End* tell humans, "We have no oceans" (130), suggesting there might be a link between their inability to gaze in awe at vast bodies of water and their inability to achieve transcendence.

"Transience" argues that the oceans and beaches played a significant role in sparking the development of technology, as children compulsively build things while playing by the shore: the boy in the present is building "sand castles" (101), and the future boy "linked the tiny pools" near the shore "with an intricate network of waterways," emulating the Martian "Cardenis, prince of engineers" (101). The adult effects of the same impulse are illustrated when the present boy observes one of the immense vehicles people built to cross the oceans, while the future boy ignores spaceships flying over his head. *Childhood's End* endorses the idea that the challenge of conquering the sea led to scientific progress by describing Professor Sullivan as "a general conducting a perpetual campaign against an enemy who never relaxed . . . the sea, and it fought him with all weapons of cold and darkness and, above all, pressure. In his turn, he countered his adversary with intelligence and engineering skill" (121).

Childhood's End is also the first Clarke story to evidence his burgeoning knowledge of the undersea world, which he previously visited only farcically in "Letters to the Editor" (Summer 1935). While Rodricks visits Sullivan's underwater Deep Sea Lab, Clarke provides the first of several enthusiastic descriptions of the undersea world in his fiction:

> He was watching the screen intently, absorbing each glimpse of this strange and unknown region as it passed before his eyes. Unknown—yes, as unknown as anything he might meet beyond the stars. . . . He was going into a realm of nightmare creatures, preying upon each other in a darkness undisturbed since the world began. It was a realm above which men had sailed for thousands of years; it lay no more than a kilometer below the keels of their ships—yet until the last hundred years they had known less about it than the visible face of the Moon. (115)

Like gazing at the ocean from the shore, observing the undersea world evokes a "sense of wonder," but it is also a "strange and unknown region."

As Clarke devoted more time to deep-sea diving, similar passages, sometimes in unlikely places, provide more details about the oceans' distinctive features and inhabitants. "The Man Who Ploughed the Sea" offers a glimpse of the undersea world as an introductory flourish when Harry Purvis rides in a private submarine and joins other guests in observing a coral reef:

> They were floating above a valley carpeted with white sand, and surrounded by low hills of coral. The valley itself was barren but the hills around it were alive with things that grew, things that crawled and things that swam. Fish as dazzling as neon signs wandered lazily among the animals that looked like trees. It seemed not only a breathtakingly lovely but also a peaceful world. There was no haste, no sign of the struggle for existence. . . . A ray, looking like some fantastic black butterfly, flapped its way across the sand, balancing itself with its long, whiplike tail. The sensitive feelers of a crayfish waved cautiously from a crack in the coral. . . . There was so much life, of so many kinds, crammed in this single spot that it would take years of study to recognise it all. (614–15)

This is precisely the sort of descriptive language that Clarke provides in nonfictional accounts of diving exploits. Yet observers are distracted by a yacht and spend the rest of their time on board two vessels, discussing the tale's inevitable invention.

"Hate" features three men who make a living by diving into coral reefs near Australia to retrieve oysters. Since venturing underwater is simply their job, Clarke speaks more prosaically about what the men observed: "there was no beauty, no underwater fairyland here. But there was money, and that was what mattered" (769). Still, he also describes the otherworldly aspects of being underwater: "There was no sense of time in this world of mist. You walked beneath the invisible, drifting ship, with the throb of the air compressor pounding in your ears, the green haze moving past your eyes" (770).

Another undersea adventure, "The Shining Ones," involves a "deep-sea engineer" (805), hired to investigate damage to an underwater facility near Sri Lanka that generates electricity from the temperature difference between the frigid sea and a lake on the surface. Though the story focuses on the squids, apparently becoming intelligent, that damaged the grid, the narrator also says, "I like to watch the luminous creatures of the sea, as they flash and flicker in the darkness, sometimes exploding like rockets just outside the observation window" (812), and is impressed by smaller squids: "Only the movie camera could do justice to these living kaleidoscopes. I do not know how long I watched them, so entranced by their luminous beauty that I had almost forgotten my mission" (814).

One novel involving humans and the sea, *Dolphin Island*, begins when orphan Johnny Clinton accidentally stows away on a "hovership" (9) and is left drifting on the sea, with little hope of rescue, when the ship sinks and its crew escapes in a lifeboat. As night falls he observes "luminous creatures in the sea" and pauses to appreciate "the wonder and mystery of the great element that covered three quarters of the globe, and which now controlled his destiny" (26).

After being escorted by friendly dolphins to Dolphin Island, where he interacts with scientists learning to speak to dolphins, Clinton is taught to dive by another boy, Mick Nauru, and has other opportunities to marvel at the undersea world: a coral reef is a "magic kingdom" (61), filled with "a score of different creatures," including "five-armed starfish," "hermit crabs," and "a thing like a giant slug, which squirted out a cloud of purple ink when Mick prodded it" (64). When he and Mick dive in the nighttime, Clinton learns about "another of the sea's many faces. Night could transform the world below the waves, as it transformed the world above. No one knew the sea who explored it only by daylight" (89). Overall, the manner in which Clinton masters diving and comes to love the ocean makes it tempting to regard *Dolphin Island* as autobiographical, since Clinton's experiences—a boy, distant from his original family, finds a new home in the sea—seem to parallel those of Clarke's in the 1950s. (As discussed below, one can argue the same about *The Deep Range*'s Franklin.)

Clarke intended to provide *2001* with underwater interludes, though they were omitted: *The Lost Worlds of 2001* shows Kelvin (not yet Frank) Poole, before joining the *Discovery* crew, at the "Cornell Underwater Lab off Bimini," where, as an "aerospace physiologist," he is researching "sleep and the rhythms which seemed to control the activities of all living creatures" (94). He finds that "the view from the window" is

> not only distractingly beautiful—it was hypnotically restful. The water was so clear that he could see almost two hundred feet, and at a guess his field of view contained ten thousand fish of fifty different species—as well as several dozen varieties of coral. At this depth [one hundred feet], though the sunlight was still brilliant, it had lost all its red and orange hues; the world of the reef was tinged a mellow blue-green, very soothing to the eyes. It looked incredibly peaceful—an underwater Eden that knew nothing of sin or death. (95)

Later, after Bowman passes through the Star Gate, he originally reaches a planet "entirely covered by sea" (200) and ventures beneath its surface to observe numerous underwater creatures.

In *Imperial Earth* Titan's Makenzie is initially frightened by one of Earth's vast bodies of water, noting, "Though it looked calm and peaceful, he found it slightly ominous—even menacing" (156). However, when predictably offered the chance to go diving, he seizes this "opportunity of a lifetime" and is soon "fascinated" by the "panorama beneath" (192–93). Later, he again dives to examine a sea urchin, the creature his late friend Karl Helmer employed as a model for his planned radio telescope in space.

In *2010* the now ethereal Bowman ventures into the underground oceans of Europa, where he observes several wonders, including "delicate, spidery structures that seemed to be the analogy of plants"; "bizarre slugs and worms"; "sturdier, most robust organisms, not unlike crabs or spiders"; and a creature that "closely resembled one of the banyan trees from Earth's tropics," which, surprisingly, "was walking" (179, 186). *The Deep Range* references another alien ocean—on Venus—describing an illustration of its "vast scaly monsters, more large and hideous than any that had lived on Earth since the Jurassic period" (168).

Also, when the *2010* astronauts are asked about their fondest memories of Earth, Maxim Brailovsky recalls "diving" as his "favorite hobby"; he particularly appreciated swimming through "one of the Japanese kelp forests" that was "like an underwater cathedral, with sunlight slanting through those enormous leaves. Mysterious . . . magical" (135).

The fact that an astronaut enjoys diving relates to another recurring theme in Clarke's fiction: similarities between being underwater and being in space. As noted, "The Road to the Sea" suggests space will replace the sea as an inspiration and stimulating challenge, but Clarke's diving experiences helped him realize, before NASA began having astronauts train for space missions underwater, that diving and life in space both involve a feeling of weightlessness in an unusual environment. Thus, stories about space often liken space to the oceans, while stories about the oceans often liken the oceans to space.

The narrator of "Maelstrom II," who is about to plummet to his doom on the lunar surface, compares his plight to that of the sailor in Edgar Allan Poe's "A Descent into the Maelstrom" (1841), trapped inside a fierce whirlpool. Poe's story demonstrates that people in the ocean, like Clarke's hero and his other astronauts, must apply scientific principles to escape from danger, as Poe's sailor ties himself to a barrel to slow down his descent, and Clarke's protagonist leaps from his vehicle to achieve a barely survivable orbit. "Transit of Earth," describing the tragic death of one of the first men to reach Mars, includes his memories of a dangerous dive into an undersea shipwreck, where the sudden closing of a hatch almost trapped him before he could reach the surface and avoid drowning. Vividly remembering running out of air, he refuses to kill himself by exposing himself to Mars's near-vacuum, a reminder that the perils of diving can be similar to the perils of space travel. Another pioneering space mission is compared to an undersea adventure in "A Meeting with Medusa": the ship that enters Jupiter's atmosphere is named the *Kon-Tiki*, after the boat that

Thor Heyerdahl piloted across the Pacific; the atmosphere's creatures are designated "mantas" and "a medusa," a sort of jellyfish; and the pilot observes "bioluminescence, very similar to that produced by microorganisms in the tropical seas of Earth" (916).

Clarke's later novels about space include references to the sea as well. *Rendezvous with Rama*'s Norton feels a connection to explorer Captain James Cook, and whenever he faces a dilemma, he asks himself, "What would the long-dead captain of that earlier *Endeavour* have done in a situation like this?" (74). In *2061* space traveler Clifford Greenberg has "done a good deal of underwater cave exploring" (90). As *3001*'s Poole first dons his Braincap, he recalls diving "down the face of a sheer cliff at the outer edge of the Great Barrier Reef" (37); and when he learns to fly with wings in a zero-gravity chamber, he says, "The nearest thing to it was scuba diving," and "he wished there were birds here, to emulate the equally colorful coral fish who had so often accompanied him over tropical reefs" (71).

Turning to stories about the sea, the similarities between life in space and life underwater are a major theme in *The Deep Range*, as discussed below, and the narrator of "The Shining Ones" likens the "diffuse glow" of an approaching giant squid to "the rising star clouds of the galaxy" as they might "appear from some world close to the heart of the Milky Way" (813). He comments that the squids "are in Trinco Deep for the same reason that there are men at the South Pole—or on the Moon. Pure scientific curiosity" (815). *Dolphin Island*'s Clinton calls the sea "a world as alien as another planet" (67) and likens a school of fish to "a fleet of spaceships from an alien world" (114). The novel, like "The Shining Ones," further populates Earth's sea with intelligent aliens—here, dolphins, as the scientist who befriends Clinton, Professor Kazan, has mastered enough of their language to carry on conversations; and when dolphins request humanity's help in resisting their chief predators, killer whales, Kazan learns they have a similarly complex language.

Though not cited specifically as a similarity to space, the undersea world shares one other quality with space: the constant possibility of death. As the diver of "Hate" notes:

> The chances were that this would be another day of uneventful drudgery, as were most of the days in the pearl diver's unglamorous life. But Tibor had seen

one of his mates die, when his air hose tangled in the *Arafura's* prop—and he had watched the agony of another whose body twisted with the bends. In the sea, nothing was ever safe or certain. You took your chances with open eyes—and if you lost, there was no point in whining. (769)

Pondering experiences when his life had been in danger, the narrator of "The Shining Ones" says, "In my business, anything out of the ordinary needs an explanation; three times I have saved my life by waiting until I had one" (812). At the end of the story, he loses his life when he encounters an enormous squid; the astronaut of "Hate" might have been killed anyway when her space capsule fell into the ocean, though she actually dies because her rescue mission is sabotaged; *Dolphin Island's* Clinton almost dies in the ocean before being rescued by dolphins; and deaths or near-deaths in the sea are recurring themes in Clarke's two major novels about the ocean, *The Deep Range* and *The Ghost from the Grand Banks*, though to varying extents.

Even without biographical information, one might guess that between writing "The Deep Range" in 1954 and expanding it into a novel in 1957, Clarke had garnered experience in deep-sea diving, for although the story—describing how warden Don Burley kills a shark preying upon the whales he protects—mentions only those creatures and the dolphins who assist him while saying little about underwater conditions, the novel is filled with descriptions of the undersea world and its inhabitants.

Before his first training voyage, former astronaut Walter Franklin and Burley pay little attention to shallow waters near the shore because "it was too familiar to them both, and they knew that the real beauty and wonder of the [Great Barrier] reef lay in the deeper waters farther out to sea" (32). In the ocean Franklin observes "a myriad brilliantly colored fish staring at him with apparent unconcern" and pronounces "the ride" "one of the most exhilarating experiences he had ever known" (35). Soon, the formerly numb and traumatized Franklin "had come to life, as he awoke to the wonder and challenge—and endless opportunity—of the element he was attempting to master" (49). Even when diving to commit suicide, Franklin finds himself "in a world of midnight blue which the pale rays of the moon could do little to illumine. Around him strange shapes moved like phosphorescent ghosts, as the creatures of the reef were attracted or scattered by the sound of his passing. Below him, no more than shadows in a deeper darkness, he could see the coral hills and valleys he had grown to know so well" (69).

Later, searching for a sea serpent, Franklin muses that

> for seven years he had roamed the oceans—one year of his life to each of the seas—and in that time he had grown to know the creatures of the deep as no man could ever have done in any earlier age. . . . He had looked upon beauty and horror and birth and death in all their multitudinous forms, as he moved through a liquid world so teeming with life that by comparison the land was an empty desert.
>
> No man could ever exhaust the wonders of the sea. (156–57)

Proceeding deeper, "Franklin thought what a pity it was that the world's most stupendous scenery was all sunk beyond sight in the ocean depths. Nothing on the land could compare with the hundred-mile-wide canyons of the North Atlantic, or the monstrous potholes that gave the Pacific the deepest soundings on Earth" (159).

Further signaling Clarke's growing familiarity with the sea is a telling difference between the story and novel: in the story, after killing a menacing shark, Burley "watched without pity as the great fish succumbed to its paralysis" (487). Yet in the novel he "watched with awe and a dispassionate pity as the great beast succumbed to its paralysis" (10), and Clarke notes that Burley's "power" to kill sea animals "would never be abused," because "he felt too great a kinship with all the creatures who shared the sea with him—even those it was his duty to destroy" (12). Indeed, the need to prevent the deaths of the whales that Franklin's agency slaughters becomes one of the novel's major messages when a Buddhist leader campaigns to end this practice, and Franklin, after acknowledging he "had found this scientific butchery extremely depressing" (150), recognizes that "he had grown to love the great beasts he guarded," and "if their slaughter could be avoided, he should welcome it, whatever the consequences to the bureau" (208).

In addition to its heightened attentiveness to, and sympathy for, sea creatures, the novel discusses another way the sea is different: its strange sounds, which Clarke himself had now heard:

> How could anyone have ever thought that the sea was silent! Even man's limited hearing could detect many of its sounds—the clashing of chitinous claws, the moan of great boulders made restive by the ocean swell, the unmistakable "flick" of a shark's tail as it suddenly accelerates on a new course. But these were merely the sounds in the audible spectrum; to listen to the full music of the sea one must go both below and above the range of human hearing. (107)

Franklin further notes, "There is no more eerie sound in all the world than the screaming of a herd of whales," so "he could imagine that he was lost in some demon-haunted forest, while ghosts and goblins closed in upon him" (108).

Although Clarke celebrates the sea's unique creatures and their attributes, *The Deep Range* is more concerned about showing how the oceans affect people, since its protagonist is comforted and healed by the sea: Franklin recovers from psychological damage caused by his horrifying accident in space by immersing himself in the sea. One can detect autobiographical resonances between Franklin's fate and Clarke's situation in 1957, as Clarke had also separated from a wife and child, came to enjoy being under the sea, and probably recognized, on his fortieth birthday, that he was unlikely to realize his adolescent dream of personally experiencing space travel; thus, also barred from space, he would have to be satisfied with the similar experience of diving.

Yet Burley, Franklin, and Clarke himself are hardly the only humans who have benefited from a "kinship" with the sea, which, the novel argues, is basic to the human condition. Explaining why they transferred Franklin to an undersea position, a psychologist tells his future wife, "You are a marine biologist and know the links we have with the sea," so people like Franklin can "feel at home" there (75). An official report notes, "At the simplest level, the fact that the sea is a continuous and sustaining fluid, in which vision is always limited to no more than a few yards, gave W. F. [Franklin] the sense of security he had lost in space" (98). Significantly, Franklin is jolted out of his growing tranquility only when he is reminded of space—by observing the Space Station and smelling the fuel used to power spacesuits—again suggesting that humans find the sea soothing, while space is disquieting.

Thus, while the novel refers to "the analogies between sea and space," which "have often been pointed out" (97), it suggests that in some respects the sea is a superior environment. Humans can more easily bond with the sea, as illustrated by Franklin's experiences. When he starts working as a sea warden, "The sea had begun to shape his life and thought, as it must that of all men who try to master it and learn its secrets," and he now "felt a kinship with all the creatures that moved throughout its length and depth" and "a sympathy, and an almost mystical reverence . . . toward the great beasts whose destinies he ruled" (116). Later, as was true of Brant in "The Road to the Sea," going to the sea enables Franklin to escape "the problems of his office," because "he could lose himself again, if only for a while, in the clear-cut and elemental simplicities of the sea" (218).

The sea further represents a larger challenge than space in that Franklin regards humanity's control over the sea as "the most daring of all man's presumptions. The sea, which had worked its will with man since the beginning of time, had been humbled at last. Not even the conquest of space had been a greater victory than this" (52). The sea is more stimulating than space, since "there was more life and wonder in the sea than in all the endless empty leagues between the planets" (116). For these reasons, Franklin is not saddened by the fact that "he had lost the freedom of space," because "he had won the freedom of the sea," and "that was enough for any man" (96–97). And as Franklin watches his son leave Earth to become an astronaut, the novel relates, "To his son, he willingly bequeathed the shoreless seas of space. For himself, the oceans of this world were sufficient" (237). Considering these assertions about the special qualities and importance of the sea, one must challenge John Hollow's claim that the novel "is, at the end, about getting the human race ready for space, about becoming worthy of the stars" (104).

While valorizing the sea and its beneficial effects, the novel acknowledges it can be deadly, and Franklin muses that it "supported and protected him—yet it would kill him in two or three minutes at the most if he made a mistake or his equipment failed" (41). The point is illustrated when Burley dies while accompanying Franklin to search for a sea serpent. Yet Franklin's "knowledge" of the sea's dangers "did not disturb him," since "he now knew and understood the challenge of the sea, and it was a challenge he wished to meet" (41). And because Franklin survives undersea perils to become a respected bureaucrat and beloved family man, one could say *The Deep Range* is a novel about one man's triumph, and all of humanity's triumph, over its ancient adversary, the sea. Later, however, Clarke published a less optimistic novel about the oceans, *The Ghost from the Grand Banks.*

Clarke's final novel about the oceans is permeated with references to people who died while confronting "the challenge of the sea." Its central event is the sinking of the *Titanic*, killing hundreds of passengers, and one result of the efforts to raise that sunken ship is the discovery of six well-preserved corpses in a locked room. The novel mentions other famous ships that sank and caused many deaths—the *Lusitania* (71), the *Mary Rose* (36, 115–18), and the *Vasa* (36)—and describes "the Casualty book—the registry of wrecks" maintained by Lloyd's of London as a "series of massive volumes" (91), emphasizing how frequently such disasters occur.

While referencing well-known tragedies at sea, the novel discusses other deaths, or potential deaths, caused by the ocean. The first chapter describes how in 1974 Jason Bradley witnessed the shipboard funerals of six Russian sailors whose bodies were recovered from a sunken submarine. The music played at the funeral, later heard again by Bradley, is Sergei Rachmaninoff's *Isle of the Dead* (1909), inspired by one of five versions of Arnold Böecklin's painting *Isle of the Dead* (1880–1886). In Venice, filled with canals, people are evidently threatened by rising sea levels, since the city is "now cowering nervously behind its Dutch-built dikes" (25). A participant in one project to raise the *Titanic*, Rupert Parkinson, "had his own account to settle with the sea," because "his beautiful twenty-five-meter yacht *Aurora* . . . had been dismasted by a freak squall off the Scillies [Isles of Sicily], and smashed to pieces on the cruel rocks that had claimed so many victims through the centuries"; "all the crew had been lost—including the skipper" (42). Bradley recalls a friend who died when he was "trapped" underwater by a "collapsed rig" (72). Although the cause of her death is a falling tree, young Ada Craig dies while in a boat on her parents' Mandelbrot Set–shaped lake. The novel concludes when Bradley is killed because his undersea rescue vehicle cannot withstand "shock waves" from an earthquake (246).

In part, all of these deaths relate to one problem: "the dangers of overconfidence, of technological hubris," described as "the most important lesson the *Titanic* can teach" (36). Thus, the attempt to raise the two parts of the *Titanic*, and, in a way, belatedly triumph over the ocean that sank it, fails because of the same earthquake that killed Bradley. And one can be confident that the future aliens similarly endeavoring to retrieve the now buried *Titanic* will be unsuccessful, as the novel ends with the alien Seeker saying only, "Let us begin" (253). I thus disagree with Robin Anne Reid, who claims "it is clear . . . that finally the 'Ghost' of the *Titanic* will be retrieved—but not by human beings" (148). Further, references to the Chernobyl disaster, the destruction of space shuttle *Challenger*, and the two imagined future tragedies of "Lagrange 3" and "Experimental Fusor One" (37) illustrate that failures and deaths extend beyond human ventures into the sea. Finally, deaths on the grandest scale possible, unrelated to the sea, are envisioned in the novel's epilogue, where a cosmic disaster dooms the entire solar system, though humans are able to escape.

Yet some passages suggest there is something especially daunting and dangerous about the oceans. When an octopus "shut[s] down" an undersea drilling operation, the novel notes, "it was no simple matter to wrest" such "hidden treasure . . . from [the sea's] grasp" (51). Bradley comments, "I've never known a major underwater operation that didn't have some surprises" (87). A similar remark he once made, "When you've thought of everything—the sea will think of something else" (189), is recalled as one of his dying thoughts (246). Scientist Franz Zwicker conveys how little we know about the sea by exclaiming, "We have photo coverage of the Moon and Mars showing everything down to the size of a small house—but most of our planet—[meaning the ocean floor] is still completely unknown!" (158). He and Bradley are developing "an automatic surveying robot" so that "we'll know the ocean as well as we know the Moon" (215). The novel thus asserts that the oceans are more unpredictable and mysterious than space.

Sporadically, the novel does compare the sea to space: a man observing a robot retrieving a body recalls Bowman's pod in *2001*; describing an underwater vehicle called Jim, which is worn like a space suit, the novel notes, "Jim had no legs—underwater, as in space, they were often more of a nuisance than they were worth" (75); and Bradley remembers "his first glimpse" of the "teeming life-forms" undersea that are "as alien as any from another planet" (129–30). Yet more attention is paid to the similarities between the sea and another otherworldly realm—the infinitely complex Mandelbrot Set—observed by means of computer images: when characters observe its "extraordinary shapes," they initially "looked like baby elephants, waving tiny trunks. Then the trunks became tentacles. Then the tentacles sprouted eyes. . . . The eyes opened up into black whirlpools of infinite depth. . . . They swept past the whirlpools, skirting mysterious islands guarded by reefs of coral. Flotillas of seahorses sailed by in stately procession" (127). Other passages compare images from the Mandelbrot Set to "the tentacles of octopoids," "microfauna in a drop of ditchwater" (10), *"tentacles," "armies of seahorses"* (82), and "waves" (127). In the novel the Mandelbrot Set also proves menacing when it maddens Helen Craig, who is "trapped in an endless loop" (10) of studying its complexities until she is jolted back to sanity. Like the sea, the Mandelbrot Set is both beautiful and deadly.

To explain the difference in tone between *The Deep Range* and *The Ghost from the Grand Banks*, one might posit that the first novel is the work of a relatively young man, approaching forty, while the second comes from an elderly man in his seventies, naturally inclined to be more pessimistic about human possibilities and more focused on the issue of death. One passage suggests that the novel represents an old man's perspective: after Ada quotes Albert Einstein's statement that "the most beautiful thing we can experience is the mysterious" (129), Bradley thinks, "I'll go along with that."

> He remembered calm nights in the Pacific, with a sky full of stars and a glimmering trail of bioluminescence behind the ship; he recalled his first glimpse of the teeming life-forms . . . gathered around the scalding cornucopia of a Galápagos mid-ocean vent, where the continents were slowly tearing apart; and he hoped that before long he would feel awe and wonder again, when the tremendous knife edge of *Titanic's* prow came looming up out of the abyss. (129–30)

As a youth, Bradley felt "awe and wonder" contemplating the sea and its inhabitants, much like characters in earlier Clarke stories; now he can only "hope" he will someday feel those emotions. Writing *The Ghost from the Grand Banks*, Clarke may have felt the same way, as suggested by Lehman, who argues that the "drastic reduction in Clarke's diving" during his later life caused "his writing . . . to have lost much of its emotional basis" (275).

Yet there is a scientific basis for Clarke's newfound pessimism about humanity's ability to learn about, and master, the sea, epitomized by the Mandelbrot Set. As Ada explains, "It contains infinite detail; you can go in anywhere you like, and magnify as much as you please—and you'll always discover something new and unexpected" (127). The Mandelbrot Set is thus an icon of human limitations: we will never fully understand it. Similarly, the sea—recalled in descriptions of the Set's features—may be something that humanity will never fully understand, and there may be many other goals that humans can never achieve, such as raising the *Titanic*. Still, Reid struggles to extract an optimistic message from the novel: "the possibility of failure does not mean that we should not dream or not attempt to make those dreams come true" (157).

Lehman, one of the few critics to discuss *The Ghost from the Grand Banks* at length, ultimately argues that, for Clarke, a fascination with the sea reflects only psychological problems, as illustrated by Bradley, whose "public heroism is paralleled by a private life devoid of emotional intimacy. . . . His risk-taking in the sea, is inspired by a fundamental neurosis also expressed in his sexuality" (275). Yet the novel conveys that Bradley, despite his fondness for sexual bondage, enjoyed a long and satisfying life while interacting with the oceans, and upon realizing he will perish underwater, his last thought is, "This is a good place to die" (246).

While not regarded as one of his greatest works, *The Ghost from the Grand Banks* uniquely brings together three of the realms that long fascinated Clarke—space (mentioned in passing references and the focus of the epilogue), the world of mathematics (represented by the Mandelbrot Set, and also central to *Imperial Earth* and *The Last Theorem*), and the undersea world (the novel's main setting)—and asserts that all of them are forever beyond humanity's grasp. Clarke had asserted in the title of a 1960 article that "We'll Never Conquer Space" (later retitled "Space, the Unconquerable"), and humanity's need to flee the solar system, and apparent extinction at the time "the Seeker" (252) visits Earth, suggests that too; the Mandelbrot Set is explicitly described as unconquerable; and as the *Titanic* has never been raised, it appears the sea is unconquerable as well. The oceans, then, were the first environment that humanity found inspiring, mysterious, and challenging, as shown by "Transience"; and like other environments that subsequently attracted humanity's attention, as shown by *The Ghost from the Grand Banks*, they may forever remain that way.

CHAPTER 8

FUTURE FAITHS

Clarke's attitudes toward religion, one can safely say, were complicated. On one hand, despite a conventional religious upbringing, he was an open and dedicated atheist, which affected his science fiction in predictable ways: protagonists display no religious beliefs and may identify themselves as nonreligious; frequent comments address the fundamental irrationality, inefficacy, and negative impact of religions; and, looking to the future, Clarke regularly anticipates that humanity will abandon all of its religions. In comments during a 1970 visit to Houston, he described himself as a "lapsed atheist," adding, "I don't believe in God, but I'm interested in Him," and listener Joseph P. Pumilia reported that he "predicted the decline of revealed religion as part of the evolution of religious thought" ("Clarke in Houston" 4). More forcefully, he told Matthew Teague in 2004, "Religion is the most malevolent of all mind viruses. . . . We should get rid of it as quick as we can."

On the other hand, even in stories reporting the future end of religious beliefs, Clarke describes the sporadic persistence of old religions, or emergence of new religions, suggesting religion may forever remain at least a minor element of the human condition. This obliges him to sometimes acknowledge that religions can have beneficial effects. This is particularly true of the one religion he consistently praises, Buddhism, though he defends his apparently contradictory admiration for the faith by labeling it a "philosophy," not a true religion.

Attempting to fit trends in Clarke's science fiction into conventional patterns, one might maintain that individuals commonly scorn religion when they are young and develop an interest in religion as they grow older and ponder their own mortality; and it is true that Clarke's earlier works usually say little or nothing about religion while later works pay more attention to religion. The difference in Clarke's case is that his growing focus on religion was unrelated to concerns about his own afterlife—something he never believed in—but rather stemmed from a realization that human religions were proving to be peculiarly persistent, a phenomenon demanding some scrutiny. It may also reflect that as an emerging author during the relatively conservative 1940s and 1950s, Clarke understood that it might be imprudent to openly criticize religion and hence tended to avoid the subject; later, having established himself as a major author, he had more freedom to comfortably express his sometimes controversial opinions regarding religion.

Only one of Clarke's stories appears to endorse Christian beliefs, as the protagonist of the final section of "Whacky" dies and apparently wakes up in either Heaven or Hell, but there is no conviction in this farcical vignette. Even three stories that accept the existence of God—"The Nine Billion Names of God," "siseneG," and "The Star"—are simultaneously attacking religion, portraying God as an evil destructive force; blithely destroying the universe in "The Nine Billion Names of God" and "siseneG"; and obliterating a civilization of benign, intelligent beings solely to herald the coming of Jesus Christ in "The Star."

Still, in the first two stories, Clarke seems more bemused than angry with the posited deity. The female God of "siseneG" merely seems capricious in arranging that "the Universe . . . never *had* existed" (929), while as Edward

James notes, "The Nine Billion Names of God" perhaps "implies a devious or jesting God." Clarke's true point, James suggests, may be that believing in simultaneously omnipotent and myopic gods like these is simply silly, because stories demonstrate "the implausibility of some of the traditional images of God" (*Science Fiction in the 20th Century* 107).

As for "The Star," its Jesuit astrophysicist defends God, maintaining, "He who built the universe can destroy it when He chooses. It is arrogance—it is perilously near blasphemy—for us to say what He may or may not do." Nevertheless, stunned by God's annihilation of a "civilisation that in many ways must have been superior to our own," he "reached" the "point when even the deepest faith must falter" (521). In a different way, then, a story that seemingly accepts the existence of a supreme being also argues against worshipping that being.

However, religion is usually conspicuous in Clarke's early fiction primarily through its absence. Characters in near-future novels like *Prelude to Space*, *Sands of Mars*, and *Islands in the Sky* make no references to religious beliefs, while other novels indicate their protagonists are atheists: *A Fall of Moondust* observes, "Father Ferraro believed in God and Man; Dr. Lawson believed in neither" (33), and *Glide Path* says, "Like most of his generation, [Alan Bishop] had no formal religion" (201). Later, Clarke planned to make the protagonist of his final novel, *The Last Theorem*, an avowed atheist, writing, "Ranjit, even as a boy, could not believe in the complex pantheon of gods and goddesses, some with an unusual number of arms, whose sculptured figures encrusted the temple walls."

Ranjit's opinion conveys one of Clarke's arguments against religions: their beliefs are obviously not true and do not merit the devotion of intelligent people. In cases like Hinduism, doctrines may be so fanciful as to seem manifestly incorrect to any thinking person, as *The Deep Range* also suggests when the narrator remarks, "The Hindu religion, with its fantastic pantheon of gods and goddesses, had failed to survive in an age of scientific rationalism" (183).

The reference to "scientific rationalism," which also "weakened" Islam (183), suggests a related argument against religions: their beliefs are illogical and hence cannot be accepted. This is why organized religions decline in the future of *The Fountains of Paradise*: the alien probe Starglider "effectively destroyed all traditional religions" (79) and "put an end to the billions of words of pious gibberish with which apparently intelligent men had addled their minds for centuries" (81), by means of logic. Presented with Thomas Aquinas's argument for the existence of God, the probe "demolish[es] Saint Thomas" within "less than an hour" (81) and announces, "The hypothesis you refer to as God . . . is unnecessary" (82). According to *The Songs of Distant Earth*, Kurt Gödel's incompleteness theorems delivered "another devastating blow" to religion by "prov[ing] that there were certain absolutely fundamental limits to knowledge, and hence the idea of a completely Omniscient Being . . . was logically absurd" (206). *Childhood's End* alludes to the irrationality of religion when an Overlord refers to "mysticism" as "the prime aberration of the human mind" (103).

In addition, the foundations of religions may be purported past events that did not actually happen, so the emergence of evidence contradicting their accounts may lead to their demise. In *Childhood's End* the Overlords bring an end to most religions by providing humans with a device that "opened up" "a window into the past": "Almost the whole of human history for the past five thousand years became accessible in an instant." Soon, "the creeds that had been based on miracles and revelations had collapsed completely" (74) as people learned these developments had never occurred. *The Deep Range* similarly reports, "Christianity, which had never fully recovered from the shattering blow given it by Darwin and Freud, had finally and unexpectedly succumbed before the archaeological discoveries of the late twentieth century" (182–83), which disproved biblical accounts of the past. More broadly, in the future of *The City and the Stars* religions vanished in part because scientific evidence "with monotonous regularity refuted the cosmologies of the prophets" (156).

Religions may also end because their deities are shown to possess no power to influence human actions, apparently one reason why Islam declined in the future of *The Deep Range*, as "the Mohammedan faith . . . had suffered additional loss of prestige when the rising Star of David had outshone the pale crescent of the Prophet" (183). Presumably, Islamic leaders assured believers that Allah would allow them to triumph over Israel and were discredited when the Jewish state instead became more powerful and prosperous than its neighbors. Again undone because of their demonstrated inefficacy, religions in *The City and the Stars* also failed because science "produced miracles which they could never match" (156). In *The Songs of Distant Earth* religions are discredited because of "a fascinating development called statistical theology" (204), which proved that "bad things happened just as often as good; as had long been suspected, the universe simply obeyed the laws of mathematical probability. Certainly there was no sign of any supernatural intervention, either for good or for ill" (206).

Finally, religions may enable, or encourage, believers to do damaging things, an additional reason for rejecting them. In *Prelude to Space* a religious fanatic who "believed that the attempt to conquer space would bring down upon humanity some stupendous metaphysical doom" (139) unsuccessfully tries to sabotage the lunar spacecraft. The protagonist of *Glide Path* was molested as a child by "the clergyman who had (very briefly) run the local scout troop" (119). Providing a detail not included in "Guardian Angel," *Childhood's End* informs readers that the leader of the opposition to the Overlords is "a clergyman," and Stormgren muses that their irrational "conflict" with the Overlords' benign rule is "a religious one, however much it may be disguised" (16). In *The Songs of Distant Earth* members of two "rival cults" (184) attempt to destroy starships that will rescue people from the impending destruction of Earth, and in "The Hammer of God" an effort to prevent an asteroid from disastrously striking Earth is sabotaged by adherents of the new religion of Chrislam, who argue that "God, Allah, is testing us" by means of the asteroid and "we mustn't interfere" (945). In Clarke's "Original Movie Outline" (1997) that became the basis of Clarke and Mike McQuay's *Richter 10*, he describes a group of "religious cultists" (340) who attack and thwart an effort to explode an underground nuclear weapon to prevent a predicted California earthquake that ultimately occurs. In a passage Clarke completed for *The Last Theorem*, Ranjit becomes alienated from his father, Ganesh, a Hindu priest, largely because while "Ranjit was Tamil" and ethnically a Hindu, his best friend "Gamini was Sinhalese" and hence Buddhist. Clarke further notes that because of "the ethnic riots of the 1980's," inspired in part by the groups' religious differences, "Ganesh had lost close relatives to rampaging mobs, and he himself had narrowly escaped death on several occasions."

Clarke condemns religions for their negative effects most strongly in *The Songs of Distant Earth* and *3001*. In the future of the earlier novel, "virtually all thinking men had finally come to agree with the harsh verdict of the great philosopher Lucretius: *all* religions were fundamentally immoral, because the superstitions they peddled wrought more evil than good" (206). In the later novel a resident of Ganymede that Poole befriends, Theodore Khan, proclaims, "Civilization and Religion are incompatible" (106), and describes religion as a form of "psychopathology" (132), "evil" (133), and "insanity" (135). That novel also explains that "religious cultists," while "mentally deranged," were able "to acquire considerable scientific knowledge," which they used to create deadly "chemical and biological agents" (213) and "computer viruses" (217) to slaughter people and disrupt society.

Overall, one could summarize Clarke's indictment of religions in this fashion: they are illogical, perhaps even silly; they are founded on falsehoods; their claims regarding divine powers to influence humanity are illusory; and they cause innumerable evils. Thus, one can reasonably predict that future societies with greater maturity and more scientific knowledge will abandon religion.

This is a recurring theme in Clarke's fiction throughout his career. The utopia crafted by the Overlords in *Childhood's End* is "a completely secular age," because "the creeds that had been based on miracles and revelations had collapsed completely" (74). The civilization of *The City and the Stars* is "a world that had no gods" (67), because "the rise of science . . . eventually destroyed all these faiths" (156). In the near future of *The Deep Range*, religious "beliefs still survived, and would linger on for generations yet" (183), but they are doomed to fade away. In *The Fountains of Paradise*, as noted, Starglider "destroyed all traditional religions." *The Songs of Distant Earth* reports that "Alpha," or "The Personal God" (203), had "faded out of the picture, more or less gracefully, in the early 2000s" (204), and officials preparing materials for space colonists had "thrown away the Veda, the Bible, the Tripitaka, the Qur'an, and all the immense body of literature—fiction and nonfiction—that was based on them" so that they could not "reinfect virgin planets with the ancient poisons of religious hatred" and "belief in the supernatural" (115–16). In the society of *3001*, "all the old religions were discredited" long ago (57).

However, while making broad statements about the future end of religion, Clarke invariably contradicts himself by stating, or indicating, that some religions still have adherents. *Childhood's End* acknowledges that "a form of purified Buddhism—perhaps the most austere of all religions—still survived" (74) during the Overlords' reign, and *The City and the Stars* notes that "all down the ages isolated cults had continued to appear and, however fantastic their creeds, they had always managed to attract some disciples. They thrived with particular strength during periods of confusion and disorder." (157). In *The Deep Range*, while other religions lost "all their power" (183), Buddhism again remained strong and popular, so much so that one of its leaders becomes "the most influential man in the East" (182) and persuades the world to stop slaughtering whales. In *The Fountains of Paradise* both Buddhism and Catholicism have survived, since the Vatican is still functioning, albeit while experiencing financial difficulties. *The Songs of Distant Earth* reports that "a few of the old faiths managed to survive, though in drastically altered forms, right up to the end of the Earth. The Latter Day Mormons and the Daughters of the Prophet even managed to build seedships of their own" (206), so they could continue practicing their religions on new worlds. In *3001*, while Indra Wallace tells the reawakened Poole that people now believe "as little as possible," she also describes them all as "either Deists or Theists," enigmatically explaining, "Theists believe there's not more than one God; Deists that there is not less than one God" (57). Khan concedes that "atheism is unprovable" (132) and is later described as "the last Jesuit" (106), an admirer of the last pope, Pius XX, and a "crypto-Deist" whose "search for God" (138) focuses on the monoliths as possible manifestations of a deity.

Further illustrating the persistence of religion, Clarke sometimes describes the emergence of new faiths in the future, such as the aforementioned Chrislam—an imagined combination of Christianity and Islam—and the "Latter Day Mormons," "Daughters of the Prophet," and "Neo-Manichees" (204) of *The Songs of Distant Earth*. In *Against the Fall of Night* and *The City and the Stars*, a space traveler called the Master inspires a terrestrial cult based on the belief that so-called "Great Ones" would someday return to Earth, and *Rendezvous with Rama* describes the future "Fifth Church of Christ," which created "an entire theology" based on the "assumption" that "Jesus Christ was a visitor from space" (55).

The paradox, then, is that Clarke powerfully argues why future humans *should* abandon religion, yet he suspects that, while its role might be diminished, people will never entirely abandon religion. Pondering that situation, he must discern something worthwhile about religion that would explain its probable endurance.

Clarke first concedes that, if nothing else, religion was useful to humanity in its past. *The Songs of Distant Earth*'s Moses Kalkor theorizes that "religion was *essential* to early human societies" because it imposed "supernatural sanctions to restrain" harmful behavior, but later, when "corrupted by power and privilege," religion became "an essentially antisocial force, the great good it had done being eclipsed by greater evils" (203). Khan, in *3001*, argues that religion was once "a necessary evil," a way for ancient people to deal with their "fear" of "a mysterious and often hostile universe" (133).

Interestingly, in the "Valediction" to *3001*, which contains Clarke's harshest attack on religion, Clarke speaks to religious friends and acknowledges that even today their beliefs might be beneficial:

> I would like to assure my many Buddhist, Christian, Hindu, Jewish, and Muslim friends that I am sincerely happy that the religion which Chance has given you has contributed to your peace of mind (and often, as Western medical science now reluctantly admits, to your physical well-being).
>
> Perhaps it is better to be un-sane and happy, than sane and un-happy. But it is best of all to be sane and happy. (262)

This compliment to religion contains a barb—the idea that having religious faith is a form of insanity—but Clarke accepts that being religious sometimes makes people happier.

In addition to improving one's physical and mental health, *3001*'s Poole maintains, "Most of the greatest works of human art have been inspired by religious devotion" (138), though Khan challenges the point, responding that "no single religion dominated" any field of art. He adds "except for music," accepting the excellence of European music inspired by Christianity, though he suggests this was unrelated to the religion's value but rather "could be due to a purely technological accident" (139). *The Songs of Distant Earth* acknowledges that the religious texts expunged from the records "contained" a "wealth of beauty and wisdom" (115).

In addition, religions have played a major role in preserving, and improving, humanity's knowledge. In *The City and the Stars* Alvin notes, "As if by a miracle," believers in the Master "saved from the past knowledge that else might have been lost forever" (228). The narrator of "The Star," both a Jesuit and a spaceship's chief astrophysicist, follows his faith's traditions by contributing to scientific knowledge, publishing "three papers in the *Astrophysical Journal*" and "five in the *Monthly Notices of the Royal Astronomical Society*" (518). Clarke's *3001* notes the Jesuits' scientific work, as Indra Wallace calls them "amazing people—often great scientists—superb scholars," "sincere and brilliant seekers of knowledge of truth," and admits they "did a tremendous amount of good as well as much harm" (106).

In one case a religion is said to make adherents better workers: *Rendezvous with Rama's* Rodrigo is one of the numerous members of the Fifth Church of Christ who "worked in space in some capacity or other," and "invariably" these individuals "were efficient, conscientious, and absolutely reliable" and hence "universally respected, and even liked" (55). Rodrigo even becomes the story's final hero, demonstrating the admirable morality of his religion by volunteering to disarm the nuclear weapon that could destroy Rama.

As another way to discern a positive attitude toward religion in Clarke, critics assert that his interest in advanced aliens with vast powers constitutes his own ersatz form of religion. Thus, despite the novel's explicit rejection of religion, David N. Samuelson argues that the Overmind of *Childhood's End* "clearly parallels the Oversoul, the Great Spirit, and various formulations of God" (Olander and Greenberg, *Arthur C. Clarke* 200), and L. David Allen concludes, "Basically, *Childhood's End* is a religious vision of the way that mankind might develop and the desirability of that direction" (55). In 1986 *Playboy* interviewer Ken Kelley said to Clarke that "a major theme in so many of your works seems to be a quest for God"; Clarke politely objected by responding, "Yes, in a way—a quest for ultimate values, whatever they are" (66). Edward James observed that Clarke "seems himself to have a strong religious streak" ("Editorial" 3).

As it happens, there is precisely one Clarke work—*3001*—that endorses the notion that advanced aliens are equivalent to the gods of ancient religions: the monolith seen by Moon-Watcher is described as "the very first of" humanity's "multitudinous gods" (55), a man's investigation of the monoliths is related to his "quest for God," and the unidentified voice in the novel's epilogue apparently identifies the monolith builders as the universe's "god," although it "is still a child" (237). The speaker is evidently so powerful as to represent a sort of god to the monolith builders, who in turn are powerful enough to function as humanity's god, suggesting, perhaps, an infinite hierarchy of grander and grander beings who are gods to beings one stage below them.

Finally, there is one religion that Clarke regularly celebrates—Buddhism—in part because, as stated in his foreword to Bhikkhu Basnagoda Rahula's *Beautiful Living: Buddha's Way to Prosperity, Wisdom, and Inner Peace* (2006), "Buddhism stands apart" from other religions "in being tolerant, accommodating, and pragmatic" (ix). *The Songs of Distant Earth* further describes Buddhism as "the only faith that never became stained with blood" (228). Clarke defended his fondness for Buddhism by asserting, as in his *Playboy* interview, that it is "not a religion, really. It's a philosophical outlook" (63), and he specifically disassociated himself from its belief in reincarnation. He evidently admired Buddhism's dedication to the preservation of all life forms—as expressed most clearly by the Mahanayake Thero's campaign to end the slaughter of whales in *The Deep Range*—and the religion improves its believers' personalities as well, as evidenced by several likable Buddhists who appear in his fiction.

In "The Nine Billion Names of God" computer experts become fond of the Buddhist monks they work for because they love their cigars, showing they "were quite willing to embrace all the minor and most of the major pleasures of life. That was one thing in their favour: they might be crazy, but they weren't bluenoses" (419). *The Deep Range*'s Mahanayake Thero is described as "reasonable and friendly" and "not a fanatic" (185), comments that could have been made about the Buddhist leader of the same name in *The Fountains of Paradise*. Indeed, one sign that Vannemar Morgan is the most unsympathetic of Clarke's protagonists is that he can never relate to this man—the "communications gap" between them "seemed in some ways greater than that between Homo sapiens and Starglider" (88)—although even the pragmatic Morgan, about to meet the leader, briefly worries that "he was attempting to destroy something ancient and noble" (75). Finally, some of Earth's remaining Buddhists, described as Moses Kalkor's "old and dear friends" (277), make their presence felt in the novel that perhaps represents Clarke's most extended meditation on religion, *The Songs of Distant Earth*.

It may seem incongruous to describe *The Songs of Distant Earth* as a novel about religion, since the subject is addressed only infrequently; yet when it does come up, religion is analyzed directly and extensively, as occurs in only one other Clarke novel, *3001*. Further, the novel intimates that the idyllic, almost utopian existence of Thalassa's inhabitants is partially due to the exclusion of religion from their culture.

The novel derives its plot from Clarke's 1958 story: the colonized world of Thalassa is visited by a starship from Earth, seeking water to repair its shield so that it can continue its journey to colonize another world, and one crew member has an affair with a Thalassan woman. In his 1981 film scenario based on the story, also called "The Songs of Distant Earth," Clarke adds two dramatic touches, retained in the novel: humans necessarily have fled from Earth because the sun was about to become a nova, and during the colonists' stay, Thalassans discover an indigenous race of sea creatures that are apparently becoming intelligent (borrowing the squids of "The Shining Ones"). Yet both versions of the story say relatively little about Thalassa's people: the story intimates that they are lazy, "content to work as much as necessary (but no more)" (665–66), and after the visitors leave, we are told the colonists "would be moving seas, levelling mountains, and conquering unknown perils" while Thalassans "would still be dreaming beneath the sun-soaked palms" (686). The film scenario indicates that people of this era are casually promiscuous, with members of either sex, without causing conflicts; the visiting astronaut "meets Loren and Marissa and falls in love with them both. Despite their cultural differences the two societies are equally civilized and sexual jealousy is (almost) extinct" (132). Expanding the story into a novel, however, Clarke elaborates at length on the ideal Thalassan civilization.

In addition to the absence of religion, other explanations for the Thalassans' apparent perfection are stated or can be inferred. Their environment—three islands enjoying a tropical climate surrounded by a global ocean—would surely strike Clarke as a veritable paradise. The robots that nurtured the embryos of the first generation of colonists and taught them human culture provided "a Jefferson Mark Three Constitution," described as "utopia in two megabytes," leading to the absence of "political crises" or "civil unrest" (77). The novel's spokesperson on religious issues—elderly colonist and former professor Moses Kalkor—offers another theory, noting that "the Thalassans were also very carefully selected genetically to eliminate as many undesirable social traits as possible" (60).

However, these comments emerge in a moment of self-doubt after Kalkor instead attributes the Thalassans' wondrous existence to "the total lack of religion in this society" (60). Initial observations demonstrate to Kalkor that

> it *is* possible to build a rational and humane culture completely free from the threat of supernatural restraints. Though in principle I don't approve of censorship, it seems that those who prepared the archives for the Thalassan colony succeeded in an almost-impossible task. They purged the history and literature of ten thousand years, and the result has justified their efforts. . . .
>
> The Thalassans were never poisoned by the decay products of dead religions, and in seven hundred years no prophet has arisen here to preach a new faith. (59–60)

As Robin Anne Reid argues, Thalassans illustrate that "human culture must be based on freedom from supernatural threats, which accompany most religions" (124).

The positive attributes of Thalassans and their civilization are stressed repeatedly. They live in a "simple, carefree world" (4), and Kalkor notes that they "seem remarkably free from such unpleasant traits as envy, intolerance, jealousy, anger" (60)—a point later repeated: "It was hard to believe that any human society, even the most enlightened and easygoing, could be totally free from jealousy or some form of sexual possessiveness" (81–82). When Kalkor "teased" Mirissa (the novel's spelling) "by saying that fidelity was almost as strange to the Lassans as jealousy, she retorted that they had gained by losing both" (242). Thalassans are casual about nudity, and as in the film scenario, both heterosexual and homosexual affairs are commonplace: though the novel's astronaut is not attracted to the woman's husband, he does, in a drunken moment, spend a night in bed with her bisexual brother, Kumar—though Kumar says, "I'm quite sure nothing happened" (166). And "the envious rumor that" Kumar "had made love to all the girls and half the boys in Tarna," while "wild hyperbole," is said to "contain a considerable element of truth" (79). Thalassans relish many simple pleasures, as they "loved" "parties" (69), "fireworks" (114), and "animals" (117), and enjoy drinking "excellent Thalassan wine" (150) and swallowing "mildly narcotic tablets" (85). Unsurprisingly, a few colonists succumb to what Kalkor terms "the *Bounty* syndrome" (174) and wish to remain on Thalassa instead of traveling to their destination, a distant and inhospitable world.

Yet there are signs that Thalassans are not entirely ideal. As in the story, they are not particularly energetic: "hard work," one colonist observes, is something that "Lassans avoid whenever possible" (107), and there is a "common Lassan tendency to procrastinate" (80). Noting the colonist Loren had "drive" and "ambition," Mirissa muses that these are "the very things that were so rare on Thalassa" and concedes her husband "Brant had no ambition" (130). Acknowledging his passivity, Mirissa concludes that "she had loved Loren for his strength," while "she loved Brant for his weakness" (245). As the starship captain plans to leave rebellious crew members on Thalassa, he expects them to "become valuable citizens—perhaps exactly the aggressive, forceful type that this society needed" (191).

Unenergetic and unambitious, Thalassans also lack the essential human traits of curiosity and creativity. A crew member notes, "Sometimes the Lassans don't seem to have any curiosity" (114), and "not enough people are interested" (123) in exploring their world's undersea life. "In all their seven hundred years of history," it is noted, "the Three Islands had produced only a handful of original thinkers" (102), though this is excused on the grounds that they were busy colonizing a new world and lacked "the minimum number of reacting minds needed to ignite fundamental research into some new field of knowledge" (103). Loren is also a "more imaginative" lover than Brant (129).

Overall, one might conclude that the disturbing passivity of Thalassans results, at least in part, from their lack of religious faith: Clarke knew that religious conflicts of the past sparked scientific progress, and his stories acknowledge that people inspired by religion had often been instrumental in preserving and expanding human knowledge. However, the novel offers only one subtle hint of such an argument. Though starship databases were purged of religious texts, they include works of literature—adaptations of Homer's *Odyssey*, Shakespeare's tragedies, and Leo Tolstoy's *War and Peace* (1869)—that were never given to Thalassans, presumably because they include references to religion. Kalkor "had to admit the wisdom of the deletions" of these works, "at least in the days the colony was founded. But now that it was successfully established, perhaps a little disturbance, or injection of creativity, might be in order" (117). In other words, Kalkor suspects that stories with intimations of religion might jolt Thalassans out of their complacency. Certainly, if nothing else, the intelligent and curious Mirissa suggests that Thalassans have the potential to achieve great things, so Steve Lehman is incorrect in dismissing them as "straw men, set up to be knocked down . . . immature and superficial, unable to confront the great scientific challenges of the universe" (275).

It is also true that, as in other Clarke works, a society purportedly free of religion has not entirely escaped it. Though a nonbeliever, Kalkor retains an attachment to, even a desire for, religious faith in that he "loved mountains" because "they made him feel nearer to the God whose nonexistence he still sometimes resented" (108), and he laments the absence of the religious works he "knew and loved" (115). Biblical stories remain on his mind as he says, "My namesake once got into a lot of trouble on a mountain," (108) and worries that while visiting a world that "often reminds me of Eden," he might represent "the Snake, about to destroy its innocence" (202).

In addition, Thalassans are not entirely unaware of religion: Kalkor notes, "The very word 'God' has *almost* vanished from their language" (60; my emphasis), and an expository chapter about religion is awkwardly provoked, in the manner of Hugo Gernsback, by having Mirissa ask, "What is God?" (202), indicating at least one Thalassan is interested in the subject. Buddhism remains an active religion until Earth's death; before he departs, Kalkor's Buddhist friends give him Buddha's preserved tooth so that it will not be destroyed, and he leaves it with Mirissa so that her society will possess at least one religious relic. And though Kalkor asserts that the version of God he terms "Alpha"— "The Personal God" (203)—had "faded out of the picture" (204), the other version of God, "Omega, the Creator of everything," has proven "not so easy to dispose of" (206–207), suggesting that even in this world, it remains possible to be a Deist, as is also true in the future of *3001*.

The novel finally intimates that even if traditional religions have faded away, there may emerge powerful belief systems that recall religion. Residents of Mars "had lived in the shadow of an illusion—almost a religion" about their indomitable spirit that "like any religion . . . had performed an essential role in their society: it had given them goals beyond themselves, and a purpose to their lives" (138). People of the future have also developed the concept of "Metalaw"—"laws and moral codes applicable to *all* intelligent creatures" (99)—which inspires a commitment to "Reverence for Life": "all life forms were worthy of respect and should be cherished" (98). One consequence of this doctrine is that "oxygen-bearing planets were placed out of bounds" for colonization because "the presence of more than a few percent oxygen in a planet's atmosphere is definite proof that life exists there" (99) and should not be disturbed. This "Reverence for Life" strongly recalls Buddhism, as Clarke conveys in *The Deep Range*.

In these ways *The Songs of Distant Earth* again illustrates the central contradiction in Clarke's attitude toward religion: even while persuasively arguing that all religions should and someday will be abandoned, he finds reasons to believe they will endure, in one form or another. If nothing else, as he acknowledged in 1970, religion is an "interesting" subject, which might in itself constitute an argument for clinging to it. Also, as suggested by interviewer Kelley, Clarke's recurring "quest for ultimate values, whatever they are" might be likened to "a quest for God" (66). Finally, as Clarke admits, religion can sometimes be beneficial, even if intelligent thinkers like Clarke cannot bring themselves to become believers. Perhaps, then, religion is a tendency that has been permanently embedded in the human psyche since the ancient times of Moon-Watcher's people, who, as noted earlier, made the monolith "the very first" of humanity's "multitudinous gods."

CHAPTER 9

THE SOLITARY OBSERVER

According to standard views, Clarke's characters are lifeless and wooden, and his works are memorable solely for their imaginative ideas. I maintain instead that Clarke's characters may represent the most fascinating, and prophetic, aspects of his fiction. True, Clarke did not give equal attention to all of his characters, and sometimes those who most engage his interest are not protagonists; thus, two prominent characters in *A Fall of Moondust*—the romantically inclined Pat Harris and Sue Wilkins—are clumsily developed, but the minor figure of astronomer Tom Lawson is more persuasive. Further, Clarke's characters are regularly reluctant to express their innermost emotions—to companions, the narrator, even themselves—so they can seem bland to readers who are focused on what they are saying, not on what they are revealingly *not* saying. Thus, only at the end of *Imperial Earth*, when Makenzie unveils a clone of Karl Helmer as his "son," does one recognize the depth of his feelings for that former friend, which he said or thought relatively little about. This explains why Clarke's characters have not received the scrutiny they deserve.

Characteristic Clarke protagonists are essentially solitary, often inclined to cast themselves as observers of, not participants in, portentous events—a trait touched upon by George Slusser, who notes that at moments of transcendence Clarke's "hero has become lyrical observer" (8), "less an actor than a spectator to the drama of evolution . . . observing but never intervening" (23, 31). I interpret stories from Clarke's early professional career collectively as his effort to come to terms with his characters' loneliness as he increasingly recognizes this as a problem and seeks to devise and articulate strategies that will alleviate their isolation without altering their basic personalities. Characters in later works tend to follow the habits Clarke introduces in the 1950s, with some refinements.

In Clarke's publications for the *Huish Magazine* and fanzines, characters almost invariably lack relatives, romantic entanglements, spouses, or children; such matters are simply not mentioned. For example, although "A Short History of Fantocracy" is essentially an assemblage of fannish in-jokes, one might imagine that an account of characters who, during a twelve-year period, become "no more than middle-aged" (Part III: 10) would note that some of them married and had children. Yet the only reference to such developments comes when William F. Temple joins the embryonic revolution "driving a gipsy caravan containing his numerous offspring (including the famous Temple Triplets)" (Part I: 7). Clarke surely comments on Temple's children solely in order to incorporate the phrase "Temple Triplets," which had a humorous meaning now lost to history.

The pattern of unattached characters continues in Clarke's first professional publications, and since they are mostly short stories, the loneliness of protagonists can go unnoticed. Only in retrospect, for example, does one notice the surprising isolation of Shervane in "The Wall of Darkness," who references no relationships while investigating his world's enormous Wall. Even when he becomes middle-aged, the story does not indicate he has a wife or family; the only person in Shervane's life we learn about is a male friend, and their relationship is not close, as they live far away from each other and meet only occasionally. Shervane seems happy to live a solitary life, sporadically contacting distant friends and devoting his energies to the mystery of the Wall.

Shervane is not unlike protagonists in *Against the Fall of Night* and "The Lion of Comarre," youths who grow impatient with complacent worlds and embark upon lonely journeys to end stagnation and reignite progress, expressing no interest in female companionship. Although Alvin describes himself as "lonely" (69), he is content to remain alone, especially since his relationship with Diaspar is antagonistic: Alvin wishes to change everything, whereas other citizens wish to change nothing. Only the Keeper of the Records and, later, his mentor Jeserac become helpful, though impersonal, allies. Similarly, in "The Lion of Comarre" Peyton breaks away from his stultifying society with the assistance of a male mentor and friend, both distant figures. Clarke recognized that his early characters were unlike other science fiction heroes in relying solely on male companions instead of seeking romance, for while summarizing the first draft of *Against the Fall of Night* in "Ego & the Dying Planet," he wryly comments, "At the point where the Hero, by long established tradition, should meet the Girl, there merely turns up another boy!" (39).

Even in the 1950s, occasional Clarke characters have no significant relationships, such as *Prelude to Space*'s Alexson. Though his age is not specified, a comment that "it's almost fifteen years since I did any science and I never took it seriously" (12) suggests he is at least in his thirties, yet he never mentions any family members, wife, girlfriend, or friends—even in the novel's coda, when he is an elderly man looking back on his life. Though he interacts with scientists, administrators, and one astronaut, he contributes nothing to the lunar mission's success and generally keeps to himself, noting that colleagues "usually . . . left him alone, knowing that that was his desire" (15). A telling moment comes when he speaks with Victor Hassell, one candidate to join the crew, and "not until Hassell had gone did Dirk realize that the young pilot had said nothing, absolutely nothing, about himself" (88–89); one might say the same thing about Alexson.

However, the historian is clearly proud that he completed a six-volume history of space flight: "Into those books had gone the greater part of his working life, and now that the task was ended, he was well content" (158). The novel thus suggests one solution to the problems of lonely men: dedicating themselves to great accomplishments. For Shervane, Alvin, Richard, and Alexson, then, their quest functions as the major relationship in their lives.

More prosaically, "Dog Star" indicates that simply having a job might be sufficient to alleviate loveliness. The story, unusually told in the first person, might be somewhat autobiographical, since Clarke's 2000 introduction to the story indicates that the lunar astronomer's late dog, Laika, is based on a dog that Clarke himself owned and loved (though the name is taken from the pioneering Russian dog sent into orbit). Like other Clarke protagonists, he is unmarried, mentions no relatives, and further comments, "I have made very few friends among human beings" (783). Recalling how he bonded with Laika, he reports, "I have been told—and I can well believe it—that I became less and less interested in human company, without being actively unsocial or misanthropic" (784). Though saddened when the dog dies shortly after he necessarily abandons him to work on the moon, he observes that his "work is a wonderful anodyne" (785), which may represent Clarke's general recommendation for those with solitary lifestyles: to find satisfaction in tasks, not companions.

Another solitary individual, *Islands in the Sky*'s Malcolm, recalls other young men in Clarke's earlier fiction: he discusses no girlfriend or close friends, expresses no interest in romance, and relies on an older male mentor—his "Uncle Jim" (6), an attorney who advises him that a contest's prize trip includes the option of Earth's Inner Station. Malcolm does not feel lonely, and at the novel's end, after Doyle offers him a permanent position at the Inner Station when he is older, Malcolm resolves to reject his offer. Instead, having interacted with Martian colonists returning to Earth, he concludes, "The space stations were too near home to satisfy me now. My imagination had been captured by that little red world glowing bravely against the stars. When I went into space again, the Inner Station would only be the first milestone on my outward road from Earth" (209). While mentioning that the "little red world" may reflect a desire to visit Mars, the concluding rhetorical flourish— "my outward road from Earth"—suggests an envisioned lifetime of constantly venturing farther and farther away from Earth on exploratory missions. He thus seems to be yet another Clarke protagonist who will find fulfillment in life by pursuing grand goals.

One Clarke protagonist—Vannemar Morgan of *The Fountains of Paradise*—explicitly chooses a life without close connections to others in order to devote himself to major projects: "Long ago, he had made that choice between work and life that can seldom be avoided at the highest levels of human endeavor" (182). While meeting a nephew makes Morgan feel "a certain bittersweet wistfulness" (182), presumably regarding the son he never had, "He had never for an instant regretted the fact that he and Ingrid," his youthful girlfriend, "had separated amicably" (119). He also notes that on Earth, "family ties had been weakening for the last two centuries," and he has only a distant relationship with his sister: they "had little in common except the accident of genetics" and "exchanged greetings and small talk perhaps half a dozen times a year" (198). Overall, Morgan's involvement in constructing the Gibraltar Bridge and space elevator more than compensated for the absence of personal relationships.

However, Morgan differs from other Clarke heroes because he wishes to be in charge of activities instead of standing on the sidelines. In this respect there is a revelatory indication that Clarke struggled to identify with the character: the fact that Duval, an observer like more typical Clarke protagonists, "did not really like" Morgan (133–34). One suspects she speaks for Clarke himself, who also preferred to write about initiatives instead of leading them. Clarke also likens Morgan to the cruel Kalidasa, suggesting that while Clarke's protagonists prefer being passive and pleasant, some accomplishments may require individuals who are assertive and unlikable.

While they sometimes have family connections, other Clarke protagonists adopt Alexson's role as observer, watching others working. In some cases, like Alexson's, this is an assignment: *Sands of Mars*'s Gibson is hired to journey to Mars and write about his experiences; *Earthlight*'s Sadler is dispatched to a lunar observatory to identify a spy; *2001*'s Floyd is sent to the moon to learn more about the monolith; and *The Ghost from the Grand Banks*'s Bradley, having declined to join efforts to raise parts of the *Titanic*, takes a job as an administrator to function as an overseeing "referee" of the competitors (148).

In other cases Clarke's protagonists are tourists, traveling to exotic places so that readers can appreciate them from a newcomer's perspective. This is literally the status of Daphne in "Holiday on the Moon," who is on a family vacation to the moon, and figuratively the situation of *Islands in the Sky*'s Malcolm, who visits the Inner Station with nothing to do but watch others' activities. In *Childhood's End* Rodricks stows away on an alien spaceship to see their world and, after being discovered, is allowed to tour its wonders. *Imperial Earth*'s Makenzie does visit Earth with tasks to perform—delivering a speech and having himself cloned—but devotes most of his sojourn to sightseeing; significantly, at a party, he fears he will be "identified for what he was—a lost and lonely outsider" (171). The space travelers of *The Songs of Distant Earth* also have work to do on Thalassa, transporting water to rebuild their spaceship's shield, but enjoy ample time to socialize with Thalassans and experience their leisurely lifestyle. In *2061* Floyd participates as a celebrity guest in a rendezvous with Halley's Comet, another sort of vacation.

A few Clarke protagonists must relocate to different environments and are assigned guides to orient them, making them tourists who evolve into residents. *The Deep Range*'s Franklin learns about Earth's undersea world with the help of Burley; *Dolphin Island*'s Clinton, upon reaching Dolphin Island, is paired with another youth, who becomes his "guide to the island" (44). After being revived in *3001*, Poole is initially supervised by historian Wallace, who helps him adjust and becomes his wife.

Finally, many of Clarke's heroes are explorers, and while they take the initiative of journeying to unfamiliar realms and sometimes act decisively, frequently they also focus merely on observing new environments. One could place in this category Clarke's youthful questers—Shervane in "The Wall of Darkness," Alvin in *Against the Fall of Night,* Peyton in "The Lion of Co-marre," and Brant in "The Road to the Sea" (discussed below). It is especially striking that Alvin, having boldly traveled to Lys and then into space, then announces he will never leave Earth again, relegating himself to the status of an observer who will obtain further information solely from a robotic space explorer. There are also the astronauts of "Jupiter Five," who venture to Amalthea to discover that it is an alien spaceship; the space travelers of *2010,* sent to investigate what happened to the first Jupiter mission; and *Rendezvous with Rama*'s Norton, assigned with his crew to explore Rama. Significantly, although Norton is Clarke's viewpoint character, he delegates the novel's most dramatic and dangerous activities—a flight to the remote far side of the craft's interior using a "sky-bike" (159), and an effort to defuse the Hermians' nuclear bomb—to subordinates Pak and Rodrigo, even though the conventions of fiction dictate that main characters should always be at the center of the action. Norton, however, is content to watch them work, realizing they are better suited to the assignments.

While fulfilling tasks and skillful observation can be rewarding for solitary individuals, as evidenced by Alexson, most people cannot be completely satisfied by their work, even if it is valuable. Thus, Clarke recognized that characters would require other ways to relieve their loneliness, and in the early 1950s he began exploring another obvious solution: a girlfriend. Clarke first road-tested this scenario in "The Road to the Sea," a story largely similar to *Against the Fall of Night* and "The Lion of Comarre" in featuring a discontented young man in a complacent society. However, unlike Alvin and Peyton, Brant is hopelessly in love with a woman, Yradne, though his friend Jon is a rival for her affections. Clarke endeavors to make Brant's passion seem strong and sincere; the character travels to Shastar hoping to find or learn something to impress Yradne, and when he copies an image of Helen of Troy in a painting, he unknowingly adds "traces of Yradne" to the portrait (297). Yet when he tells one visitor from the stars that he only wants to "settle down with Yradne," the man responds, "Great art and domestic bliss are mutually incompatible. Sooner or later, you'll have to make your choice" (298). The statement is odd, because the story originally foregrounds the question of Yradne's choice: will she select Brant or Jon? Now the unresolved situation is Brant's choice: will he continue pursuing Yradne or become a solitary artist? In the context of Clarke's early career, Brant seemingly must become either a happily married man or someone who, like Alexson, focuses solely on his avocation. Significantly, instead of the expected conclusion of Brant winning Yradne's heart, the story ends with Brant still alone, pondering his future.

"The Awakening" (1952) briefly indicates that protagonist Marlan had a tepid romantic relationship, for when he departed to enter suspended animation, "Roweena wept, but not for long" (84). *The City and the Stars* also provides Alvin with a longtime girlfriend, Alystra, but Alvin has lost interest in her, despite her continuing affection, and Clarke eventually provides a disingenuous explanation for Alvin's change of heart:

He understood now why he had never loved Alystra, or any of the women he had known in Diaspar. . . . Diaspar had forgotten many things, and among them was the true meaning of love. In Airlee he had watched the mothers dandling their children on their knees, and had himself felt that protective tenderness for all small and helpless creatures that is love's unselfish win. Yet now there was no woman in Diaspar who knew or cared for what had once been the final aim of love.

There were no real emotions, no deep passions, in the immortal city. Perhaps such things only thrived because of their very transience. (183)

Yet if Alvin believes he can find true love only with a woman who is capable of having and loving children, many such women are available in Lys, but he is never attracted to them. Instead, as in *Against the Fall of Night*, the only resident of Lys he bonds with is Seranis's son.

A failed romantic relationship is an element in Clarke's most poignant exploration of male loneliness, the autobiographical *Glide Path*. True, Clarke asserts in his preface that *"all* the characters in the following pages (except the Mark I) are entirely imaginary" [ix], but one cannot read a novel about a man doing exactly what Clarke did during World War II without regarding it as a sort of self-portrait. Further, without the distractions of futuristic technology and environments, Clarke necessarily focuses more on the personality of protagonist Alan Bishop and emphasizes the issue of his loneliness, matters that might have been marginalized amid more fantastic events.

While we learn about three persons who played significant roles in his life, Bishop feels little attachment to his deceased mother; the matronly spinster Miss Hadley, who took him under her wing; or his alcoholic father, who cut himself off from his son after his ship was lost during the Dunkirk evacuation: "all the love that had not followed his wife to the churchyard had gone with his lost ship. There was nothing left for his son" (30). At times he bitterly resents his father's distance and Miss Hadley's decision to end Bishop's budding romance with a local woman. Bishop reports on various occasions that "he did not feel at all sociable" (12); he sought "privacy" as "a rare and valued gift" (74); "he was driven by a blind urge to get away from people, to find some place where he could be alone with his thoughts" (159); and he "wanted no part . . . not even as a spectator," of the "music and gaiety" of a party (226–27). After his father's death, he concludes, "He had outgrown his home. . . . There was no longer any place where he really belonged" (161).

Bishop also feels a visceral antagonism toward pilot Dennis Collins, who is more handsome, attractive to women, and born into a higher class. Since his reaction to Collins extends beyond simple jealousy, he speculates about why he so dislikes Collins and concludes vaguely, "It had to be some complex or other, and it probably stemmed from his childhood. (After all, what didn't?)." Yet the novel reports that Bishop "knew very little about psychology, least of all his own," and while his thoughts about his childhood are "very near the truth," he cannot understand his problem, because "the mind carefully focuses upon its blind spots" (177–78).

Recognizing his need for companionship, a coworker takes Bishop to a brothel, where he develops feelings for his regular consort, Lucille. Eventually, however, he recognizes that she "had been no more than a delightful plaything, toward whom he would always feel gratitude—and nothing else" (177), a woman who "had not given him love" (229). Still, he "suspected, a little uncomfortably, that her memory would warp and color his emotions for years to come" (229). His only moment of intense emotion comes at the novel's end when he visits the abandoned machine he had worked so hard to perfect: "He had not cried at his father's grave, but now the tears were trickling down his cheeks. How strange—indeed, how perverse—to weep for a machine!" (228). Like Alexson, Bishop forges his strongest relationship with his work, and describes his "sorrow" as "that which every man must know when a chapter of his life closes" (228).

Seeking conventional romances in Clarke's fiction, one notes occasional lighthearted stories like "Patent Pending" and "Cosmic Casanova" involving amorously inclined men who receive their comeuppance. When Clarke endeavors to tell a conventional "boy meets girl" story, however, he has only limited success, as illustrated by *A Fall of Moondust*'s Harris and Wilkins. Their budding relationship is presented flatly, even ineptly, particularly when the couple incongruously decides to consummate their relationship in a chamber within a vehicle trapped under mounds of lunar dust.

Wisely, Clarke relegates other romances to the status of subplots, exemplified by *The Deep Range*'s Franklin and Indra and *3001*'s Poole and Wallace. In these three instances, couples first encounter each other as matters of business;

the woman takes a leading role in pursuing the man and forging a connection; and the romance concludes with the man and woman distancing themselves from each other. Harris becomes a spaceship pilot, which will require long absences from his new wife; Franklin's job as an undersea administrator often keeps him away from his wife; and Poole and Wallace amicably separate after fifteen years of marriage. Overall, Clarke's preferred narrative features a man who gets married and then spends much of his life isolated from his wife and family—a situation recalling Clarke's life in the 1950s, when he separated from his wife, Marilyn, after one year but remained married for a decade.

One exception to this pattern is in Clarke's outline and completed passages of *The Last Theorem*, wherein protagonist Ranjit Subramanian was to enjoy a long, happy marriage to Myra de Souza, spending almost all of his time with her until her death. As a sign of his devotion, an interviewer asks Ranjit, "Would you like to go" into space? He replies, "Only if Myra comes with me." Another unexpected theme is Ranjit's estrangement from, and reconciliation with, his father, a Hindu priest; indeed, in two scenes originally projected to begin and end the novel, his father shows young Ranjit the Sri Lankan observatory used by astronomer Percy Molesworth, and an elderly Ranjit lays a lock of Myra's hair on the Martian crater named after Molesworth. This singular focus on traditional family values may represent Clarke's intended tribute to the people of Sri Lanka—particularly the close-knit family of Hector Ekanayake, who long lived with him and whose lifestyle contrasted with that of Clarke and his other protagonists.

Clarke's later narratives typically feature mature men who have already married, eliminating any need to persuasively describe their courtship; yet like Franklin, they spend most of their time away from their families. One rationale for this is space travel, which temporarily separates men from spouses and children during lengthy journeys and may permanently separate them if the men and their families adjust to different gravities.

An early instance of such an isolated husband occurs in "Breaking Strain," wherein astronaut Grant rationalizes that he deserves to live because he "had a wife and three children," though he indicates their relationship is not close: he is "moderately fond" of his family but notes that "for some obscure reason they responded with little more than dutiful affection" (180), perhaps because they saw each other so seldom. In "Holiday on the Moon" astronomer John Martin spends most of his time working on the moon, only occasionally seeing his wife and two children on Earth, though they visit him for a brief vacation.

Unlike other visiting observers in Clarke's fiction, *Earthlight*'s Sadler also has a wife, to whom he seems committed, and the couple plans to have a son; the final chapter reveals that thirty years later that son has given them a grandson. Still, the novel focuses exclusively on an isolated Sadler, and the accountant does not seem particularly depressed by the extended separation from his wife. This surely struck Clarke as an ideal way to craft suitable protagonists: provide them with wives and children so that no questions are raised about their loneliness or sexuality, but keep family members mostly offstage so that the stories can describe essentially solitary men.

Oddly, some novels involve men who are isolated from two different families. The *Deep Range*'s Franklin, permanently unsuited for space travel, can no longer visit his first wife and family on Mars, and his job requires frequent separations from his second wife and family. In *2001* Floyd speaks only briefly to a housekeeper on Earth (in the novel) and his daughter (in the film) while traveling to the moon. We learn in *2010* that after his wife and daughter died in an accident, he married again and had a son, but his second marriage ends because he journeys to Jupiter, leading his wife to divorce him. *Rendezvous with Rama*'s Norton has two families—one in Australia, one on Mars—but his space voyages provide only limited opportunities for visits. *The Hammer of God*'s Robert Singh leaves his wife and child on Earth and relocates to Mars, where he marries again and starts another family, though space missions again allow only occasional contact. These novels, then, feature married men only when they are alone; we learn about families solely through memories and occasional messages. Thus, Clarke's secret to a happy marriage is for men to be mostly alone, spending little time with their families and keeping in touch by means of long-distance communication.

While this scenario suggests that Clarke was less than enthusiastic about the virtues of marriage, the sentiment surfaces only rarely. In *The Deep Range*, as Franklin becomes romantically involved with Indra, he "was impressed by her thoroughness, and was amused to find himself thinking that so competent a woman would be very useful to have around the house. Then he reminded himself hastily that women who were too efficient were seldom happy unless they ran their husbands' lives as well as their own" (57). This concern does not deter Franklin from marrying her, and their relationship proves blissful—"quarrels were rare, and after the birth of Peter they were rarer" (116)—but the remark may reflect Clarke's less than blissful experiences as a married man. Another reference to unpleasant wives comes in *Dolphin Island* when a female killer whale trained to avoid attacking dolphins is observed nudging her boyfriend to stop bothering dolphins as well. Clinton concludes, "He had just seen a ferocious monster converted into a henpecked husband, forbidden to take snacks between meals" (168–69). It is not an opinion one expects from a sixteen-year-old boy lacking experience with marriage, so he may be expressing Clarke's own attitudes.

Still, on one occasion Clarke describes a man who laments his distance from his family and resolves to prioritize them above other considerations. In "Death and the Senator" Martin Steelman long focuses on political ambitions, spending little time with family members or friends. Yet told he is dying of heart disease, Steelman (belying the coldness suggested by his name) reaches out to his estranged wife, daughter, son-in-law, and grandchildren and finds, for the first time, "he felt at peace with the world" (744). Inspired by this new closeness to family members, he rejects an opportunity to be cured in an orbiting space hospital, choosing to spend his remaining time with his family and old friends. As he dies, he reflects, "In the last few weeks he had known contentment, and for that no price was too great" (757).

While it seems noble for Steelman to reject the chance for an extended life to devote time to his family, there is some egotism in his decision, since Steelman recognizes that the men offering medical assistance—an American scientist whose proposal for a space hospital had been opposed by Steelman, and Russian scientists in charge of their own facility—want to gain a political advantage by curing a prominent official. Steelman acknowledges that "his stubborn pride . . . was too much a part of his personality to vanish even under the shadow of death" (745), and while refusing treatment, he reflects, "he had no wish to be a pawn" (755). One might, then, interpret Steelman's newfound appreciation for his family primarily as a rationale for a decision based more on a determination to avoid benefiting former enemies.

There is also ambiguity in another story involving a man who seems attached to his family, "Maelstrom II." Imperiled Cliff Leyland almost immediately thinks about "the faces of his wife and children" (787) while contemplating his impending death; speaking to his wife, Leyland reports he "would willingly have given these last few hours of his life to have seen their faces once again" (790); after the conversation, "He wept for his family, and for himself. He wept for the future that might have been" (791); and when he realizes his life has been improbably saved, "with thankfulness and joy, he could make that second call to Earth, to the woman who was still waiting in the African night" (797). Yet, paradoxically, Leyland is yet another of Clarke's heroes who chooses a career of space travel that necessarily involves regular and lengthy separations from the wife and family he professes to love.

Other than distant marriages, Clarke explores two other methods for relieving loneliness in *Sands of Mars*: identifying oneself with a larger community and forging strong bonds with other men that, while nonsexual, offer as much fulfillment as marriage. This novel seems a transitional work—on one hand, Gibson is much like Alexson: he is not a young man, though "still on the right side of forty-five" (15); his job is to observe and record the work of others; he embraces his status as "an outsider," said to be "the rôle he had always preferred to play" (121); and he never married or raised a family. On the other hand, unlike *Prelude to Space*, *Sands of Mars* is openly concerned about its protagonist's "inner loneliness—the loneliness of the bachelor facing the approach of middle age" (115), and Gibson acknowledges that "perhaps he had been afraid to show his deeper feelings and had hidden them behind banter and even occasional sarcasm" (174). The novel's focus, more than revelations about Mars, becomes Gibson's quest to understand the reasons for his loneliness and alleviate his condition.

The novel reveals that Gibson aspired to become a scientist but while in college fell in love with a woman; preoccupied with the romance, he neglected his studies and was dismissed from the university. Blaming the woman for his failure—which he later admits was unjustified—Gibson distanced himself from her, and after he "had a breakdown and was advised not to return to college," a psychologist "persuaded him to take up writing during his convalescence" and thus launched his writing career. But Gibson's success does not compensate for "the future that had been lost," and ongoing bitterness about his lover's harmful effects explains why he "had never fallen in love again, and . . . realised that he never would" (70). His perceived mistreatment by another person makes him a loner and perpetual "outsider," and unlike Bishop, Gibson understands how youthful events warped his personality.

Eventually, Gibson eases his loneliness by joining and identifying with a larger community as he feels more and more a part of the Martian colonists' world. After he delivers a report to Earth, leader Warren Hadfield notes his "change of attitude": "When you started, we were 'they.' Now we're 'we'" (128). "Becoming a part of the Martian community" (170), he asks to remain on Mars and is assigned to "lead a small section which, frankly, will be our propaganda department" (202).

A second, perhaps more significant solution to Gibson's issues takes the form of one crewmate on the voyage to Mars—"cabin-boy" Jimmy Spencer (18)—who is actually his illegitimate son, born to his lover after they separated. Upon figuring this out, Gibson does not inform Spencer but assumes a fatherly role in traveling with Spencer around Mars and aiding and abetting his burgeoning romance with Hadfield's daughter. Though the novel provides no details, we are told that his relationship with Hadfield will also become important, because Gibson will later "identify" a key "moment" as "the beginning of his friendship with Hadfield—the first man to whom he was ever able to give his unreserved admiration and respect" (187–88).

Little about Gibson's story seems autobiographical: it is unlikely that Clarke was wounded by an unrevealed adolescent romance; he actually graduated from college and completed graduate work in astronomy before voluntarily leaving because, as reported in *Ascent to Orbit: A Scientific Autobiography: The Technical Writings of Arthur C. Clarke* (1984), "terminal boredom" was about to "set in" (117); and he obtained a science-related position, as assistant editor of *Physics Abstracts*, until income from writing allowed him to quit and become a full-time writer. Yet Clarke's original goal, like Gibson's, had been to become a scientist, and even after becoming a famous writer he may have felt bitter about circumstances that made a scientific career impossible: a class society that, due to Clarke's lowly status, did not allow him to enter college at a younger age, perhaps, or the professor who drove him away from astronomy by focusing "introductory lectures" on "a boring and specialised subject, the errors of the telescope" (*Ascent to Orbit* 83–84).

In addition, the ways Gibson addresses his loneliness eerily foreshadow Clarke's life in the late 1950s and thereafter. First, whatever his original reasons were for relocating to Sri Lanka, he became deeply attached to the country and its people, and its culture was central to *The Fountains of Paradise* and the projected focus of *The Last Theorem*. Second, in the late 1950s Clarke forged strong relationships with two younger men—photographer Mike Wilson and business associate Hector Ekanayake—and effectively functioned as a surrogate father to both men, since they went on to marry in the manner of Spencer. Indeed, Neil McAleer notes, "throughout his long career" Clarke "figuratively became the father to many sons, in his literary work as well as in his life" (73).

Still, perhaps because he had not yet taken these steps in 1951, there remains something inauthentic about Gibson's personal dramas. It is implausible that he happens to encounter a long-lost son serving as part of a six-man spaceship crew; nothing about their intermittent conversations suggests any real intimacy is developing; and Gibson's efforts to promote Jimmy's romance seem motivated more by a sense of duty than true affection. Only later would Clarke be able, or willing, to address such personal matters effectively.

A more persuasive version of Gibson's transformation occurs in *A Fall of Moondust*. The story's true heroes are the men who rescue the passengers— Lawson and Chief Engineer Lawrence—and Lawson at times is central to the novel. Like Bishop and Gibson, he was scarred by youthful experiences— a "loveless, institutionalized childhood" in an orphanage—and despite his brilliance, the people he works with uniformly find the "very neurotic" (56) Lawson cold and unlikable; after first talking to him, Lawrence reports, he "hasn't done anything, except nearly make me lose my temper" (65). Yet after playing a key role in locating the trapped vehicle, he unexpectedly becomes a beloved television personality, with Harris referring to "his irascible TV talks on scientific subjects." Harris himself still "found it impossible to like him. It seemed, however, that some millions of people did" (246–47). Thus, like Gibson, Lawson has become a part of a larger community.

Yet Lawson's transformation is also attributed to a strong bond forged between two men during a crisis. When Lawson joins Lawrence to identify the location of the buried vehicle, the astronomer "felt as if he were on a tightrope walking across an abyss, or feeling his way along a narrow path through a quaking quicksand. All his life he had been uncertain of himself, and had known security and confidence only through his technical skills—never at the level of personal relations. Now the hazards of his present position were reacting upon those inner fears. He felt a desperate need for solidity, for something firm and stable to which he could cling" (99). When he has a panic attack, Lawrence shakes him and says, "You've got a brain—a damn good brain—so don't waste it by behaving like a scared kid. . . . I'll get you out of here all right—don't you worry about *that*" (100–101). After he "saw Lawson slowly relax," Lawrence observes that "the astronomer sat quite motionless, obviously in full control of himself but apparently listening to some inner voice. What was it telling him? wondered Lawrence. Perhaps that he was part of mankind, even though it had condemned him to that unspeakable orphans' home when he was a child. Perhaps that, somewhere in the world, there might be a person who could care for him, and who would break through the ice that had encrusted his heart" (101). Only after this experience does Lawson, while still "irascible," become friendly and talkative enough to become a celebrity.

There are briefer references to similar male bonding experiences in *Glide Path* and *The Ghost from the Grand Banks*. In the first novel, after Collins and Bishop survive a harrowing landing on a stormy night, the narrator reports:

> They had shared an experience that they could never talk about, except jokingly, in the days to come. Yet each knew that from now on their relationship was wholly altered.
>
> They would never really like each other, but they would never again be enemies. They were linked now in a comradeship as strong and deep as love itself, though springing from different roots. (216)

And we are told that *The Ghost from the Grand Banks*'s Donald Craig "would often wonder about the relationship that had developed between himself and Jason Bradley. Though they had met only half a dozen times, and then almost always on business, he had felt that bond of mutual sympathy that sometimes grows between two men, and can be almost as strong as a sexual one, even when it has no erotic content. . . . In any event, they enjoyed each other's company, and met even when it was not strictly necessary" (207).

In *Dolphin Island* Clarke provides Clinton—unlike Malcolm, the untroubled hero of his previous juvenile novel—with the same sorts of personal issues that plagued Gibson, Bishop, and Lawson, and addresses them similarly. After Clinton's parents die and he begins living with an unwelcoming aunt and her family, he feels "he had no home; there was no place where he really belonged" (14). He happily stows away on a hovership and, upon reaching Dolphin Island, has no desire to return to his aunt. Soon, he feels he is becoming part of the island community: "It was as if a new chapter had opened in his life. . . . Having lost those he loved while he was so young, he had been scared of making fresh attachments; worse than that, he had become suspicious and self-centered. But now he was changing as the warm communal life of the island swept away the barriers of his reserve" (75).

He also forges bonds with male companions. The boy assigned to serve as his guide, Mick, becomes "the first really close friend that Johnny had ever made" (107). And the older Professor Kazan takes an interest in Clinton because of his affinity with dolphins and comes to personally like him. When Kazan's life is threatened, Clinton realizes that "the island had become the home he had never known, and the Professor a replacement for the father he could scarcely remember. Here he had felt the security which he had longed for and unconsciously striven to find" (155).

The experiences of *The Deep Range*'s Franklin summarize all of Clarke's proposed solutions to the problem of male loneliness; perhaps these were required because the astronaut endured an unusually traumatic sort of solitude after his space accident left him "millions of miles from anywhere . . . completely alone . . . absolutely isolated " for "four hours" (73–74). Unable to work in space, Franklin is first provided with the satisfying new job of monitoring the Earth's oceans. While he sporadically communicates with the wife and family on Mars that he can never see again, he marries again and raises two more children. He forges strong relationships with the people he works with and the sea itself, especially the whales he becomes determined to preserve. And while he and mentor Burley initially maintain an "impersonal relationship" (32), they eventually become close friends, as "Franklin felt an inexpressible gratitude toward him" (93), and they spend so much time together that Franklin's wife regards him as "practically a member of the family" (132). At one emotional moment, Franklin describes precisely how all these factors have finally given him a satisfying life:

> Franklin was as happy now as he had ever hoped to be. His family gave him the emotional security he needed; his work provided the interest and adventure which he had sought in space, only to lose again. There was more life and wonder in the sea than in all the endless empty leagues between the planets. . . . The sea had begun to shape his life and thought, as it must that of all men who try to master it and learn its secrets. He felt a kinship with all the creatures that moved throughout its length and depth. (116)

Given Clarke's known sexual preferences, one might suspect that his fore-grounded male friendships are actually homosexual relationships, even if this is discreetly not mentioned. Yet Clarke himself formed deep but platonic bonds with other men; there is no evidence that characters advanced their relationships beyond that level; and *The Ghost from the Grand Banks* carefully specifies that the bond between Craig and Bradley was nonsexual. Indeed, explicit references to homosexuality in Clarke's fiction are relatively rare.

There is, first, a provocative moment in *The City and the Stars* when Alvin and his friend Hilvar settle down for the night during their journey: "Hilvar had stripped off his clothes, and for the first time Alvin saw how much the two branches of the human race had diverged. Some of the changes were merely ones of emphasis or proportion, but others, such as the external genitals and the presence of teeth, nails, and definite body hair, were more fundamental" (138). One can say, accurately enough, that Alvin finds himself close to a naked man and stares at his body with great interest, perhaps erotic interest, but it seems more likely that, as the novel asserts, his fascination with Hilvar's body stems purely from scientific curiosity, and nothing in the novel suggests the men were ever more than friends. (There are other brief references to male nudity in Clarke's fiction: *The City and the Stars* explains that Diaspar's men have retractable genitals; *The Songs of Distant Earth*'s Kumar freezes to death while naked and sporting an erection [221]; *The Hammer of God* mentions a naked lunar athlete; and an interested woman abruptly refuses to sleep with *3001*'s Poole upon discovering he has been "mutilated" [80], or circumcised.)

Second, homosexuals sometimes appear in Clarke's works as minor characters. "I Remember Babylon" generally describes such individuals as commonplace: the producer planning to bombard America with damaging pornography comments, "We've had a lot of fun planning the feature I've christened 'Queer Corner.' Don't laugh—no go-ahead agency can afford to ignore *that* audience. At least ten million, if you count the ladies—bless their clogs and tweeds. If you think I'm exaggerating, look at all the male art mags on the newsstands" (709). In *2010* Floyd learns that two crewmates—Max Brailovsky and Walter Curnow—have become homosexual lovers, and rebukes Curnow solely because their affair is hurting the feelings of a female crewmate who is "in love with Max" (139). In *2061* two of Floyd's friends are a stereotypically bickering homosexual couple, George and Jerry, who sometimes have affairs with younger men; Floyd "often envied the long-term stability of their relationship, apparently quite unaffected by the 'nephews' from Earth or Moon who visited them from time to time" (37).

In "The Songs of Distant Earth" (1981) the visiting astronaut "falls in love" (132) with both a woman and her husband, and the novel, while omitting this development, introduces another character, Kumar, who is bisexual and is briefly in bed with the astronaut. Another man from Earth, Lieutenant Horton, "had fallen in with a gang of hairy hunks on North Island," though Loren comments, "I'd have sworn you were ninety percent hetero" (159).

In *The Ghost from the Grand Banks* Craig's wife, Edith, after recovering from mental problems, leaves her husband to live with another woman, her nurse Dolores. Her doctor tells Craig, "Edith's prime orientation isn't toward men—and Dolores actively disliked them. . . . She was able to connect to Edith on the physical level even before we connected on the mental one. They will be very good for each other" (223). In *The Hammer of God* one member of Singh's crew is bisexual: "lovesick young scientists of all genders were more likely to confide in him than in the SHIPDOC-PSYCH program" (115).

Finally, in a few novels Clarke indicates that his heroes had homosexual experiences when they were young. One of these was brief and nonconsensual, as *Glide Path*'s Bishop, while reviewing his minimal sexual experience, mentions "a highly refined encounter with the clergyman who had (very briefly) run the local scout troop" (119). Since he mentions it only once, the incident apparently had no traumatizing effects.

Imperial Earth's Makenzie had many sexual encounters with his friend Helmer while they were teenagers, commenting, "His love-making often lacked tenderness and consideration; there were even times when he had scared Duncan into something approaching impotence. And to do *that* to a virile sixteen-year-old was no mean feat" (45–46). Yet Duncan and Karl later become rivals for the affections of a woman, Calindy, and Clarke states clearly that Duncan was not homosexual, only a "normal" bisexual, when the man "remembered—for the first time in years—a boy who had fallen in love with him in his late teens. It is hard to reject anyone who is devoted to you, but although Duncan had good-naturedly succumbed a few times to Nikki's blandishments, he had eventually managed to discourage his admirer, despite torrents of tears. . . . Duncan could never feel quite happy with someone whose affections were exclusively polarized toward one sex" (189). Still, the reason for Makenzie's journey to Earth—to have himself cloned—relates to a male homosexual's presumed desire to give birth to a child without a woman, and his lingering affection for Karl becomes evident when he creates a clone of Karl, not himself, as his successor.

Finally, in a passage completed for *The Last Theorem*, Ranjit is interrupted while enjoying a sexual encounter with his friend Gamini, but though the men remain friends, Ranjit goes on to marry a woman and have two children.

Overall, Clarke's fiction indicates that young male friends might engage in sexual experiments but will naturally abandon the practice as they mature into adulthood and develop long-standing relationships with women. And since Clarke's married men usually spend long periods of time away from their wives, it is evident that for Clarke's characters, as for Clarke himself, sexual activity was never the most important aspect of their lives.

Certainly, Clarke's most famous characters are Heywood R. Floyd, Dave Bowman, and Frank Poole, observed in the novel and film *2001* and Clarke's sequels. The screenplay and novel indicate that Clarke intended to make them much like other protagonists: loners who employ various strategies to alleviate their isolation. The novel's Floyd is a widower living with his three children and a housekeeper, and Bowman, Poole, and their hibernating crewmates are "unmarried," chosen to journey to Saturn because "it was not fair to send family men on a mission of such duration" (103). Yet Bowman and Poole each have at least one girlfriend, for the novel reports they "had been making intimate personal calls at least once a week," though later "the warmth and frequency of the conversations with their girls on Earth had begun to diminish" (103).

Generally, all three men seem happy with their lives, as like other Clarke characters they primarily focus on their work and are reasonably communicative: in the novel Floyd talks to stewardesses during both flights, speaks at some length with Russian colleagues on the space station, and has extended conversations on the moon with Administrator Ralph Halvorsen and chats briefly with Halvorsen's daughter. Bowman and Poole frequently talk with each other, to colleagues on Earth, and to HAL 9000, and their conversations, among other things, provide a complete picture of precisely why the computer becomes unhinged. While Poole is glad he does not have to respond to his family's birthday message, noting he had "moved into a new dimension of remoteness, and almost all emotional links had been stretched beyond the yield point" (120), he is apparently attentive to their message. Bowman's close relationship to his family is revealed in *The Lost Worlds of 2001* when he contacts his astronomer father upon reaching Phobos.

However, the screenplay includes one passage describing two lunar residents having an unwritten, "very banal administrative conversation in low tones" (b59), and Stanley Kubrick seemingly took those words as guidelines when he altered the screenplay while filming. Not only did he eliminate the screenplay's narration, but he also removed some conversations and made others briefer and blander: Floyd now spends most of his travel time sleeping, his conversations are consistently perfunctory and uncommunicative, and Bowman and Poole say relatively little while journeying to Jupiter. Aside from smatterings of small talk, conversations in the film are matters of business, and only HAL seems to convey genuine emotions. Other changes were made to emphasize the isolation of the film's characters: while Floyd is given a wife, she is never seen; Halvorsen's daughter never appears, and there is no indication that people on the moon have families; there are no references to Bowman's and Poole's girlfriends; and during Poole's birthday greeting, actor Gary Lockwood has clearly been instructed to act completely bored, indicating he feels little if any affection for his family.

Since his other films feature conventionally talkative characters who communicate their feelings, Kubrick's unusual approach in *2001* can be interpreted as his response to the special circumstances of its creation: he was in constant contact with Arthur C. Clarke and regularly reading Clarke's fiction, both published works and the scenarios he drafted that were presented in *The Lost Worlds of 2001*. My theory is that Kubrick perceived Clarke's characters, and perhaps Clarke himself, as being peculiarly lonely individuals; he did not regard Clarke's ameliorative solutions as a sufficient response to their unsatisfactory isolation; and he transformed his film into the story of how the aliens behind the monolith recognize and correct their fundamental problem.

In Clarke's novel the primary drawback to humanity's use of tools is violence, as evidenced by the way Moon-Watcher and fellow primates start wielding their tools to attack and murder members of a rival tribe, and by the threatening nuclear bombs orbiting Earth in the year 2001. The aliens' transformation of Bowman into the Star Child addresses this issue, since the pacifistically inclined Star Child immediately eliminates Earth's nuclear weapons. In the film, however, the primary drawback to humanity's growing dependence on the advanced tools known as machines is that they are turning people into machines, unable to feel or convey genuine emotions; John Hollow notes while describing the film's Poole, "The astronaut has become more a part of the machine than he realizes" (140). The aliens' transformation of Bowman into the Star Child, then, represents their effort to restore people's genuine human nature, visually indicated by replacing the space-suited Bowman with a naked human fetus—what Hollow terms "the ultimate symbol of human potential" (142). The film, in other words, can be viewed as Kubrick's commentary on the characteristic Clarke hero and his need for radical, revolutionary change.

The intelligent Clarke, watching *2001*, must have recognized that, at least in part, Kubrick was critiquing the characters he created, though this is not something he would discuss; like his characters, Clarke was not inclined to communicate his feelings. However, several subsequent works can be regarded as Clarke's efforts to respond to Kubrick's message.

Rendezvous with Rama mildly rebukes Kubrick by repeatedly describing, and defending, characters who are disinclined or reluctant to engage in conversation. When crew members enter Rama, "no one had spoken . . . as if everyone realized that this was a moment for history, not to be spoiled by unnecessary small talk. That suited Norton, for at the moment he, too, had nothing to say" (39). Later, descending a ladder, Norton "wasted no time in conversation" (55). Walking across a Raman plain, "apart from an occasional consultation with the ship, they marched on in silence" (80). When people have important business, the novel asserts, there is nothing wrong with limited communication. Only the presence of a larger audience mandates extended discourse, so when Norton tersely reports, "Everyone in fine shape—no problems. Proceeding as planned," he is upbraided by a crewmate: "Skipper, this isn't good enough. You know the news services have been screaming at us for the last week. I don't expect deathless prose, but can't you do better than that?" (74–75).

Further, almost defiantly, Clarke returns to the figure of the absolutely solitary observer in two major stories—"Transit of Earth" and "A Meeting with Medusa"—as if to validate their isolated lifestyles. The protagonist of "Transit of Earth," which Clarke described as his best story, is identified only as "Evans," a man whose doomed crewmates have sacrificed their lives so he can observe a rare alignment of the sun, Earth, and Mars. The only time the dying narrator mentions his family is while recalling, "As a kid, I used to do a lot of skin diving, when my family went to the Caribbean for vacations" (884). He strangely says nothing, though, about how much he will miss his family, he mentions no other loved ones, and the only indication of affection for dead crewmates comes when he resolves to rearrange one of their awkwardly positioned corpses. He desires to die in solitude, for when "a tiny light" indicates that "someone must be trying to talk to me," he does not respond, saying, "Sorry, everyone, I've said all my goodbyes, and don't want to go through that again" (889).

The only people Evans talks about are people he never knew: he recalls a photograph of Robert Scott and members of his doomed expedition, other explorers who lost their lives; says, "I am one with Captain Cook, back in Tahiti in 1769, watching the transit of Venus" (891); mentions composers he is listening to—Edvard Grieg, Sergei Rachmaninoff, and Johann Sebastian Bach; and lists writers who speculated about Mars—H. G. Wells, Percival Lowell, Edgar Rice Burroughs, Stanley G. Weinbaum, and Ray Bradbury. These individuals apparently mean more to him than any person he interacted with; he consoles himself with the thought that his fate connects him to famous figures from the past, indicating that, like other Clarke protagonists, he sees his work as the most important aspect of his life. And by having him describe his dying moments in a poignant, emotional manner, Clarke demonstrates that a solitary individual can also be completely human.

"A Meeting with Medusa" is one of Clarke's most revelatory stories; apparently about an explorer's encounter with aliens in Jupiter's atmosphere, it ultimately focuses on the man himself—who, it transpires, is not a man. For pilot Howard Falcon has been so grievously injured in an airship crash that it became necessary to effectively turn him into a machine: he "unlocked his undercarriage so that it no longer formed a chair, and rose on his hydraulics to his full seven feet of height" (926). Only such a cyborg, it transpires, could have survived the close encounter with Jupiter.

Though Clarke is vague about the physical nature of Falcon's mechanical body—save that it is a "metal cylinder that had replaced his fragile body" (926)—his mental transformation becomes more interesting. A colleague is surprised to hear him refer to "men" as if he were no longer a man: "He said 'men.' He's never done that before. And when did I last hear him use the word 'we'? He's changing, slipping away from us" (926). Falcon himself is aware of his special nature: "Some day the real masters of space would be machines, not men—and he was neither," and "he took a sombre pride in his unique loneliness—the first immortal midway between two orders of creation" (926). Clearly, Falcon has perfectly adjusted to a special, and intense, form of loneliness, necessarily separated from humans with normal bodies.

One might conservatively interpret Falcon as only an exaggerated portrait of all disabled people—like Clarke in a wheelchair—who depend on machinery to survive and hence may feel alienated from people who move without assistance. Yet such individuals live in societies that increasingly strive to ease their isolation by ensuring that all human experiences—entering tall buildings, soaking in spas, enjoying amusement park rides, competing in athletic events—are accessible to them. Falcon's situation is so extreme—he not only depends on machinery but also is part of the machinery—that ameliorative steps are ineffectual, making distance from people inevitable.

"A Meeting with Medusa," then, offers yet another response to Kubrick's film. If Floyd, Bowman, and Poole, surrounded by machines, figuratively become machines, Falcon has *literally* become a machine. And his resulting separation from human beings, far from representing a flaw, is a natural development in the evolution of human intelligence, a step toward the human-constructed "machines" that will become the true "masters of space." The protagonists of *2001*, then, might be defended as cyborgs-in-training, and the true future of humanity is best represented not by the Star Child but by the HAL 9000 computer. Indeed, in *2061* HAL is resurrected to become the ethereal Bowman's companion, and in *3001* the entities have merged to become Halman, another version of the combination of human and machine that Falcon represents.

Finally, if Kubrick stripped Floyd, Bowman, and Poole of their humanity to emphasize their problematically solitary nature, Clarke makes a concerted effort, in sequels to *2001*, to restore their humanity. In *2010*, although Floyd's wife and daughter died in an accident, he remarries and has a son, and while his voyage to Jupiter leads to divorce, he forges strong relationships with crewmates, especially a man he previously disliked, Curnow, and has a brief affair with a female cosmonaut.

The novel also reveals why Bowman never married: he had been traumatized by the accidental death of his older brother and an abortive relationship with Betty Fernandez that he could never forget. Demonstrating the strength of his lingering emotional attachments to former companions, the Star Child, even while wondering, "Why had he come here, returning like an unquiet ghost to the scene of ancient anguish?" (160), visits and speaks with Betty. Then, in a touching moment, he enters his elderly mother's apartment and figures out how to "control . . . obdurate matter" to comb her hair: "Ten-year-old Dave Bowman had finished the chore which he always hated but which his mother loved" (169–70). Evidently eager for company, he silently asks his alien overseers to resurrect HAL to become his colleague.

In *2061* the elderly Floyd is alone, having never married for a third time, and has little contact with his ex-wife, two daughters, or grandson Chris (whose father has died). Nevertheless he enjoys socializing with George and Jerry; while traveling to Halley's Comet, he befriends several passengers and becomes close to enigmatic actress Yva Merlin; and he develops a new relationship with his grandson while rescuing him and other crewmates on Europa. The briefly glimpsed Bowman has bonded with HAL, and they add a duplicate of Floyd to their circle to provide his "knowledge and experience," or "wisdom" (268), and better serve as Europa's "administrators of the unforeseen" and "guardians" (271).

When Poole is revived in 3001, he cannot reunite with long-dead family members, though he recalls "everyone he had ever loved[:] Mother, Father (before he had gone off with that Other Woman), dear Uncle George and Aunt Lil, brother Martin—and, not least, a succession of dogs, beginning with the warm puppies of his earliest childhood and culminating in Rikki" (85–86). He also remembers Helena, the woman he planned to marry upon returning from Jupiter, who perhaps employed his sperm to have his child; he befriends several men; after traveling to Jupiter, he reconnects with Bowman; and he has several sexual encounters with women before marrying Wallace, who provides him with two children before they separate. He concludes the novel anticipating the opportunity "to cradle his first grandson in his arms" (236).

In sum, Kubrick may have endeavored to present Floyd, Bowman, and Poole as robotic functionaries, drained of human emotions by all-encompassing machines, but Clarke's sequels argue that they were in fact living, breathing human beings, even if they did not express themselves well. Like other Clarke characters, they spend much of their time alone but are sustained by satisfying jobs, strong friendships, and relationships with distant family members, which make them content with their lives.

The typical Clarke protagonist, then, may be generally described in this fashion: almost invariably male, he may be alienated from his family and without any sexual partners or friends, but he never laments their absence while focusing his energies on fulfilling work. His primary task often involves intense scrutiny of the world, not active engagement with it. While he may maintain contact with his family or have a wife and children, he mostly spends his time separated from them, ostensibly due to extenuating circumstances. He may forge connections to some larger community or nonsexual relationships with male friends.

This is also a description of Clarke's lifestyle. Moving to Sri Lanka, he separated himself from family members and friends, though he kept in touch with occasional visits and long-distance communication. He grew close to the family of Hector Ekanayake, who lived with him, but clearly spent most of his days alone in his office, writing, reading, and corresponding via email. Clarke was a keen observer of the world, first as a traveler and skin diver and later as a constant reader of nonfiction. He forged connections to two communities: the science fiction community, which he contributed to by establishing the annual Arthur C. Clarke Award to honor the year's outstanding science fiction novel published in the United Kingdom, and his adopted nation of Sri Lanka, which he repeatedly praised. He was known for close relationships with male friends, particularly photographer Wilson and Hector's younger brother Leslie, whose death in 1977 devastated Clarke, while fulfilling his sexual urges with impersonal homosexual encounters.

More significantly, Clarke's characters anticipate how more and more people now live their lives. Like Clarke, young people regularly move far away from families and friends while sometimes remaining connected by means of vacations and correspondence. People increasingly choose to remain unmarried and live alone, and increasing numbers of married couples, because of their work, must live far apart. The internet provides users with the enticing ability to become spectators of events and entertainment from around the world, and same-sex relationships, both sexual and nonsexual, are arguably more important than ever. Clarke's characters, then, may someday be regarded as his most significant prediction of the future.

Arthur C. Clarke's professional writing career might be divided into two phases. Throughout the 1940s, 1950s, and 1960s, he wrote occasional novels and numerous stories that typically focused on one major interest—that is, we find humorous stories, stories about new inventions, stories about space travelers, stories presenting alternative futures for humanity, stories that foreground aliens, stories involving the undersea world, and, rarely, stories that explore religious issues or provide character studies. Then, beginning with *2001: A Space Odyssey* and *Rendezvous with Rama*, Clarke devoted himself almost exclusively to writing leisurely paced episodic novels, with brief chapters touching upon several of his interests—sometimes all of them.

Consider the novel that Clarke identified as his finest, *The Songs of Distant Earth*. The novel has moments of wry, even cruel humor, as the doggedly amorous Kumar, accidentally elevated into space while stark naked, freezes to death sporting an enormous erection: "in death, the Little Lion was even more male than he had been in life" (221). Several inventions are described, including the "quantum drive" (42) that enables humans to send manned spaceships to other solar systems. The novel looks back at humanity's initial progress in conquering the solar system, mentioning among other initiatives "the Louis Pasteur satellite hospital" (35) and a Martian colony. The novel describes how discovering that the sun was about to become a nova forced humans to rapidly develop a program to colonize other solar systems, first with robotic ships carrying human embryos and later with manned spaceships. The Thalassans discover sea creatures, the "scorps," that wear bracelets and maintain undersea farms, suggesting they are becoming intelligent. The novel's setting is a world covered by an ocean, and there are descriptions of diving expeditions. The novel explains why humans excluded all references to religion in the material employed to educate their colonists. And its viewpoint character, Loren Lorenson, visits Thalassa primarily as an observer, though he bonds with its people by having an affair with a native woman and fathering a child.

While *The Songs of Distant Earth* and Clarke's other novels were successful in their day, it remains uncertain whether they will remain popular in the future. In the short term, Clarke's works are doing reasonably well: one always finds several Clarke novels in bookstores; the Syfy Channel invested heavily in miniseries based on *Childhood's End* (2015) and *3001: The Final Odyssey* (originally announced for 2017), which will keep his memory alive; and other Clarke works may be adapted as films, including the long-delayed but recently relaunched project to film *Rendezvous with Rama*. Only a few novels, like *Prelude to Space*, seem completely outdated, and Jules Verne and H. G. Wells demonstrate that science fiction writers do not necessarily lose their appeal after their predictions are realized or invalidated. In sum, when his private diaries are made public in 2038, and long thereafter, the world will likely remain interested in Clarke.

Those future individuals who still read novels may feel a special affinity with Clarke for two reasons. First, though progress in conquering space remains agonizingly slow, more and more people will be traveling to and living in space, and they may regard Clarke as unusually and insightfully prophetic in describing both the general nature and specific aspects of everyday life in space. Second, as intimated, people may be increasingly leading largely solitary lifestyles, distant from partners and free to engage in brief sexual affairs, and such readers may be discomfited by other twentieth-century novels describing societies that consist almost entirely of married heterosexual couples and young men and women seeking to become heterosexual couples. Clarke's comfortably detached characters, in contrast, may better accord with their own situation, making him seem more like a twenty-first-century writer than a twentieth-century writer—perhaps the greatest compliment one can imagine for a science fiction writer.

Still, in one respect Clarke's works were already starting to seem old-fashioned when he died in 2008, as evidenced by the contrast between his characters and those created by his younger "collaborators." Their characters are very modern in their constant attentiveness to their own psychological traumas, weakness in the face of adversity, and sense of being cruelly victimized by others. Yet while Clarke's characters have problems and sometimes think about their problems, they are never obsessed with or consumed by their problems; they remain resolutely focused on their responsibilities—to their jobs, to their friends and family members, to their aspirations and goals. Psychologists might conclude that they are unhealthily bottling up emotions and employing work as a substitute for the personal fulfillment they really need, and future readers might regard them, in their own jargon, as not "relatable" to their own lives. However, they might also admire their strength of character, their calmness during crises, and the way others can rely on them. Certainly, for example, if asked to choose a crew to explore an immense alien spacecraft, any sane person would opt for Clarke's coolly competent Norton and his colleagues, not the deeply disturbed and distracted individuals of Gentry Lee's *Rama II*, who are focused more on their personal issues than the alien spaceship.

For another reason, then, Clarke's characters seem central to any understanding and appreciation of his works and may someday be cherished more than his admirable scientific speculations or his cosmic perspectives.

CLARKE'S "COLLABORATIONS"
WITH OTHER AUTHORS

While Clarke and Gentry Lee's *Cradle* was his first official "collaboration,"
twelve other texts might be placed in this category, as they represent the work
of other authors acknowledging their use of Clarke's ideas. First, a forgotten
story in a 1938 fanzine, D. R. Smith's "Cosmic Case #4," is described as based
"upon an idea suggested by Arthur C. Clarke" (8).

Second, the anthology *Three for Tomorrow* (1969) contains novellas written
by Robert Silverberg, Roger Zelazny, and James Blish in response to an essay
by Clarke, published as the book's foreword, offering this question: "With
increasing technology goes increasing vulnerability. . . . How is the society
of the future going to protect itself from an increasing spectrum of ever
more horrendous disasters, particularly those made possible by new devices
(high-powered lasers? drugs?) in the hands of madmen?" (9). Clarke did no
other work for the volume, though he has been incorrectly cited as its editor
(it was actually edited by an uncredited Silverberg).

Six novels published under the umbrella title *Arthur C. Clarke's Venus Prime*—*Breaking Strain* (1987), *Maelstrom* (1988), *Hide and Seek* (1989), *The Medusa Encounter* (1990), *The Diamond Moon* (1991), and *The Shining Ones* (1991)—are credited solely to Paul Preuss, though each is based on a Clarke story. Clarke's plots are reworked to feature a new female protagonist, a spacefaring investigator named Sparta, and Clarke's only contribution to the books was to write their afterwords.

Beyond the Fall of Night (1990) was initially promoted as a collaborative work by Clarke and Gregory Benford; in fact, as readers could quickly discover, the book consists of the republished text of Clarke's *Against the Fall of Night* and Benford's original sequel. Thus, there was no pretense that any actual "collaboration" occurred.

Most recently, there is Stephen Baxter and Alastair Reynolds's authorized sequel to "A Meeting with Medusa," *The Medusa Chronicles* (2016), which may become the first of several new sequels to Clarke stories.

Cradle involves a benevolent alien race that visits underdeveloped planets, captures specimens of promising life forms, creates improved versions of those creatures, and deposits "cradles" on those planets containing the modified beings' embryos and robot instructors to help them mature. When a spaceship delivering such a package to Earth is damaged after encountering a satellite, it lands off the Florida coast to make repairs, diverting an American cruise missile. When a female journalist, a boat owner, and his crewmate undertake to locate the missile, they contact the submerged vehicle, assist with repairs, and persuade the departing aliens to take their cradle with them instead of leaving it to alter Earth's natural development. Complicating matters are an investigating navy commander, his overzealous subordinate, and a duplicitous treasure hunter. The novel is weakened by lengthy, unpersuasive explorations of each character's personal traumas, and the fact that Lee's characters, here and in the Rama trilogy, regularly smoke cigarettes contrasts with Clarke's aversion to smoking, expressed in *The Ghost from the Grand Banks* by the predicted emergence of technology to edit smoking out of old movies.

The Rama trilogy, beginning with *Rama II*, is credited to Clarke and Lee. Soap opera is again prioritized over science as Lee improbably posits that when a second Raman spacecraft approaches, authorities would dispatch an exploratory mission consisting of only twelve people, including two un-qualified journalists, who all suffer from severe psychological problems and a proclivity to personal conflicts. As characters squabble and conspire against one another, they seem inattentive to the alien spacecraft they should be investigating. Yet *Rama II* belatedly sputters to life when physician Nicole des Jardins and engineer Richard Wakefield investigate a Raman "city" and discover a race of intelligent bird-like aliens called "avians" and replicas of objects left behind by explorers of the first spacecraft, suggesting the vehicles have been in contact. When the Raman vehicle alters its course to approach Earth, Nicole, Richard, and crewmate Michael O'Toole warn the spaceship to protect itself against Earth's nuclear missiles, and they remain inside the craft when it leaves the solar system.

In *The Garden of Rama* Nicole, Richard, and Michael spend twelve years traveling to Sirius; Nicole has three daughters with Richard (effectively her husband) and two sons with Michael (to provide offspring with genetic diversity). Near Sirius they rendezvous with an immense processing facility, the Node, where they meet a human-like "biot" who tells them that Rama's mission is to locate and retrieve specimens of spacefaring species. One male and one female are asked to remain at the facility as potential parents, so one daughter marries Michael to stay behind; the others return to Earth's solar system, hibernating in a redesigned Rama, to join a recruited colony of two thousand humans to live within the spacecraft for "observation." Implausible conflicts emerge because officials, not believing Nicole's message requesting colonists for Rama, instead recruit people to join a Mars colony; discovering that Nicole was truthful, they suddenly inform colonists they will be living in a space habitat. Further, unable to find enough volunteers, they include convicted felons, including the particularly unsavory Nakamura, who takes control of the colony, dangerously tinkers with its specially prepared environment, attacks and slaughters nearby avians, and imprisons opponents. The monitoring masters of Rama are displeased by these activities but take no action as Richard escapes and Nicole faces a death sentence.

In *Rama Revealed* Nicole is rescued and joins her husband and other family members in taking refuge with aliens they call "octospiders," who are friendly, intelligent, and amazingly advanced in biological technology. They are imperiled by Nakamura, who launches an unprovoked war, and when

Richard and one octospider attempt to negotiate a settlement, Nakamura murders them. The octospiders reluctantly retaliate by unleashing the first of a planned series of bioengineered diseases, which kills all humans over forty years old. At this point, Raman overseers intervene and put the spacecraft's residents to sleep until they reach the Node, now positioned near Tau Ceti. There, Nicole is reunited with Michael, her daughter, and their children and completely informed about Rama's purpose: it is part of a mission launched by a being termed the Creator—or God—to intensely study the innumerable universes He created to find the one model that naturally evolves toward complete harmony—a quasi-religious vision that pleases the Catholic Michael but is at odds with Clarke's own beliefs. Though the dying Nicole is offered mechanical replacements for failing organs to keep her alive indefinitely, she declines treatment but is allowed to visit a "Knowledge Module" and receive a virtual tour of the universe.

Richter 10, credited to Clarke and Mike McQuay, is the weakest Clarke "collaboration" and seems the least like Clarke's work in focusing not only on characters' personal issues but high-level political maneuvers as well. After his parents are killed in a 1994 California earthquake, Lewis Crane becomes obsessed with predicting earthquakes and as an adult achieves a successful system with the assistance of African American colleague Dan Newcombe. As conspiracies unfold involving Crane's foundation, the Chinese company controlling America's government, and Islamic African Americans seeking to expand their enclaves into a separatist state, Crane is discredited when falsified data leads him to incorrectly predict an earthquake in the southern United States but then vindicated when a subsequent prediction of an earthquake in the same region proves accurate. He resolves to prevent the earthquake destined to devastate California by audaciously employing nuclear bombs to fuse together two plates beneath the state, but the Islamists, now aided by Newcombe, thwart his plans, kill his wife and son, and make Crane an international pariah. Crane remarries and sets up a projected utopian community on the moon; however, bringing their lives to a fitting conclusion, Crane reunites with Newcombe to calmly die while they personally witness the earthquake that destroys California.

The Trigger, credited to Clarke and Michael Kube-McDowell, begins promisingly as researchers accidentally discover a device that detonates nitrate explosives at a distance, potentially making it impossible for anyone to employ guns or other weapons for violent purposes. A pro-disarmament senator persuades them to reveal their invention, called the Trigger, to idealistic President Breland, who soon makes them available to governments and citizens everywhere. No facility protected by a Trigger can be violently assaulted, as would-be perpetrators' weapons are destroyed before they can act. An improved version of the technology, the Jammer, prevents explosives from exploding instead of igniting them. A growing emphasis on politics seems unlike Clarke, as the novel devolves into an extended diatribe in favor of gun control, with saintly advocates of the new technology interminably arguing against sinister, sometimes homicidal, opponents who are determined to eliminate the Trigger and Jammer to protect their Second Amendment rights. But proponents of the technology prevail, and in an epilogue set twenty years in the future, the scientist who crafted the Trigger ponders his newest discovery, a device that selectively kills individuals based on their DNA.

As an established writer of hard science fiction, Stephen Baxter, credited coauthor of all remaining texts discussed here (except *The Last Theorem*), was the most capable of Clarke's "collaborators," though he also generally fails to emulate his style. "The Wire Continuum" soberly considers the idea Clarke treats farcically in "Travel by Wire!"—a system to instantly teleport people and goods by means of wires or radio waves. Baxter creates an alternate history (a genre Clarke avoided) wherein postwar scientists, continuing research launched by Nazi Germany, achieve such teleportation in 1962, leading to various revolutionary effects, including instantaneous space travel to other planets. The protagonists are married couple Henry Forbes and Susan Maxton Forbes, who maintain a troubled relationship while pilot Henry improbably advances from airplanes to space flights and, eventually, a flight to another solar system, and Susan assists in perfecting and improving the system.

In "Hibernaculum 46" a utopian future world enjoys limitless energy and resources, yet numerous individuals, bored with their ideal world, are having their bodies frozen in suspended animation within underground "hibernacula." One woman, convinced this process is draining the planet of innovative, energetic citizens, seeks to sabotage one hibernaculum, but her attempt is detected and thwarted. The hibernaculum's head then persuades her that it is beneficial to have people placed in suspended animation to awaken at a time when humans can finally travel to other solar systems, a development that will spark a human renaissance requiring capable, motivated participants.

The Light of Other Days describes a remarkable invention: a device that locates and makes use of tiny, transitory wormholes, initially employed for instantaneous long-distance communication. But the driven tycoon who developed the machine, Hiram Patterson, recruits his estranged son, David, a physicist, to improve the technology so that it enables people to observe any event, anywhere in the world. This technology gradually becomes accessible to everyone, eliminating privacy and exposing corrupt activities. It is further enhanced to enable people to view past events, so people can compile an entirely factual historical record. Complicating matters are the impending arrival, in five hundred years, of a huge traveling world that will strike and destroy Earth, and Hiram's machinations to control his other son, Bobby, to end his relationship with a female journalist, and to protect himself from people whose lives were ruined by his invention. Eventually Hiram learns how to employ wormholes to extract limitless energy from Earth's core, enabling the world to achieve a utopia and prevent Earth's destruction; others adapt the technology to become "Joined" as a group intelligence; and a project is launched to use the technology to resurrect all people and beings who ever lived on Earth. Despite melodramatic touches and questionable speculations, this is the best of Clarke's "collaborations."

In the Time Odyssey trilogy, beginning with *Time's Eye: Book One of a Time Odyssey*, the first intelligent species to emerge in the cosmos, the Firstborn, determines that the universe has a finite amount of energy and resolves to preserve its energy at all costs. Since advanced civilizations consume large amounts of energy, they begin annihilating intelligent species whenever they are detected. Before doing so, they have the poorly explained habit of first constructing a pocket universe containing a duplicate of the doomed planet, composed of fragments from various times in its history, and such a duplicate Earth, called Mir, is the setting for *Time's Eye*. There, while the aliens' spherical, floating Eyes observe events, twenty-first-century United Nations soldiers interact with prehistoric australopithecines, the armies of Alexander the Great and Genghis Khan, and nineteenth-century British soldiers, including Rudyard Kipling. After inconsequential adventures, UN worker Bisesa

Dutt is mysteriously transported back to Earth (due to the intervention, we later learn, of other aliens, the Lastborn, who oppose the Firstborn).

In *Sunstorm: A Time Odyssey: 2* the aliens undertake to obliterate humanity by hurling a distant planet into the sun, causing a "sunstorm" of radiation to kill all life on Earth. To avoid this fate, scientists construct an enormous, ultra-thin shield to partially protect Earth from the radiation and mitigate its impact. Descriptions of how the shield is designed, built, and deployed represent the only part of the trilogy that resembles Clarke's writing. Dutt contacts authorities with the key information that this is not a natural event, so scientists recognize that humanity will soon face another threat.

In *Firstborn: A Time Odyssey: 3* the aliens attempt to destroy Earth in another way: by transforming an Eye into a "Q-bomb" of dark energy. But it is learned that millennia ago, an extinct race of Martians discovered how to disable the Eyes, and when Dutt is transported back to Mir, she discovers that its pocket universe also contains a duplicate of ancient Mars. Thomas Edison contacts the Martians with huge burning ditches forming Martian symbols, and upon receiving his message, a Martian scientist somehow "squeezes" an Eye, inspiring it to emit a distress signal that inexplicably confuses the Eye designed to destroy the real Earth, causing it to destroy the real Mars instead. The novel concludes with the Lastborn contacting Dutt, presumably to enlist humanity's assistance in further efforts against the Firstborn. To put matters mildly, none of these events really make any sense, as explained in my "The Endless Odyssey."

One must, however, praise Baxter for a credible addition to the White Hart series, "Time Gentlemen Please" which recaptures its spirit and tone by describing a contemporary reunion of the pub's attendees, including David Kyle, James MacCreigh, John Christopher, and Ken Slater. Clarke, as "Charles Willis," participates by means of television, as arranged by brother "Bill" (Fred Clarke); a new visitor, a thinly disguised Gregory Benford ("Benjamin Gregford"), is considered "at sixty-six a sprightly youth" (193); and everyone pays tribute to "those who could no longer join us" (194): the deceased John Wyndham, Charles Eric Maine, George Whitley, William F. Temple, and John Brunner. Harry Purvis, now in a wheelchair, arrives to tell an outlandish story about an Australian scientist who develops a "temporal flux accelerator" (199) enabling him to experience three hours of time in one second (recalling the device in "All the Time in the World"). But in his accelerated state, he discovers that light and heat move too slowly to affect him, so he freezes to death. Purvis concludes by claiming that problems with the device were later corrected, so it is being used to create phony antiques, including "seventeenth-century English pewter tankards" (208)—a barb directed at Gregford, who proudly displayed such an item as his recent purchase.

Finally, although scattered passages of Clarke's prose are embedded in *The Last Theorem*, it is almost entirely the work of Frederik Pohl. Clarke provided its basic plot in an outline: a young Sri Lankan mathematician, Ranjit Subramanian, discovers a short proof of Fermat's Last Theorem; he then works for the United States government; he marries a woman named Myra and has two children, daughter Natasha and a mentally disabled son, Robert; his wife dies; and he eventually travels into space. In a later introductory passage, largely identical to the novel's "The First Preamble," Clarke mentions an alien race, the Grand Galactics, who detect evidence of humanity's existence. From this, Pohl devises an elaborate subplot involving advanced aliens who first resolve to destroy humanity but, upon discovering evidence of tremendous progress, change their minds, allow humanity to survive, and eventually anoint them as their successors. Pohl also creates almost all of Ranjit's adventures, including experiences as a university student; his abduction by pirates (replacing a sequence involving Tamil rebels that Pohl removed at Clarke's insistence); his activities as a professor and government employee; Natasha's participation in a race involving solar-powered spacecraft (borrowing language from "The Wind from the Sun"); Myra's death while diving; and Ranjit's final transition to virtual life as a computer program, visited by far-future humans crafting a narrative of his career.

This edited bibliography lists all of Clarke's novels; story collections and omnibuses; screenplays and plays; short fiction; poetry; artwork; work as editor,
advisor, or consultant; and nonfiction books. Subsequent sections list the
articles, introductions, afterwords, letters, and interviews cited in the text;
selected film and television appearances; and selected books, music, films and
television programs based on his works. (I exclude audiobooks, podcasts, and
video interviews.) I hope to add to my World of Westfahl website, https://
www.sfsite.com/gary/intro.htm, a longer version of this bibliography, providing all of Clarke's short nonfiction, film appearances, and related works,
and a comprehensive bibliography of secondary sources.

NOVELS

1951   *Prelude to Space: A Compellingly Realistic Novel of Interplanetary Flight.* New York:
        World Editions, 1951. Revised and republished as *Prelude to Space.* London:
        Sedgwick & Jackson, 1953. New York: Gnome Press, 1954. Also published as
        Master of Space and *The Space Dreamers.*
        The Sands of Mars. London: Sidgwick & Jackson, 1951. Republished as *Sands of
        Mars.* New York: Gnome Press, 1952.

1952   *Islands in the Sky.* Philadelphia: John C. Winston, 1952. London: Sidgwick &
        Jackson, 1952.

1953   *Against the Fall of Night.* New York: Gnome Press, 1953. Originally published in
        Startling Stories 18 (November 1948): 11–70.
        Childhood's End. New York: Ballantine, 1953. Expansion of "Guardian Angel."
        Republished with revised prologue, identified as first chapter. London: Pan
        Macmillan, 1990. Original prologue restored, again as first chapter, with revised
        version included as untitled appendix. New York: Del Rey/Ballantine, 2001.

1955   *Earthlight.* New York: Ballantine, 1955. Expansion of "Earthlight."

1956   *The City and the Stars.* New York: Harcourt, Brace, and Company, 1956. Revision
        and expansion of *Against the Fall of Night.*

1957   *The Deep Range.* New York: Harcourt, Brace, and Company, 1957. Expansion of
        "The Deep Range."

1961   *A Fall of Moondust*. New York: Harcourt, Brace & World Inc. 1961.

1963   *Dolphin Island: A Story of the People of the Sea*. New York: Holt, Rinehart, and
        Winston, 1963. Also serialized in *Worlds of Tomorrow* 1 (April 1963): 6–56, and
        (June 1963): 114–62.

        Glide Path. New York: Harcourt Brace Jovanovich, 1963.

1968   *2001: A Space Odyssey*. New York: New American Library, 1968. "Based on a
        screenplay by Stanley Kubrick and Arthur C. Clarke."

1973   *Rendezvous with Rama*. New York: Harcourt Brace Jovanovich, 1973.

1975   *Imperial Earth: A Fantasy of Love and Discord*. London: Gollancz, 1975. Republished
        as *Imperial Earth*. New York: Harcourt Brace Jovanovich, 1976.

1979   *The Fountains of Paradise*. New York: Harcourt Brace Jovanovich, 1979.

1982   *2010: Odyssey Two*. New York: Del Rey/Ballantine, 1982.

1986   *The Songs of Distant Earth*. New York: Del Rey/Ballantine, 1986. Expansion of
        "The Songs of Distant Earth" (1958) and "The Songs of Distant Earth" (1981).

1987   *2061: Odyssey Three*. New York: Del Rey/Ballantine, 1987.

1988   *Cradle* (with Gentry Lee). New York: Warner, 1988. This novel and later
        "collaborations," except *The Last Theorem*, were written entirely by the credited
        coauthor, with ideas and input from Clarke.

1989   *Rama II* (with Gentry Lee). New York: Bantam, 1989.

1990   *The Ghost from the Grand Banks*. New York: Bantam, 1990.

1991   *The Garden of Rama* (with Gentry Lee). New York: Bantam, 1991.

1993   *The Hammer of God*. New York: Bantam, 1993. Expansion of "The Hammer of God."

1994   *Rama Revealed* (with Gentry Lee). New York: Bantam, 1994.

1996   *Richter 10* (with Mike McQuay). New York: Bantam, 1996.

1997   *3001: The Final Odyssey*. New York: Del Rey/Ballantine, 1997.

1998   *The Fate of Fu Manchu*. Rochester, MI: Portentous Press, 1998. A 1935 story
        published as a chapbook.

1999   *The Trigger* (with Michael P. Kube-McDowell). London: HarperCollins/Voyager,
        1999. New York: Bantam Spectra, 1999.

2000   *The Light of Other Days* (with Stephen Baxter). New York: Tor, 2000.

2004   *Time's Eye: Book One of a Time Odyssey* (with Stephen Baxter). New York: Del Rey/
        Ballantine, 2004.

2007   *Sunstorm: A Time Odyssey: 2* (with Stephen Baxter). New York: Del Rey/Ballantine,
        2007.

2008   *Firstborn: A Time Odyssey: 3* (with Stephen Baxter). New York: Del Rey/Ballantine,
        2008.

        The Last Theorem (with Frederik Pohl). London: HarperCollins/Voyager, 2008.
        New York: Del Rey/Ballantine, 2008. Almost entirely written by Pohl, though
        based on Clarke's outline and incorporating passages by Clarke.

SHORT STORY COLLECTIONS AND OMNIBUSES

1953   *Expedition to Earth: Eleven Science-Fiction Stories*. New York: Ballantine, 1953.

1956   *Reach for Tomorrow*. New York: Ballantine, 1956.

1957   *Tales from the White Hart*. New York: Ballantine, 1957. Republished with one
        additional story. Hornsea, England: PS Publishing, 2007.

1958	*The Other Side of the Sky*. New York: Harcourt, Brace & World, 1958.
1959	*Across the Sea of Stars: An Omnibus Containing the Complete Novels of* Childhood's End *and* Earthlight. New York: Harcourt, Brace & World, 1959. Introduction by Clifton Fadiman.
1961	*From the Ocean, From the Stars: An Omnibus Containing the Complete Novels* The Deep Range *and* The City and the Stars *and Twenty-Four Short Stories*. New York: Harcourt, Brace & World, 1961.
1962	*Tales of Ten Worlds*. New York: Harcourt, Brace & World, 1962.
1965	*An Arthur Clarke Omnibus*. London: Sidgwick & Jackson, 1965. Three previously published books, separately paginated.
	Prelude to Mars: An Omnibus Containing the Complete Novels Prelude to Space *and* Sands of Mars *and Sixteen Short Stories*. New York: Harcourt, Brace & World, 1965.
1967	*The Nine Billion Names of God: The Best Short Stories of Arthur C. Clarke*. New York: Harcourt Brace Jovanovich, 1967.
1968	*An Arthur Clarke Second Omnibus*. London: Sidgwick & Jackson, 1968. Three previously published books, separately paginated.
	The Lion of Comarre and Against the Fall of Night. New York: Harcourt, Brace & World, 1968.
1972	*The Lost Worlds of 2001*. New York: Signet, 1972. Sometimes classified as nonfiction, intermingling a nonfiction account of filming *2001: A Space Odyssey* with fictional vignettes based on material developed for, but not used in, the film and novel.
	Of Time and Stars: The Worlds of Arthur C. Clarke. Edited by J. B. Priestley. London: Gollancz, 1972.
	The Wind from the Sun: Stories of the Space Age. New York: Harcourt Brace Jovanovich, 1972. Republished with three additional stories. New York: New American Library, 1987.
1973	*The Best of Arthur C. Clarke: 1937–1971*. Edited by Angus Wells. London: Sidgwick & Jackson, 1973. Republished in two volumes: *The Best of Arthur C. Clarke, 1932–1955*. London: Sphere, 1976. *The Best of Arthur C. Clarke, 1956–1971*. London: Sphere, 1977.
1978	*Four Great SF Novels*. London: Gollancz, 1978.
1983	*The Sentinel: Masterworks of Science Fiction and Fantasy*. New York: Berkley Books/ Byron Preiss Visual Publications, 1983. Illustrations by Lebbeus Woods.
1987	*2001: A Space Odyssey; The City and the Stars; The Deep Range; A Fall of Moondust; Rendezvous with Rama*. New York: Octopus Books/Heinemann, 1987.
1988	*A Meeting with Medusa*. Published dos-à-dos with *Green Mars* by Kim Stanley Robinson. New York: Tor, 1988.
1989	*Tales from Planet Earth*. London: Century Hutchinson, 1989. Edited by Martin H. Greenberg, uncredited.
1990	*Beyond the Fall of Night* (with Gregory Benford). New York: Ace/Putnam, 1990.
	Against the Fall of Night, retitled "Part I" of purported two-part novel with a "Part II" that is an original sequel by Benford. Republished as *Against the Fall of Night—Arthur C. Clarke/Gregory Benford—Beyond the Fall of Night*. London: Victor Gollancz, 1991.
1991	*More Than One Universe: The Collected Stories of Arthur C. Clarke*. New York: Harcourt Brace Jovanovich, 1991.

1996	*Childhood Ends: The Earliest Writings of Arthur C. Clarke.* Edited by David Aronovitz. Rochester, MI: Portentous Press, 1996.
2000	*The Collected Stories of Arthur C. Clarke.* London: Gollancz, 2000. New York: Tor, 2001.
2001	*The Ghost from the Grand Banks and The Deep Range.* New York: Warner Aspect, 2001. *The Space Trilogy.* London: Orion/Gollancz, 2001.
2004	*3001: The Final Odyssey/The Songs of Distant Earth.* London: Grafton, 2004. Two previously published books, separately paginated.
2005	*The Dark Blue Depths: Adventures from Inner to Outer Space.* New York: iBooks, 2005.
2006	*Clarke's Universe: Two Stories from a Master of Science Fiction.* New York: iBooks, 2006.
2011	*Rama: The Complete Rama Omnibus* (with Gentry Lee). London: Victor Gollancz, 2011.
2014	*Arthur C. Clarke's Early Short Stories.* CreateSpace Independent Publishing Platform, 2014.
2016	*The Selected Works of Arthur C. Clarke* (with Michael P. Kube-McDowell and Mike McQuay). New York: RosettaBooks, 2016. Kindle edition. *A Collection of Short Stories.* VintReads, 2016. Kindle edition.

SCREENPLAYS AND PLAYS

1933	*Two Hours in a Lab: A One-Act Drama* (as by "Clericus"). *Huish Magazine* 22 (Christmas 1933); page numbers unknown. Unproduced play. Republished in *Childhood Ends,* 9–10.
1934	*Jule Gets His: A New Super-Drama by a Well-Known Author* (as by "Clericus," also attributed to "W. Shakespeare"). *Huish Magazine* 23 (Summer 1934): 41–43. Unproduced screenplay. Republished in *Childhood Ends,* 19–21.
1935	*The Mystic Potion* (as by "DIL"; written by unidentified Huish students). *Huish Magazine* 24 (Autumn 1935): 46–51. Unproduced play, included for completeness, although Clarke in *Childhood Ends* declined to confirm he was one of its authors. Republished in *Childhood Ends,* 50–56.
1949	Note: Clarke denied he wrote episodes of the television series *Captain Video* in 1949, stating he had merely worked for the series as an advisor; it is also believed he assisted as a set designer.
1952	"All the Time in the World." *Tales of Tomorrow.* New York: ABC-TV, June 13, 1952. Adaptation of "All the Time in the World."
1959	*Beneath the Seas of Ceylon.* Sri Lanka: Ceylon Tea Board, 1959.
1964	"Treasure of the Great Reef." *Adventure.* London: BBC, January 6, 1964. Episode of documentary series, narrated by Clarke.
1968	"Meteor 02." *Jännitysnäytelmä.* Finland: March 3, 1968. Translated by Toini Havu-Ollikainen. Adaptation of "Breaking Strain." Referenced as Clarke's screenplay, translated by Havu-Ollikainen, but more likely a screenplay written entirely by Havu-Ollikainen, based on Clarke's story. *2001: A Space Odyssey* (with Stanley Kubrick). MGM, 1968. Screenplay published as *2001: A Space Odyssey: Screenplay.* Utrecht: Stichting De Roos, 2001.
1993	*Arthur C. Clarke: Before 2001* (with Robert Lewis Knecht). Southern Cross Entertainment Group, 1993. Documentary about Clarke's discovery of undersea treasure.

1995   *The Colours of Infinity* (with Nigel Lesmoir-Gordon). Gordon Films, 1995.
        Documentary about fractals. Screenplay published as "The Colours of Infinity:
        The Film Script." In *The Colours of Infinity: The Beauty and Power of Fractals*,
        edited by Nigel Lesmoir-Gordon, 148–74. Bath, England: Clear Books, 2004.

SHORT FICTION

1932   "Correspondence" (as by "One-Time 6th Former"). *Huish Magazine* 21 (Autumn
        1932): 51–52. Purported letter from former student. Republished in *Childhood
        Ends*, 4–5.
        "Interviews with Celebrities VIII" (as by "Clericus"). *Huish Magazine* 21 (Autumn
        1932): page numbers unknown. Purported interview with "unspoiled rustic";
        publication in this issue deduced from position in *Childhood Ends*. Republished in
        Childhood Ends, 1–3.
1933   "The Jon Bloc Soc." *Huish Magazine* 22 (Christmas 1933): 41–42. Fictionalized
        account of club meeting. Republished in *Childhood Ends*, 11–12.
        "Our Correspondence Column" (as by "A Real Old 6th Former"). *Huish Magazine*
        22 (Spring 1933): 42–43. Purported letter from former student. Republished in
        Childhood Ends, 6.
        "News from the Torrid Zone" (as by "Ex-Sixth Former"). *Huish Magazine* 22
        (Christmas 1933): 34–35. Purported letter from former student. Republished in
        Childhood Ends, 7–8.
1934   "Answers to Correspondents" (as by "Clericus"). *Huish Magazine* 23 (Summer 1934):
        44–45. Clarke's answers to purported letters. Republished in *Childhood Ends*,
        22–23.
        "French without Tears" (as by "Clericus"). *Huish Magazine* 23 (Summer 1934): 47–48.
        Farcical description of numerical way to render French. Republished in *Childhood
        Ends*, 24–25.
        "Letters to the Editor" (as by "Batsin Belphry"). *Huish Magazine* 23 (Autumn 1934):
        29. Farcical letter. Republished in *Childhood Ends*, 26.
        "Octogenarian Observations" (as by "Clericus"). *Huish Magazine* 22 (Christmas
        1934): 41–42. Purported interview with former students. Republished in *Childhood
        Ends*, 13–14.
1935   "The Fate of Fu-Manchu" (as by "Clericus"). *Huish Magazine* 24 (Spring 1935): 33–37.
        Republished in *Childhood Ends*, 33–36.
        "Letters to the Editor" (as by "A. Munchhausen"). *Huish Magazine* 24 (Spring 1935):
        39–40. Purported letter from former student. Republished in *Childhood Ends*,
        37–38.
        "Letters to the Editor" (as by "De Profundis"). *Huish Magazine* 24 (Summer 1935):
        50–52. Purported letter from former student. Republished in *Childhood Ends*,
        40–41.
1936   "In Darkest Somerset" (as by "Clericus"). *Huish Magazine* 25 (Summer 1936): 41–43.
        Fictional account of journey to Somerset. Republished in *Childhood Ends*, 71–72.
        "Interviews with Notorieties—No. 1" (as by "Ego"). *Huish Magazine* 25 (Spring
        1936): 47–50. Purported interview with "the Professor." Republished in *Childhood
        Ends*, 68–70.

1937   "Travel by Wire!" *Amateur Science Stories* 1.2 (1937): 9–11.

1938   "How We Went to Mars." *Amateur Science Stories* 1.3 (1938): 2–6, 13.
        "Retreat from Earth." *Amateur Science Stories* 1.3 (1938): 7–13.

1939   "Into the Past." *Satellite* 3.1 (1939): 3–6.

1940   "At the Mountains of Murkiness, or Lovecraft-into-Leacock." *Satellite* 3.4 (1940):
        2–7. Republished as "At the Mountains of Murkiness, or, From Lovecraft to
        Leacock." In *At the Mountains of Murkiness, and Other Parodies*, edited by George
        Locke, 94–111. London: Ferret Fantasy, 1973.
        "Ego's Review." *Gargoyle*, no. 2 (April 1940): 7–9. Reviews of fictitious books.
        Note: The purported story "Court News" (1940) is listed in bibliographies as
        appearing in the June 1940 *Gargoyle*, but the issue never appeared. This is
        possibly an early title for the nonfictional "Ego & the Dying Planet" (1941),
        published in a later issue of *Gargoyle*.

1941   "Letters to a Secretary of an Interplanetary Society" (as by "Arthur 'Ego'
        Clarke"). *Fantast* 2.2 (1941): 17. Farcical letters.
        "A Short History of Fantocracy—1948–1960: Part I" (as by "Arthur Ego Clarke").
        Fantast 2.7 (1941): 6–8. "Part II." *Fantast* 3.1 (1942): 21–24. "Part III." *Fantast* 3.2
        (1942): 8–11.

1942   "The Awakening." *Zenith*, no. 4 (February 1942): 57–59. Revised version. *Future
        Combined with Science Fiction* 2 (January 1952): 83–85. Elements of story
        incorporated into "Nemesis."
        "Whacky." *Fantast* 3.2 (1942): 25.

1946   "Loophole." *Astounding Science-Fiction* 37.2 (1946): 57–61.
        "Rescue Party." *Astounding Science-Fiction* 37.3 (1946): 36–60.
        "Technical Error." *Fantasy: The Magazine of Science Fiction* 1.1 (1946): 56–68.

1947   "The Castaway" (as by "Charles Willis"). *Fantasy: The Magazine of Science Fiction*
        1.2 (1947): 72–76.
        "Nightfall." *King's College Review* 46 (December 1947): 9–10.
        "The Fires Within" (as by "E. G. O'Brien"). *Fantasy: The Magazine of Science
        Fiction* 1.3 (1947): 72–77.
        "Inheritance" (as by "Charles Willis"). *New Worlds* 1.3 (1947): 54–57.

1948   "The Forgotten Enemy." *King's College Review* 47 (December 1948): 20–24.

1949   "Breaking Strain" (as "Thirty Seconds—Thirty Days"). *Thrilling Wonder Stories*
        35.2 (1949): 106–122.
        "Critical Mass." *Lilliput* 24.3 (1949): 43–45. Revised to include Harry Purvis in *Tales
        from the White Hart*, 38–45.
        "Hide-and-Seek" (as "Hide and Seek"). *Astounding Science-Fiction* 44.1 (1949): 68–77.
        "History Lesson." *Startling Stories* 19 (May 1949): 137–41.
        "The Lion of Comarre." *Thrilling Wonder Stories* 34.3 (1949): 44–69.
        "Transience." *Startling Stories* 19.3 (1949): 125–28.
        "The Wall of Darkness." *Super Science Stories* 5.3 (1949): 66–78.

1950   "Guardian Angel." *Famous Fantastic Mysteries* 11 (April 1950): 98–112, 127–29.
        "Nemesis" (as "Exile of the Eons"). *Super Science Stories* 6 (March 1950): 86–96.
        "Silence, Please!" (as by "Charles Willis"). *Science-Fantasy* 1.2 (1950): 47–56.
           Republished as "The Secret Weapon" and "The Strange Sound of Dying."
        "Time's Arrow." *Science-Fantasy* 1.1 (1950): 31–42.

"A Walk in the Dark." *Thrilling Wonder Stories* 36.3 (1950): 134–40.

1951   "The Broken Circuit." *Sketch* 240 (November 7, 1951): 484.

"Earthlight." *Thrilling Wonder Stories* 38.3 (August 1951): 56–86.

"Holiday on the Moon" (as by "Charles Willis"). *The Heiress* (January 1951): 38–43; (February 1951): 27–30, 60–61; (March 1951): 40–44, 66; (April 1951): 58–61, 74.

"'If I Forget Thee, Oh Earth . . . '" *Future Combined with Science Fiction Stories* 2.3 (1951): 66–69.

"The Road to the Sea" (as "Seekers of the Sphinx"). *Two Complete Science-Adventure Books* 1 (Spring 1951): 106–142.

"Second Dawn." *Science Fiction Quarterly* 1.2 (1951): 104–130.

"The Sentinel" (as "Sentinel of Eternity"). *10 Story Fantasy* 1 (Spring 1951): 41–47.

"Superiority." *Magazine of Fantasy and Science Fiction* 2.4 (1951): 3–11.

"Trouble with the Natives" (as "The Men in the Flying Saucer"). *Lilliput* 28 (February 1951): 73–78. Republished as "Captain Wyxtpthll's Flying Saucer."

1952   "All the Time in the World." *Startling Stories* 26.3 (1952): 69–76.

1953   "Encounter in the Dawn." *Amazing Stories* 27.5 (1953): 4–16. Republished as "Expedition to Earth."

"Jupiter Five." *If* 2.2 (1953): 4–28, 75.

"The Nine Billion Names of God." In *Star Science Fiction Stories*, edited by Frederik Pohl, 195–202. New York: Ballantine, 1953.

"The Other Tiger." *Fantastic Universe Science Fiction* 1.1 (1953): 116–18.

"The Parasite." *Avon Science Fiction and Fantasy Reader* 1.2 (1953): 118–28.

"The Possessed." *Dynamic Science Fiction* 1 (March 1953): 85–88.

"Publicity Campaign." *The Evening News* [London] (June 9, 1953), 6.

1954   "Armaments Race." *Adventure* 127.6 (1954): 34–36, 57–58.

"The Deep Range." In *Star Science Fiction Stories No. 3*, edited by Frederik Pohl, 36–45. New York: Ballantine, 1954.

"No Morning After." In *Time to Come*, edited by August Derleth, 75–85. New York: Farrar, Straus and Young, 1954.

"Patent Pending" (as "The Invention"). *Argosy* 339.5 (1954): 34–37, 85–86.

1955   "Refugee" (as "?"). *Magazine of Fantasy and Science Fiction* 9 (July 1955): 114–24.

"The Star." *Infinity Science Fiction* 1.1 (1955): 120–27.

1956   "Big Game Hunt" (as "The Reckless Ones"). *Adventure* 131.4 (1956): 40–41, 58–60.

"The Pacifist." *Fantastic Universe Science Fiction* 6.3 (1956): 4–12.

"The Reluctant Orchid." *Satellite Science Fiction* 1.2 (1956): 114–22.

"Venture to the Moon." Six-part series published in the *Evening Standard* [London]: "The Starting Line" (as "Double-Crossed in Outer Space") (May 23, 1956): 17; "Robin Hood, F.R.S." (as "Saved! . . . by a Bow and Arrow") (May 24, 1956): 17; "Green Fingers" (as "Death Strikes Surov") (May 25, 1956): 17; "All That Glitters" (as "Diamonds! . . . and Then Divorce") (May 26, 1956): 11; "Watch This Space" (as "Who Wrote That Message to the Stars? . . . In Letters a Thousand Miles Long") (May 28, 1956): 17; and "A Question of Residence" (as "Alone on the Moon") (May 29, 1956): 17.

"What Goes Up" (as "What Goes Up . . ."). *Magazine of Fantasy and Science Fiction* 10.1 (1956): 26–34.

1957   "Cold War." *Satellite Science Fiction* 1.4 (1957): 86–92.

         "The Defenestration of Ermintrude Inch." In *Tales from the White Hart*, 142–48. New York: Ballantine, 1957.

         "Let There Be Light" (as "Dazzled to Death"). *Dundee Evening Telegraph*, September 5, 1957, 7. Republished in *Playboy* 4.2 (1958): 51, 54, 70. Revised to include Harry Purvis in *Tales of Ten Worlds*, 105–113.

         "The Man Who Ploughed the Sea." *Satellite Science Fiction* 1.5 (1957): 104–119.

         "Moving Spirit." In *Tales from the White Hart*, 73–83. New York: Ballantine, 1957.

         "The Next Tenants." *Satellite Science Fiction* 1.3 (1957): 103–111.

         "The Other Side of the Sky." Six-part series published in *Infinity Science Fiction* 2: "Special Delivery" (September 1957): 6–9; "Feathered Friend" (September 1957): 10–13; "Take a Deep Breath" (September 1957): 14–17; "Freedom of Space" (October 1957): 56–59; "Passer-by" (October 1957): 59–62; and "The Call of the Stars" (October 1957): 63–66.

         "Security Check." *Magazine of Fantasy and Science Fiction* 12 (June 1957): 114–17. Unverified prior publication in the *Evening News* [London], January 13, 1956.

         "Sleeping Beauty" (as "The Case of the Snoring Heir"). *Infinity Science Fiction* 2.2 (1957): 26–38.

         "The Ultimate Melody" (as "Ultimate Melody"). *If* 7.2 (1957): 70–75. Revised to include Harry Purvis in *Tales from the White Hart*, 45–52.

1958   "Cosmic Casanova." *Venture Science Fiction* 2.3 (1958): 23–29.

         "Out of the Sun" (as "Out from the Sun"). *If* 8.2 (1958): 77–81, 112–13.

         "A Slight Case of Sunstroke" (as "The Stroke of the Sun"). *Galaxy* 16.5 (1958): 71–77.

         "The Songs of Distant Earth." *If* 8.4 (1958): 6–29.

         "Who's There?" (as "The Haunted Spacesuit"). *This Week*, May 11, 1958, 18, 20–21.

1959   "Out of the Cradle, Endlessly Orbiting" (as "Out of the Cradle"). *Dude* 3 (March 1959): 55–57.

         "Report on Planet Three" (as "From Mars: A Report on Earth"). *Holiday* 25 (May 1959): 39–43. Purported translation of Martian document; usually classified as nonfiction.

1960   "I Remember Babylon." *Playboy* 7.5 (1960): 73, 94–100.

         "Into the Comet" (as "Inside the Comet"). *Magazine of Fantasy and Science Fiction* 19.4 (1960): 30–38, 46.

         "Summertime on Icarus" (as "The Hottest Piece of Real Estate in the Solar System"). *Vogue* 136 (June 1960): 54–55.

         "Trouble with Time" (as "Crime on Mars"). *Ellery Queen's Mystery Magazine* 36.1 (1960): 107–111.

1961   "Before Eden." *Amazing Stories* 35.6 (1961): 36–46, 66.

         "Death and the Senator." *Analog Science Fact/Science Fiction* 67.3 (1961): 33–50.

         "Hate" (as "At the End of the Orbit"). *If* 11.5 (1961): 84–99.

         "Saturn Rising." *Magazine of Fantasy and Science Fiction* 20.3 (1961): 44–53.

1962   "An Ape about the House." *Dude* 6 (May 1962): 37–39, 62.

         "Dog Star" (as "Moondog"). *Galaxy* 20.4 (April 1962): 188–93.

1963   "The Secret" (as "The Secret of the Men in the Moon"). *This Week* (August 11, 1963): 8–11.

1964   "The Food of the Gods." *Playboy* 11.5 (1964): 113–14.

"The Shining Ones." *Playboy* 11.8 (1964): 100–101, 108–111, 113–14.

"The Wind from the Sun" (as "The Sunjammer"). *Boys' Life* 54 (March 1964): 15–18, 67–70.

1965   "Dial F for Frankenstein" (as "Dial 'F' for Frankenstein"). *Playboy* 12.1 (1965): 148–49, 215–16.

"The Last Command." *Bizarre! Mystery Magazine* 1.2 (1965): 29–31.

"Maelstrom II." *Playboy* 12.4 (1965): 84, 90, 178, 180.

1966   "The Light of Darkness." *Playboy* 113.6 (1966): 113, 174–76.

"The Longest Science-Fiction Story Ever Told" (as "A Recursion in Metastories"). *Galaxy* 25.1 (1966): 78–79.

"Playback." *Playboy* 13.12 (1966): 220–27.

1967   "The Cruel Sky." *Boys' Life* 57 (July 1967): 22–23, 49, and (August 1967): 46–48, 56.

"Love That Universe" (as "A Desperate and Universal Shout"). *Escapade* 12.5 (1967): 60–end page. Listed incorrectly elsewhere as 1961 publication.

1968   "Crusade." In *The Farthest Reaches*, edited by Joseph Elder, 103–108. New York: Trident, 1968.

1969   "Coming Distractions." *Penthouse* 11 (July 1969): 36, 38. Reviews of fictitious books.

1970   "Neutron Tide." *Galaxy* 30.2 (1970): 82–85.

1971   "A Meeting with Medusa." *Playboy* 18.12 (1971): 160–64, 270–72, 274–76, 278–80.

"Reunion." In *Infinity Two*, edited by Robert Hoskins, 231–32. New York: Lancer, 1971.

"Transit of Earth." *Playboy* 18.1 (1971): 109–111, 210, 272–74.

1972   "Abyss." In *The Lost Worlds of 2001*, 200–205. New York: Signet, 1972. This and other items below from this book are vignettes based on material developed for, but not used in, *2001: A Space Odyssey*.

"Alone." *The Lost Worlds of 2001*, 152–61.

"Ancestral Voices." *The Lost Worlds of 2001*, 107–113.

"Ball Game." *The Lost Worlds of 2001*, 182–85.

"Cosmopolis." *The Lost Worlds of 2001*, 206–213.

"Discovery." *The Lost Worlds of 2001*, 130–32.

"Farewell to Earth." *The Lost Worlds of 2001*, 71–75.

"Final Orbit." *The Lost Worlds of 2001*, 168–73.

"First Encounter." *The Lost Worlds of 2001*, 53–58.

"First Man to Jupiter." *The Lost Worlds of 2001*, 144–48.

"Flight Pay." *The Lost Worlds of 2001*, 128–29.

"From the Ocean, From the Stars." *The Lost Worlds of 2001*, 88–96.

"Gift from the Stars." *The Lost Worlds of 2001*, 66–70.

"The Impossible Stars." *The Lost Worlds of 2001*, 174–76.

"Into the Night Land." *The Lost Worlds of 2001*, 230–36.

"Joveday." *The Lost Worlds of 2001*, 162–64.

"Jupiter V." *The Lost Worlds of 2001*, 165–67.

"Last Message." *The Lost Worlds of 2001*, 186–87.

"The Long Sleep." *The Lost Worlds of 2001*, 133–37.

"Man and Robot." *The Lost Worlds of 2001*, 80–87.

"Midnight, Washington." *The Lost Worlds of 2001*, 117–23.

"Moon-Watcher." *The Lost Worlds of 2001*, 59–65.

"Oceana." *The Lost Worlds of 2001*, 226–29.

"The Question." *The Lost Worlds of 2001*, 114–16.

"Reunion." *The Lost Worlds of 2001*, 192–99.

"Runaway." *The Lost Worlds of 2001*, 138–43.

"Scrutiny." *The Lost Worlds of 2001*, 214–17.

"Second Lesson." *The Lost Worlds of 2001*, 237–38.

"Skyrock." *The Lost Worlds of 2001*, 218–25.

"The Smell of Death." *The Lost Worlds of 2001*, 149–51.

"Something Is Seriously Wrong with Space." *The Lost Worlds of 2001*, 177–81.

"Universe." *The Lost Worlds of 2001*, 100–106.

"View from the Year 2000." *The Lost Worlds of 2001*, 13–16.

"When the Twerms Came." *Playboy* 19.5 (1972): 120–121. Comic strip, illustrated by Skip Williamson. Text without illustrations republished in *The View from Serendip*, 179–181.

"With Open Hands." *The Lost Worlds of 2001*, 97–99.

1977   "Quarantine." *Isaac Asimov's Science Fiction Magazine* 1.1 (1977): 49–50.

1981   "The Songs of Distant Earth." *Omni* 3.12 (1981): 76–79, 132. Film treatment, derived from "The Songs of Distant Earth."

1984   "sisteneG." *Analog Science Fiction/Science Fact* 104.5 (1984): 174–77.

1986   "On Golden Seas." *DSB Newsletter* (Pentagon Defense Science Board) (August 1986), pages unknown.

"The Steam-Powered Word Processor." *Analog Science Fiction/Science Fact* 106.9 (1986), 175–79.

1990   "Tales from the 'White Hart,' 1990: The Jet-Propelled Time Machine." In *Drabble II: Double Century*, edited by Rob Meades and David Wake, 84. Boston: Beacon, 1990.

1992   "The Hammer of God." *Time*, Special Issue, 140.27 (1992): 83–87.

1997   "Appendix: Original Movie Outline." In *Richter 10*, by Arthur C. Clarke and Mike McQuay, 339–41. London: Vista, 1997.

1998   "The Wire Continuum" (with Stephen Baxter). *Playboy* 45.1 (1998): 76–78, 170–78. This and two later "collaborative" stories were written entirely by Baxter, with ideas and input from Clarke.

1999   "Droolings from My Second Childhood: 2." *Altair*, no. 4 (Aussiecon III edition) (August 1999): 36–37.

"Improving the Neighbourhood." *Nature* 402, no. 6757 (November 4, 1999): 19.

2000   "Hibernaculum 46" (with Stephen Baxter). In *Voyager 5: Collector's Edition*, editor unidentified, 99–108. London: HarperCollins/Voyager, 2000.

"Move Over, E.R.!" *Altair*, no. 5 (February 2000): 67.

2007   "Time Gentlemen Please" (with Stephen Baxter). In *Tales from the White Hart*, 193–208. Hornsea, England: PS Publishing, 2007. Introduction by Stephen Baxter.

POETRY

1938   "Prelude to the Conquest of Space" (as by "Arthur C. 'Ego' Clarke"). *Novae Terrae* 2 (April 1938): 20.

1939   "The Twilight of a Sun." *Fantast* 1.1 (1939): 2–3.
1972   "Kubrick, Stan." In *The Lost Worlds of 2001*, 190. Incorporated into text.

ARTWORK

1938   "The Conquest of Space." *Novae Terrae* 3.3 (1938): Cover (with William F. Temple).
1949   *Captain Video and His Video Rangers.* New York: Dumont Television Network, 1949–1955. Clarke at some time assisted as a set designer.

WORK AS EDITOR, ADVISOR, OR CONSULTANT

1932–36 *Huish Magazine*, Autumn 1932 through Summer 1936. Clarke was a member of the magazine's editorial committee and sub-editor from Autumn 1935 to Summer 1936.
1937–39 *Novae Terrae*, beginning with *Novae Terrae* 2.6 (November 1937) through 3.5 (January 1939). Maurice K. Hanson listed as editor; Clarke and Ted Carnell (as Edward J. Carnell) listed as associate editors.
1939   *Bulletin of the British Interplanetary Society* 3 (1939). Editor.
        New Worlds 1.2 (April 1939), and 1.3 (May 1939). Ted Carnell listed as editor; Ken G. Chapman as assistant editor; Maurice K. Hanson, Frank Arnold, Clarke, and Harold Kay listed as associates; William F. Temple added as an associate in the May issue.
        New Worlds 1.4 (June 1939). Ted Carnell listed as editor; Clarke listed as his assistant.
1940   *Fanmail* 1.1 (1940). Editor. Fanzine; unseen; only five copies produced.
1949   *Captain Video and His Video Rangers.* New York: Dumont Television Network, 1949–1955. Clarke at some time worked as an advisor.
        Physics Abstracts 52 (1949). Assistant editor.
1950   *Dan Dare, Pilot of the Future.* Syndicated comic strip by Frank Hampson. Clarke credited as "Scientific Advisor," though by some reports he assisted in writing stories and scripts.
1966   *Time Probe: The Sciences in Science Fiction.* New York: Delacorte Press, 1966. Credited as editor; actually edited by Robert Silverberg, uncredited.
1967   *The Coming of the Space Age: Famous Accounts of Man's Probing of the Universe.* New York: Meredith Press, 1967. Editor.
1981   *The Science Fiction Hall of Fame Volume Four.* London: Gollancz, 1981. Editor (with George W. Proctor, uncredited). Republished as *The Science Fiction Hall of Fame, Volume III*. New York: Avon, 1982.
1990   *Project Solar Sail.* New York: New American Library/Roc, 1990. Credited as editor; actually edited by "Managing Editor" David Brin.

NONFICTION BOOKS AND COLLECTIONS

1950   *Interplanetary Flight: An Introduction to Astronautics.* London: Temple Press, 1950. New York: Harper & Row, 1950. Second edition. New York: Harper & Brothers, 1960. Preface attributes all revisions to J. G. Strong.
1951   *The Exploration of Space.* New York: Harper & Brothers, 1951.

1954 *The Exploration of the Moon*. London: Frederick Muller, 1954. New York: Harper & Brothers, 1954. Illustrations by Robert Allan Smith.

 The Young Traveller in Space. London: Phoenix House, 1954. Also published as *Going into Space*. Revised by Robert Silverberg as *Into Space: A Young Person's Guide to Space*. New York: Harper & Row, 1971.

1956 *The Coast of Coral*. New York: Harper & Brothers, 1956. Photographs by Mike Wilson.

1957 *The Making of a Moon: The Story of the Earth Satellite Program*. New York: Harper & Row, 1957.

 The Reefs of Taprobane: Underwater Adventures around Ceylon. New York: Harper & Brothers, 1957. Photographs by Mike Wilson.

1958 *Boy beneath the Sea*. New York: Harper & Row, 1958. Photographs by Mike Wilson.

 Voice across the Sea. New York: Harper & Row, 1958. Revised edition. London: Luscombe Mitchell Beazley, 1974. New York: Harper & Row, 1974.

1959 *The Challenge of the Spaceship: Previews of Tomorrow's World*. New York: Harper & Brothers, 1959.

1960 *The Challenge of the Sea*. New York: Holt, Rinehart, and Winston, 1960. Introduction by Wernher von Braun. Illustrations by Alex Schomburg.

 The First Five Fathoms: A Guide to Underwater Adventure. New York: Harper & Brothers, 1960. Photographs by Mike Wilson. Introduction by Jacques-Yves Cousteau.

1961 *Indian Ocean Adventure*. New York: Harper & Brothers, 1961. Photographs by Mike Wilson.

1962 *Profiles of the Future: An Inquiry into the Limits of the Possible*. New York: Harper & Row, 1962. Revised edition. London: Pan, 1973. New York: Harper & Row, 1973. Third edition. London: Pan, 1983. New York: Holt, Rinehart, and Winston, 1984. Millennial edition. London: Gollancz, 1999.

1964 *Indian Ocean Treasure* (with Mike Wilson). New York: Harper & Row, 1964. This and *The Treasure of the Great Reef* are credited to "Arthur C. Clarke and Mike Wilson," but Wilson contributed only photographs, as in other books.

 Man and Space (with the editors of Time-Life Books). New York: Time-Life Books, 1964. Consulting editors René Dubos, Henry Margenau, and C. P. Snow.

 The Treasure of the Great Reef (with Mike Wilson). New York: Harper & Row, 1964.

1965 *Voices from the Sky: Previews of the Coming Space Age*. New York: Harper & Row, 1965.

1968 *The Promise of Space*. New York: Harper & Row, 1968.

1970 *Space the Unconquerable*. Colombo, Sri Lanka: Lake House Investments, 1970. Editor unidentified.

1972 *Beyond Jupiter: The Worlds of Tomorrow*. Boston: Little, Brown, and Company 1972. Paintings by Chesley Bonestell.

 Report on Planet Three and Other Speculations. New York: Harper & Row, 1972.

1973 *Mars and the Mind of Man* (with Ray Bradbury, Bruce Murray, Carl Sagan, and Walter Sullivan). New York: Harper & Row, 1973. Transcript of panel discussion, accompanied by speakers' afterthoughts.

1975 *Technology and the Frontiers of Knowledge* (with Saul Bellow, Daniel Bell, Edmundo O'Gorman, and Sir Peter Medawar). Foreword by Daniel J. Boorstin. Garden City, NY: Doubleday, 1975.

1977   *The Telephone's First Century—and Beyond: Essays on the Occasion of the 100th Anniversary of Telephone Communication* (with Michael L. Dertouzos, Morris Halle, Ithiel de Sola Pool, and Jerome B. Wiesner). New York: Thomas Y. Crowell, in cooperation with American Telephone and Telegraph Company, 1977. Preface by John D. deButts. Introduction by Thomas E. Bolger.

The View from Serendip. New York: Random House, 1977.

1981   *New Communications Technologies and the Developing World.* Colombo, Sri Lanka: Government Printing Service, 1981. Republished in *Media Asia: An Asia Mass Communication Quarterly* 8.4 (1981): 185–90. Republished as "New Communications and the Developing World."

1984   *Ascent to Orbit: A Scientific Autobiography: The Technical Writings of Arthur C. Clarke.* Hoboken, NJ: John Wiley, 1984.

1984: Spring: A Choice of Futures. New York: Del Rey/Ballantine, 1984.

1985   *The Odyssey File* (with Peter Hyams). Edited by Steven Jongeward. New York: Del Rey/Ballantine, 1985. Clarke's electronic correspondence with Hyams during the filming of *2010: The Year We Make Contact.*

1986   *Arthur C. Clarke's July 20, 2019: Life in the 21st Century* (with Patrice Adcroft, Douglas Collins, Owen Davies, T. A. Heppenheimer, Judith Hooper, Erik Larson, Tim Onosko, Kathleen Stein, G. Harry Stine, Mark Teich, Dick Teresi, Robert Weil, Pamela Weintraub, and Richard Wolkomir). New York: Macmillan, 1986.

1989   *Astounding Days: A Science Fictional Autobiography.* London: Gollancz, 1989.

1992   *The Fantastic Muse.* Huddersfield, West Yorkshire, UK: Hilltop Press, 1992. Article and poem.

How the World Was One: Beyond the Global Village. New York: Bantam, 1992. Revision of *Voice across the Sea.*

1993   *By Space Possessed: Essays on the Exploration of Space.* London: Gollancz, 1992. Edited by John Burke, credited only in introduction.

1994   *Frontline of Discovery: Science on the Brink of Tomorrow* (with Carole Douglis, Robert Friedel, Stephen S. Hall, Richard Restak, Dava Sobel, and Walter Sullivan). Washington, DC: National Geographic Society, 1994. Clarke contributed only the epilogue but is credited as "Contributing Author."

The Snows of Olympus: A Garden on Mars. London: Gollancz, 1994. New York: Norton, 1995.

1998   *Arthur C. Clarke & Lord Dunsany: A Correspondence* (with Lord Dunsany). Edited by Keith Allen Daniels. San Francisco: Anamnesis Press, 1998.

1999   *Greetings, Carbon-Based Bipeds! Collected Essays, 1934–1998.* Edited by Ian T. Macauley. New York: St. Martin's Press, 1999.

2003   *From Narnia to a Space Odyssey: The War of Ideas between Arthur C. Clarke and C. S. Lewis* (with C. S. Lewis). Edited by Ryder W. Miller. New York: iBooks, 2003.

2005   *Asteroid* (with Patrick Moore). Introduction by Martin Rees. Exeter, Great Britain: Canopus Press, 2005. Credited to Moore and Clarke, though Moore states he "wrote most of the text" [iii].

SHORT NONFICTION CITED IN TEXT

1938   "The Fantastic Muse." *Novae Terrae* 2.11 (May 1938): 18–20.

1939   "We Can Rocket to the Moon—Now!" *Tales of Wonder*, no. 7 (Summer 1939): 84–88.

1941   "Ego & the Dying Planet" (officially credited to unknown author). *Garygoyle* 2.2 (April 1941): 38–39. Summary of draft of *Against the Fall of Night*.

1943   "Congratulations." *Futurian War Digest* 3.7 (July 1943): 8. Includes quotation from Clarke letter.

        "Fan News." *Futurian War Digest* 4.1 (October 1943): 6–7. Includes quotation from Clarke letter.

1945   "Extra-Terrestrial Relays." *Wireless World* 51 (October 1945): 305–308.

1946   "The Challenge of the Spaceship." *Journal of the British Interplanetary Society* 6 (December 1946): 66–78. Republished as "Spaceships." *Omni* 1.5 (February 1979): 77–85.

1949   "You're on the Glide Path—I Think" (as by "A.C.C."). *The Aeroplane* 77 (September 23, 1949): 441–42.

1960   "Space, the Unconquerable" (as "We'll Never Conquer Space"). *Science Digest* 47 (June 1960): 53–58.

1961   Revised preface to *The Challenge of the Spaceship: Previews of Tomorrow's World*. New York: Ballantine Books, 1961, 7–8.

1963   Untitled preface. *Glide Path*. New York: Harcourt Brace Jovanovich, 1963, [ix].

1968   "Clarke's Third Law on UFO's." (Letter) *Science* 159 (January 19, 1968): 255.

1969   Foreword to *Three for Tomorrow: Three Original Novellas of Science Fiction*, by Robert Silverberg, Roger Zelazny, and James Blish, ix–x. New York: Meredith Press, 1969. Edited by Silverberg, uncredited.

1970   Pumilia, Joseph F. "Clarke in Houston." *Mathom*, no. 4 (March 1970): 3–6. Features quotations from unrecorded Clarke question-and-answer session as recalled by Pumilia.

1983   "Introduction: Of Sand and Stars." In *The Sentinel*, 9–15.

        "Last and First Books" (as "Introduction"). *Nebula Maker and Four Encounters*, by Olaf Stapledon, vii–x. New York: Dodd, Mead, 1983.

1985   "Note on 1985 Printing." In *Interplanetary Flight: An Introduction to Astronautics*, by Arthur C. Clarke, ix–xi. New York: Berkley, 1985.

1986   Kelley, Ken. "Arthur C. Clarke: A Candid Conversation about the Future of Space Travel—and about Sex, Immortality and '2001'—with the Witty Dean of Science Fiction Writers." *Playboy* 33.7 (July 1986): 49, 52–60, 62–63, 65–66.

1990   Foreword to *Childhood's End*. London: Pan Macmillan, 1990, [v–viii].

1993   Letter. *Interzone*, no. 76 (October 1993): 4.

1994   Epilogue to *Frontline of Discovery: Science on the Brink of Tomorrow*, 190–95.

1996   "Arthur C. Clarke and Gentry Lee Online Chat." Transcript of question-and-answer session conducted via instant messages. Originally posted at SciFi.com on November 1, 1996.

1997   "Foreword: The Birth of HAL." *HAL's Legacy: 2001's Computer as Dream and Reality*, edited by David G. Stork, xi–xvi. Cambridge: MIT Press, 1997.

2000   Untitled introduction to "Dog Star." *The Collected Stories of Arthur C. Clarke*, 782.

2001   Foreword to *The Space Trilogy*. London: Gollancz, 2001, [xi–xii].

        "Foreword: Coming Home." *Literary Trips: Following in the Footsteps of Fame, Volume Two*, edited by Victoria Brooks, ix–x. Vancouver, BC: GreatestEscapes .com Publishing, 2001.

| 2003 | Foreword to *Beyond: Visions of the Interplanetary Probes*, by Michael Benson, 9–11. New York: Harry N. Abrams, 2003. |

2003   Foreword to *Beyond: Visions of the Interplanetary Probes*, by Michael Benson, 9–11. New York: Harry N. Abrams, 2003.

"Foreword 1." *To the Edge of Doom*, by Tyronne Fernando, 9. London: Athena, 2003.

2004   Teague, Matthew. "From the Archives: A Day with Arthur C. Clarke." *Popular Science* website, posted August 19, 2004.

2005   Foreword to *Science Fiction Quotations: From the Inner Mind to the Outer Limits*, edited by Gary Westfahl, ix–xi. New Haven, CT: Yale University Press, 2005.

2006   Foreword to *Beautiful Living: Buddha's Way to Prosperity, Wisdom, and Inner Peace*, by Bhikkhu Basnagoda Rahula, ix. Houston: Vimamsa Publishers, 2006.

2007   Foreword to *The Rise of Animals: Evolution and Diversification of the Kingdom Animalia*, by Mikhail A. Fedonkin, James G. Gehling, Kathleen Grey, Guy M. Narbonne, and Patricia Vickers-Rich, xi. Baltimore: John Hopkins University Press, 2007.

FILM AND TELEVISION APPEARANCES (SELECTED)

1971   "Arthur C. Clarke in Conversation." Episode of *Camera Three*. CBS Productions, January 3, 1971.

1980   *Arthur C. Clarke's Mysterious World*. London: ITV, September 2 through November 25, 1980. Documentary series hosted by Clarke.

1981   *Village in the Jungle (Beddegama)*. National Film Corporation of Sri Lanka, 1981. Clarke plays Leonard Woolf.

1985   *Arthur C. Clarke's World of Strange Powers*. London: ITV, April 3 through July 10, 1985. Documentary series hosted by Clarke.

1988   *God, the Universe, and Everything Else*. Central Independent Television, 1988. Video discussion featuring Clarke, Stephen Hawking, and Carl Sagan.

1992   *Arthur C. Clarke Royal Television Society Lecture*. Toronto: York University Television, 1992.

1994   *Arthur C. Clarke's Mysterious Universe*. London: ITV, January 1 through June 26, 1994. Documentary series hosted by Clarke.

Without Warning. New York: WB Network, October 30, 1994. Clarke appeared as interviewed expert in fictional movie.

1995   "Arthur C. Clarke." Episode of biographical series *This Is Your Life*. Thames Television International, January 11, 1995.

Conferment by Satellite Link of an Honorary Degree on Dr Arthur C Clarke CBE and the Science Fiction Foundation Collection. Liverpool: University of Liverpool Central Television and Photographic Service, 1995. VHS tape.

1997   "Arthur C. Clarke." Episode of documentary series *Masters of Fantasy*. Sci-Fi Channel, April 22, 1997.

"The Man Who Saw the Future." Episode of *The Works*. London: BBC-TV, July 13, 1997.

2001   *Stanley Kubrick: A Life in Pictures*. Warner Brothers, 2001. Documentary.

2001: HAL's Legacy. InCA Productions, 2001. Documentary.

2001: The Making of a Myth. Atlantic Celtic Films, January 13, 2001. Short documentary.

2004   *Arthur C. Clarke*. Films for the Humanities, 2004. Documentary.

2007   *Vision of a Future Passed: The Prophecy of 2001.* Leva Filmworks, October 23, 2007. Short documentary.

              We Love "The Sky at Night." London: BBC-TV, May 6, 2007. Documentary.

BOOKS AND STORIES BASED ON CLARKE'S WORKS (SELECTED)

1938   Smith, D. R. "Cosmic Case 4." *Novae Terrae* 3.3 (November 1938): 6–8.

1961   *A Fall of Moondust.* In *Reader's Digest Condensed Books, Volume 4, 1961: Autumn Selections,* editor in chief DeWitt Wallace, 344–404. Pleasantville, NY: Reader's Digest Association, 1961. Condensed version of Clarke's novel.

1967   *A Fall of Moondust.* London: Nelson, 1967. Adapted by Stanley Donald Kneebone. Republished. Sunbury-on-Thames: Nelson, 1978.

1976   *Islands in the Sky.* Hong Kong: Oxford University Press, 1976. Retold by Suzan Davies.

              Kirby, Jack, writer and artist. "Beast-Killer." *2001: A Space Odyssey,* no. 1 (December 1976): 1–3, 6–7, 10–11, 14–17, 22–23, 26–27, 30–31. Comic book, first of ten (others listed below) inspired by *2001: A Space Odyssey.*

              ———. "The Capture of X-51." *2001: A Space Odyssey,* no. 8 (July 1977): 1–3, 6–7, 10–11, 14–17, 22–23, 26–27, 30–31.

              ———. "Hotline to Hades." *2001: A Space Odyssey,* no. 10 (September 1977): 1–3, 6–7, 10–11, 14–17, 22–23, 26–27, 30–31.

              ———. "Inter-Galactica: The Ultimate Trip." *2001: A Space Odyssey,* no. 6 (May 1977): 1–3, 6–7, 10–11, 14–17, 22–23, 26–27, 30–31.

              ———. "Marak!" *2001: A Space Odyssey,* no. 3 (February 1977): 1–3, 6–7, 10–11, 14–17, 22–23, 26–27, 30–31.

              ———. "Mister Machine." *2001: A Space Odyssey,* no. 9 (August 1977): 1–3, 6–7, 10–11, 14–17, 22–23, 26–27, 30–31.

              ———. "The New Seed." *2001: A Space Odyssey,* no. 7 (June 1977): 1–3, 6–7, 10–11, 14–17, 22–23, 26–27, 30–31.

              ———. "Norton of New York 2040 A.D." *2001: A Space Odyssey,* no. 5 (April 1977): 1–3, 6–7, 10–11, 14–17, 22–23, 26–27, 30–31.

              ———. *2001: A Space Odyssey.* Marvel Treasury Special. New York: Marvel Comics Group, 1976. 83pp. Comic book adaptation of film.

              ———. "Vira the She-Demon." *2001: A Space Odyssey,* no. 2 (January 1977): 1–3, 6–7, 10–11, 14–17, 22–23, 26–27, 30–31.

              ———. "Wheels of Death." *2001: A Space Odyssey,* no. 4 (March 1977): 1–3, 6–7, 10–11, 14–17, 22–23, 26–27, 30–31.

1979   *Rendezvous with Rama.* Oxford: Oxford University Press, 1979. Adapted by David Fickling.

1980   Welfare, Simon, and John Fairley. *Arthur C. Clarke's Mysterious World.* New York: A & W Visual Library, 1980. Based on Clarke-hosted documentary series.

1984   Fairley, John, and Simon Welfare. *Arthur C. Clarke's World of Strange Powers.* New York: G. P. Putnam's Sons, 1984. Based on Clarke-hosted documentary series.

1987   Welfare, Simon, and John Fairley. *Arthur C. Clarke's Chronicles of the Strange and Mysterious.* London: Collins, 1987. Nine chapters, one written by Clarke and others, including his comments; inspired by two Clarke-hosted documentary series.

Preuss, Paul. *Breaking Strain*. New York: Avon, 1987. Arthur C. Clarke's Venus Prime 1. Based on "Breaking Strain."

1988   Preuss, Paul. *Maelstrom*. New York: Avon, 1988. Arthur C. Clarke's Venus Prime 2. Based on "Maelstrom II."

1989   Preuss, Paul. *Hide and Seek*. New York: Avon, 1989. Arthur C. Clarke's Venus Prime 3. Based on "Hide-and-Seek."

1990   Benford, Gregory. "Part II." *Beyond the Fall of Night*, by Arthur C. Clarke and Gregory Benford, 145–298. New York: Ace/Putnam, 1990. Benford's sequel to *Against the Fall of Night*.

Preuss, Paul. *The Medusa Encounter*. New York: Avon, 1990. Arthur C. Clarke's Venus Prime 4. Based on "A Meeting with Medusa."

1991   Preuss, Paul. *The Diamond Moon*. New York: Avon, 1991. Arthur C. Clarke's Venus Prime 5. Based on "Jupiter V."

———. *The Shining Ones*. New York: Avon, 1991. Arthur C. Clarke's Venus Prime 6. Based on "The Shining Ones."

1992   *Tales of Ten Worlds*. Oxford: Macmillan, 1992. Retold by Helen Reid-Thomas.

1993   Welfare, Simon, and John Fairley. *Arthur C. Clarke's A-Z of Mysteries: From Atlantis to Zombies*. Foreword by Arthur C. Clarke. London: HarperCollins, 1993. Seventy-three brief chapters, one written by Clarke; inspired by two Clarke-hosted documentary series.

1995   Lee, Gentry. *Bright Messengers*. New York: Bantam Spectra, 1995. Set in same universe as *Rama II* and its sequels.

1996   *The Songs of Distant Earth: Short Stories*. Oxford: Oxford University Press, 1996. Retold by Jennifer Bassett.

1999   Lee, Gentry. *Double Full Moon Night*. New York: Bantam Spectra, 1995. Set in same universe as *Rama II* and its sequels.

2000   Fairley, John, and Simon Welfare. *Arthur C. Clarke's Mysteries*. Foreword by Arthur C. Clarke. Amherst, NY: Prometheus, 2000. Omnibus of chapters from *Arthur C. Clarke's Mysterious World*, *Arthur C. Clarke's World of Strange Powers*, and *Arthur C. Clarke's Chronicles of the Strange and Mysterious*. The book references an earlier, unseen edition: London: Michael O'Mara Books, 1998.

Lee, Gentry. *The Tranquility Wars*. New York: Bantam Spectra, 2000. References universe of *Rama II* and its sequels.

2001   *2001: A Space Odyssey*. Harlow: Pearson Education, 2001. Retold by David Maule.

2003   *Rendezvous with Rama*. Oxford: Macmillan Heinemann ELT, 2003. Retold by Elizabeth Walker.

2004   Benford, Gregory. *Beyond Infinity*. New York: Warner Aspect Books, 2004. London: Orbit Books, 2004. Expansion of "Part II" with references to Clarke's text removed.

2016   Baxter, Stephen, and Alastair Reynolds. *The Medusa Chronicles*. New York: Saga Press/Simon & Schuster, 2016. Sequel to "A Meeting with Medusa."

2001: A Space Odyssey. Los Angeles: KinderGuides/Moppet Books, [2016]. Retold by Fredrik Colting and Melissa Medina.

MUSIC BASED ON CLARKE'S WORKS

1973   Bedford, David. *The Tentacles of the Dark Nebula*. London: Decca Records, 1973. Vocal music using lyrics from "Transience." Score published in 1975. London: Universal Edition, 1975.

1994   Oldfield, Mike. *The Songs of Distant Earth*. London: Mike Oldfield Music, 1994. Includes music based on Clarke's novel.

2001   Bedford, David. *The City and the Stars*. Vocal music based on Clarke's novel. Performed in 2001. No information found on CD release.

FILMS AND TELEVISION PROGRAMS BASED ON CLARKE'S WORKS (SELECTED)

1977   *Rescue Party* (short). Santa Monica, CA: BSA Educational Media, 1977. Based on "Rescue Party."

1984   *2010: The Year We Make Contact*. MGM, 1984. Based on *2010: Odyssey Two*. Clarke makes cameo appearance.

1985   "The Star." *Twilight Zone*. New York: CBS-TV, December 20, 1985. Based on "The Star."

1994   *Trapped in Space*. Paramount Pictures/Village Roadshow Productions, 1994. Based on "Breaking Strain."

2015   *Childhood's End*. Syfy Channel, December 14 through December 16, 2015. Miniseries based on *Childhood's End*.

2017–   Note: A miniseries based on *3001: The Final Odyssey* has been announced for 2017. A long-standing project to film *Rendezvous with Rama* was revived in 2016, with no anticipated date of release.

Agel, Jerome, ed. *The Making of Kubrick's 2001*. New York: New American Library, 1970.

Allen, L. David. *"Childhood's End*, Arthur C. Clarke, 1953." *Science Fiction: An Introduction*. Lincoln, NE: Cliff's Notes, 1973. 47–55.

Arnold, Frank. "Mordecai of the White Horse." *Eye*, no. 3 (Christmas, 1954), page numbers unknown. Retitled "Tales from the White Horse" and online at http://www .fiawol.org.uk/FanStuff/THEN%20Archive/Horse/HorseTales.htm.

Baxter, John. *Stanley Kubrick: A Biography*. New York: Carroll & Graf, 1997.

Benford, Gregory, and George Zebrowski, eds. *Sentinels in Honor of Arthur C. Clarke*. Overland Park, KS: Hadley Rille Books, 2010. Stories and essays.

Blackford, Russell. "Future Problematic: Reflections on *The City and the Stars*." In *Earth Is but a Star: Excursions through Science Fiction to the Far Future*, edited by Damien Broderick, 35–46. Crawley: University of Western Australia Press, 2001.

Campbell, John W., Jr. Introduction to *Who Goes There?* by John W. Campbell Jr., 3–6. Chicago: Shasta Press, 1948.

Clarke, Fred. "Arthur C. Clarke: The Early Days." *Foundation: The Review of Science Fiction*, no. 41 (Winter 1987): 9–14.

Clarke, Fred, with Mark Stewart, Kelvin F. Long, and Robert Godwin. *Arthur C. Clarke: A Life Remembered*. Burlington, Ontario: Apogee Prime, 2013. Foreword by Gregory Benford. Introduction by Angie Edwards.

Goldman, Stephen H. "Wandering in Mazes Lost; or, The Unhappy Life of Arthur C. Clarke's 'Childhood's End' in Academia." *Foundation: The Review of Science Fiction*, no. 41 (Winter 1987): 21–29.

Hollow, John. *Against the Night, the Stars: The Science Fiction of Arthur C. Clarke*. New York: Harcourt Brace Jovanovich, 1983.

Hume, Kathryn. "The Edifice Complex: Motive and Accomplishment in *The Fountains of Paradise*." *Extrapolation* 24.4 (1983): 380–88.

James, Edward. "Arthur C. Clarke." In *A Companion to Science Fiction*, edited by David Seed, 431–40. Malden, MA: Blackwell, 2005.

———. "Clarke's Utopian Vision." In *A Celebration of British Science Fiction*, edited by Andy Sawyer, Andrew M. Butler, and Farah Mendlesohn, 26–33. Guildford, UK: Science Fiction Foundation, 2005.

———. "Editorial." *Foundation: The Review of Science Fiction*, no. 41 (1987): 3.

———. *Science Fiction in the 20th Century*. Oxford: Oxford University Press, 1994.

Lehman, Steve. "Sounding the Science Fiction of Arthur 'Sea' Clarke." *Paradoxa* 4.10 (1998): 269–76.

McAleer, Neil. *Arthur C. Clarke: The Authorized Biography*. Chicago: Contemporary, 1992. Revised and updated as *Sir Arthur C. Clarke: Odyssey of a Visionary: A Biography*. New York: Rosetta Books, 2013.

Moylan, Tom. "Ideological Contradiction in Clarke's *The City and the Stars*." *Science-Fiction Studies* 4.2 (1977): 150–57.

Nicholls, Peter, and John Clute. "Arthur C Clarke." *The Encyclopedia of Science Fiction*. Third edition. Edited by John Clute, David Langford, Peter Nicholls, and Graham Sleight. London: Gollancz, last updated March 2, 2017. Accessed August 8, 2017. http://sf-encyclopedia.com/entry/clarke_arthur_c.

Olander, Joseph D., and Martin Harry Greenberg, eds. *Arthur C. Clarke*. New York: Taplinger, 1977. Cited contributors: Peter Brigg, Robert Plank, and David N. Samuelson.

Rabkin, Eric S. *Arthur C. Clarke*. Mercer Island, WA: Starmont House, 1980.

Reid, Robin Anne. *Arthur C. Clarke: A Critical Companion*. Westport, CT: Greenwood Press, 1997.

Ruddick, Nicholas. "The World Turned Inside Out: Decoding Clarke's *Rendezvous with Rama*." *Science-Fiction Studies* 12.1 (1985): 42–50.

Samuelson, David N. *Arthur C. Clarke: A Primary and Secondary Bibliography*. Boston: G. K. Hall, 1984.

———. "Sir Arthur C. Clarke." Revised and updated by Gary Westfahl. *Science Fiction Writers: Critical Studies of the Major Writers from the Early Nineteenth Century to the Present Day*. Second edition. Edited by Richard Bleiler. New York: Charles Scribner's Sons, 1999. 203–212.

Seeley, Nicholas. "The Wizard in the Space Station: A Look Back at the Works of the Late Sir Arthur C. Clarke." *Strange Horizons*, April 14, 2008. http://www.strangehorizons.com/2008/20080414/seeley-a.shtml.

Slusser, George. *The Space Odysseys of Arthur C. Clarke*. San Bernardino, CA: Borgo Press, 1978.

Westfahl, Gary. *Cosmic Engineers: A Study of Hard Science Fiction*. Westport, CT: Greenwood Press, 1996.

———. "The Endless Odyssey: The *2001* Saga and Its Inability to Predict Humanity's Future." In *Science Fiction and the Prediction of the Future: Essays on Foresight and Fallacy*, edited by Westfahl, Wong Kin Yuen, and Amy Kit-Sze Chan. Jefferson, NC: McFarland, 2011. 135–70.

Wollheim, Donald A. *The Universe Makers: Science Fiction Today*. New York: Harper & Row, 1971.

Zivkovic, Zolan. "The Motif of First Contact in Arthur C. Clarke's 'A Meeting with Medusa.'" *New York Review of Science Fiction*, no. 150 (February 2001): 1, 8–13, and 151 (March 2001): 10–17.

atomic energy, 24–25, 32, 35, 49, 56, 58, 74–75
"Awakening, The" (1942) (Clarke), 17, 77–78, 90, 98
"Awakening, The" (1952) (Clarke), 37, 65, 66, 77–78, 79, 90, 98, 155

Babbage, George, 26
Bach, Johann Sebastian, 171
Baxter, John, 14
Baxter, Stephen, 2–3, 182, 185
Beautiful Living: Buddha's Way to Prosperity, Wisdom, and Inner Peace (Rahula), 143
"Before Eden" (Clarke), 99
Bell, Alexander Graham, 68
Benford, Gregory, 1, 6–7, 12–13, 16, 82, 182, 187
Beyond the Fall of Night (Clarke and Benford), 182
Beyond: Visions of the Interplanetary Probes (Benson), 78
Bible, the, 91, 139, 147
"Big Game Hunt" (Clarke), 33–34, 34–35
Blackford, Russell, 5, 83, 86
Blish, James, 91, 181
Blue Danube Waltz, The (Strauss), 107
Body of Glass (aka *He, She and It*) (Piercy), 4
Böecklin, Arnold, 130
Bradbury, Ray, 171
"Breaking Strain" (Clarke), 58, 59, 60, 158–59
Breaking Strain (Preuss), 182
Bretnor, Reginald, 25
Brigg, Peter, 17, 74, 77
Brightfount Diaries, The (Aldiss), 27
British Interplanetary Society, 13
Broderick, Damien, 82
"Broken Circuit, The" (Clarke), 32
Brunner, John, 187 ·
Buddhism, 101, 127, 134, 138, 139–40, 141, 143, 147, 148
Burke, John F., 20
Burroughs, Edgar Rice, 26, 171

Caesar, Julius, 23
Campbell, John W., 3, 89
"Castaway, The" (Clarke), 99, 102
"Challenge of the Spaceship, The" (Clarke), 48
Challenge of the Spaceship, The (Clarke), 30
Chandler, A. Bertram (pseudonym of George Whitley), 26, 187
Childhood Ends: The Earliest Writings of Arthur C. Clarke (Clarke), 3, 7, 19, 20, 31
Childhood's End (miniseries), 178
Childhood's End (novel) (Clarke), 1, 6, 14, 43, 45, 115, 118, 120–21, 178; aliens, 71–72, 93, 95–96, 98, 100, 102, 103, 105, 109; characters, 24, 154; "Foreword," 43, 89; human destinies, 28–29, 42, 65, 82, 87–89, 106; and religion, 90–92, 137, 138, 139–40, 142
Christianity, 90–91, 114, 135, 137–42, 184
Christopher, John (pseudonym of Sam Youd), 20, 26, 187
City and the Stars, The (Clarke), 6, 37, 41, 80, 82–87, 93, 95, 119, 137–38, 139–40, 141, 155–56, 166
Clarke, Arthur C.: biography, 9–16, 30, 50, 72, 102, 123, 128, 152, 156, 158, 162–63, 174–75; characters, 3, 6, 60–61, 149–75, 177–79; "collaborations," 2–3, 6, 11, 189, 181–88; and disabilities, 6, 15, 172; and fandom, 3, 9, 12, 13, 20, 22, 87; and homosexuality, 6, 13, 14, 15, 20–21, 145, 166–68, 175; involvement with films, 1–2, 15; juvenilia, 5, 6, 17–24; knighthood, 2, 15; and literature, 3, 4, 5–6; scientific work, 9–10, 13, 30, 31–32, 36, 162–63; Third Law, 5, 28
Clarke, Charles, 10–11
Clarke, Fred, 3, 9, 187
Clement, Hal, 94
Clute, John, 4–5
"Cold Equations, The" (Godwin), 56
"Cold War" (Clarke), 33
Coleridge, Samuel Taylor, 25

Fu Manchu stories (Rohmer), 18

Wilson, Mike, 13, 117, 163, 175
"Wind from the Sun, The" (Clarke), 51, 188
"Wire Continuum, The" (Clarke and Baxter), 2–3, 185
Wollheim, Donald A., 73
Wyndham, John (pseudonym of John Beynon Harris), 26, 187

Youd, Sam (pseudonym John Christopher), 20, 26, 187
"You're on the Glide Path—I Think" (Clarke), 13

Zelazny, Roger, 181
Zivkovic, Zolan, 77

GARY WESTFAHL, formerly of the University of La Verne and the University of California, Riverside, has now retired to focus exclusively on research and writing. His many books on science fiction include *William Gibson* and *Hugo Gernsback and the Century of Science Fiction*.

MODERN MASTERS OF SCIENCE FICTION

THE UNIVERSITY OF ILLINOIS PRESS

is a founding member of the

Association of American University Presses.

University of Illinois Press

1325 South Oak Street

Champaign, IL 61820-6903

www.press.uillinois.edu